formal specification
of
programming languages

a panoramic primer

FRANK G. PAGAN

Department of Computer Science
Southern Illinois University at Carbondale

PRENTICE-HALL, INC., Englewood Cliffs, New Jersey　07632

Library of Congress Cataloging in Publication Data

Pagan, Frank G
    Formal specification of programming languages.

    Bibliography: p. 235
    Includes index.
    1. Programming languages—Syntax. 2. Program-
ming languages—Semantics. I. Title.
QA76.7.P33   001.64'24   80-23516
ISBN 0-13-329052-2

© 1981 by PRENTICE-HALL, INC.,
Englewood Cliffs, New Jersey 07632

Prentice-Hall Software Series
Brian W. Kernighan, advisor

Editorial/production supervision
    and interior design by Linda Mihatov Paskiet
Cover design by Edsal Enterprises
Manufacturing buyer: Joyce Levatino

Printed in the United States of America

10 9 8 7 6 5

PRENTICE-HALL INTERNATIONAL, INC., *London*
PRENTICE-HALL OF AUSTRALIA PTY. LIMITED, *Sydney*
PRENTICE-HALL OF CANADA, LTD., *Toronto*
PRENTICE-HALL OF INDIA PRIVATE LIMITED, *New Delhi*
PRENTICE-HALL OF JAPAN, INC., *Tokyo*
PRENTICE-HALL OF SOUTHEAST ASIA PTE. LTD., *Singapore*
WHITEHALL BOOKS LIMITED, *Wellington, New Zealand*

contents

LIST OF TABLES   v

PREFACE   vii

1
PROLOG   1

2
FORMAL SYNTAX   7

  2.1 Backus–Naur Form *8*
      2.1.1 The BNF Metalanguage 8
      2.1.2 The Language Pam 14
      2.1.3 The Language Eva 16
  2.2 Variations on BNF *21*
  2.3 Attribute Grammars *27*
      2.3.1 Concepts and Characteristics 27
      2.3.2 A Complete Syntactic Specification for Eva 37
  2.4 Two-Level Grammars *49*
      2.4.1 Another Notation for Context-Free Grammars 50
      2.4.2 Context-Sensitivity—Hyper-Rules and Metanotions 52
      2.4.3 Another Complete Syntactic Specification for Eva 60

3
FROM SYNTAX TO SEMANTICS   73

3.1 Syntax, Semantics, and Abstract Syntax *74*
3.2 Translational Semantics Using Attribute Grammars—
     A Complete Definition of Pam *79*
3.3 Interpretive Semantics Using Two-Level Grammars *99*
     3.3.1 A Complete Definition of Pam 100
     3.3.2 A Complete Definition of Eva 122

4
FORMAL SEMANTICS   133

4.1 The Operational Approach—Vienna Definition Language *135*
     4.1.1 Notation for Objects and Abstract Syntax 135
     *4.1.2 Control Mechanism and Notation for Instruction
             Definitions—A Semantic Specification for Pam 143*
     4.1.3 A Semantic Specification for Eva 155
4.2 The Denotational Approach *167*
     4.2.1 Concepts and Characteristics 167
     4.2.2 The Denotational Semantics of Pam 173
     4.2.3 The Denotational Semantics of Eva 180
4.3 The Axiomatic Approach *193*
     4.3.1 Concepts and Characteristics 193
     4.3.2 The Axiomatic Semantics of Pam 199
     4.3.3 The Axiomatic Semantics of Eva 205

5
PROGRAMMING LANGUAGES AS METALANGUAGES   217

5.1 Definition of One Programming Language by Another *218*
5.2 Self-Definition *227*

6
EPILOG   231

BIBLIOGRAPHY   235

INDEX   241

list of tables

2.1   BNF Grammar for Pam *15*
2.2   BNF Grammar for Eva *17*
2.3   Grammar for Pam Using Extended BNF *23*
2.4   Grammar for Eva Using Extended BNF *24*
2.5   Attribute Grammar for the Syntax of Eva *44*
2.6   Grammar for Pam in Two-Level Grammar Notation *51*
2.7   Two-Level Grammar for Eva *69*
3.1   Attribute Grammar Mapping Pam into a Simple Symbolic Machine Language *92*
3.2   Two-Level Grammar Defining the Syntax and Semantics of Pam *116*
3.3   Two-Level Grammar Defining the Syntax and Semantics of Eva *125*
4.1   VDL Definition of the Semantics of Pam *152*
4.2   VDL Definition of the Semantics of Eva *162*
4.3   Denotational Definition of the Semantics of Pam *178*
4.4   Denotational Definition of the Semantics of Eva *190*
4.5   Axiomatic Definition of the Semantics of Pam *204*
4.6   Partial Axiomatic Definition of the Semantics of Eva *214*
5.1   Operational Semantics of Pam Expressed in Algol 68 *224*

preface

What I have tried to do in this book is to offer a wide-ranging and gentle introduction to the important area of techniques and metalanguages for the formal specification of the syntax and semantics of computer programming languages, from BNF to axiomatic semantics. Formal language definition has often appeared to be a complex, arcane art, a general knowledge of which could only be obtained by finding and reading a large number of highly scattered, specialized publications. This book draws together in one place basic information on, and examples of the use of, a wide variety of prominent definition methods. In order to minimize the amount of complex mathematical discourse and formalism, the description of the various meta-languages, although detailed, is informal. Emphasis is placed on the actual use of the metalanguages in defining programming languages as opposed to their theoretical bases or mathematical underpinnings. In analogy to the several existing books which informally survey a selection of programming languages for the formal specification of algorithms (i.e., the coding of programs), the present book informally surveys a selection of metalanguages for the formal specification of programming languages.

Various subsets of the material will be found useful by most computer scientists with an interest in high-level programming languages. The reader is assumed to have a general knowledge of programming, preferably including familiarity with two or more high-level languages, and of related aspects of computer science such as trees and other data structures and the concept of recursion. Some knowledge of various topics in discrete mathematics, such as set theory, functions, logic, and modern algebra, is also desirable. As a text, the book can be used by graduate students or senior undergraduates studying the structure, design, or theory of programming languages.

The principal expository device employed throughout is the use of two small, specially designed languages as the objects of case studies of the various specification techniques. One of these languages ("Pam") has elementary facilities for integer arithmetic and flow-of-control (conditional and loop structures), while the other ("Eva") has block structure, recursive procedures, and a structured data type (character strings). All these features are similar to some of the features of widely known real languages such as Pascal and PL/I, and the two languages together provide a fairly comprehensive basis for illustrating the use of the various metalanguages. The fact that, individually, they are also unrealistically small and weak is necessary in order to prevent the case studies from becoming overly long or complex.

There are brief guides to sources of further information at the ends of sections. Wherever possible, I have only referenced publications that are fairly readily accessible. In many cases, more complete sets of references may be found in those publications.

There is little in the way of precedent or prescription to suggest an order of presentation for the subject matter, and the organization I have chosen reflects the fact that this work necessarily represents just one person's view of the complex landscape of formal language specification. Chapter 2 deals with the formal specification of syntax, where the latter term is taken to include all context-sensitive properties of program texts, and covers BNF and its variants (Secs. 2.1, 2.2), attribute grammars (Sec. 2.3), and two-level grammars (Sec. 2.4). The languages Pam and Eva are introduced in the context of BNF. Chapter 4 deals with formal semantics, introducing the operational approach and Vienna Definition Language (Sec. 4.1), the denotational approach (Sec. 4.2), and the axiomatic approach (Sec. 4.3). The transition from formal syntax to formal semantics is made in Chapter 3, which includes descriptions of techniques for specifying semantics by means of grammars. Chapter 5 discusses the concept of using a programming language as a metalanguage, possibly the same language as is being defined.

I have tried to allow as much flexibility as possible with respect to the order in which the various sections may be read. The prerequisite structure relating all the sections is shown in the accompanying diagram; a particular section should not be read until all earlier sections connected to it with lines leading downward have been read. Thus, someone who was primarily interested in the use of two-level grammars for the specification of semantics could follow the sequence 1, 2.1.1, 2.1.2, 2.1.3, 2.4.1, 2.4.2, 2.4.3, 3.1, 3.3.1, 3.3.2, with the option of reading 3.1 immediately after 2.1.3. Many other paths are

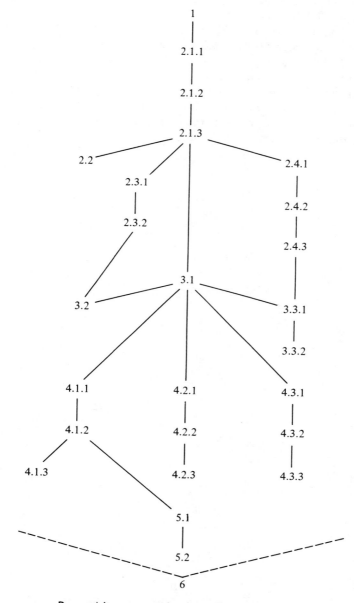

Prerequisite structure for the sections of the text

possible, depending on one's interests or course description. The Epilog (Chapter 6) makes mention of all other sections but may be read even if less than the whole book is covered.

Financial support for research connected with parts of this work was provided by the National Research Council of Canada while I was affiliated with Memorial University of Newfoundland. I would like to acknowledge the contributions of Donna Batten and Michael Rayment in helping to construct and verify some of the two-level grammars. Donna Batten also ably assisted in the isolation and correction of numerous errors, omissions, and lapses of clarity in other parts of the initial manuscript. Any and all shortcomings that remain are my fault alone.

F. G. PAGAN
Carbondale, Illinois

1

prolog

Given that programming languages are strictly artificial entities created to facilitate the preparation of computer programs and the representation and communication of algorithms, their diversity, complexity, and often unfathomed depth of structure and concept are truly remarkable. After three decades of intense research and development, there is still no end in sight to the stream of useful innovations in language design and valuable theoretical insights into language structure. It therefore seems appropriate that computer scientists have adopted the term 'language' to describe these media which are so much more than mere 'notations' and have borrowed some of the concepts and terminology used by linguists in the study of natural language.

When we are concerned with language description, the terms *syntax, semantics,* and *pragmatics* provide a basic categorization of the various aspects. Roughly speaking, syntax deals with questions of superficial *form* of a language, semantics with its underlying *meaning,* and pragmatics with its practical *use.* This is a very general and rather vague characterization, as different approaches to language description are based on different interpretations of these concepts; this is especially true in the case of semantics, for there is definitely more than one meaning of 'meaning'.

To take as an example the common assignment statement, of which

$$a := b + sin\ (x) + 2$$

might be a particular instance, an informal description might include the following statements:

- *Syntax.* An assignment statement consists of a variable followed by the symbol ':=' followed by an expression.

- *Semantics.* The execution of an assignment statement consists of evaluating the expression on its right side and causing the resulting value to be associated with the variable on its left side, thus superseding any value previously associated with the variable.

- *Pragmatics.* An assignment statement may be used to compute and retain the value of an invariant expression that is needed at more than one point in a program, or to update the value of a variable in terms of its previous value, or . . . .

Of course, descriptions of "variable" and "expression" would also have to be supplied. The following are two possible alternatives to the second statement in the list above:

- *Semantics.* Given any logical assertion that holds after executing the statement, the assertion obtained by substituting the expression for all free occurrences of the variable in the given assertion holds before executing the statement.

- *Semantics.* An assignment statement denotes a function that maps memory states into memory states, such that the memory state resulting from an application of the function to a particular state is the same as the given state except that the value associated with the variable is given by the application of the function denoted by the expression to the given state.

The majority of language descriptions have always been informal, i.e., expressed in a narrative form instead of using a rigorous notation, and for some purposes this is perfectly satisfactory. After all, formal notations are inherently esoteric (some more than others), whereas natural language is universally understood. In teaching introductory programming, for example, it is probably not even desirable to distinguish sharply between syntax, semantics, and pragmatics. When it comes to the writing of a *definitive specification* or *standard definition* of a language, however, the informal approaches have some well-known disadvantages. The main problem is lack of clarity and precision: natural language is simply too vague and imprecise to express the intricate and detailed properties of a programming language completely, exactly, and unambiguously, and experience has shown that this is what we require. The more we try to achieve such exactitude, the more cumbersome and verbose is the phraseology. Conciseness of specification is a virtue (up to a point, at least) that is not realized in a narrative description. These deficiencies are evident even in the short examples given above, where some effort has been made to be precise.

Thus we must turn to formal methods if there is to be any hope of being able to write language specifications with the qualities of *completeness, consistency, precision, absence of ambiguity, conciseness, understandability,* and *usefulness,* bearing in mind that it may be impossible to achieve all of these simultaneously. A great deal of work has been done, and much remains to be done, on the development and application of general, formal methods for specifying the syntax and semantics of programming languages. We shall confine our attention to syntax and semantics from now on, for at the present time it is not at all clear that pragmatics can or should be formalized.

We may well ask what is meant by the *usefulness* of a language specification; in other words, why do we want such precise definitions of programming languages anyway? Almost every book and article on the subject of formal definition has included a discussion of this basic question, and there is, more or less, a consensus that the aims and advantages of formal specification are as follows:

1. *Standardization of programming languages.* The need to define standard versions and standard extensions of "old" languages has long been recognized, and special committees have spent much time and effort on the task of standardizing such languages as Fortran, Cobol, and PL/I, which are widely used but which were originally defined by mostly informal means. Standardization, if effectively conceived and implemented, can inhibit the unruly proliferation of ill-defined and incompatible dialects provided by different implementations and described in different expositions, thus increasing the language's value as a medium of communication and a tool for writing portable programs. It is now generally accepted that standardization efforts can be really successful only if they are provided with an adequate technical basis, and this means that they must employ formal specification techniques to one extent or another.

2. *Reference for users.* The users of a programming language need a definitive document to which they can refer for completely detailed and accurate information on questions of legality and meaning of the language's facilities. In principle, a formal specification technique is the best means of providing such a document.

3. *Proofs about programs.* In view of the generally recognized inadequacy of the debugging and testing process, it is often desirable to verify facts about programs, especially their *correctness,* by means of rational proof. If the proofs are to be mathematically rigorous, the properties of the language constructs to which they refer must be rigorously formalized. A further

possibility is the use of computational tools to aid the checking or even the generation of the proofs. On a somewhat different tack, a formal definition of a language might suggest a very systematic methodology for constructing programs that are guaranteed to conform to their specifications, so that, in effect, the correctness proof is inherent in the description of the construction process.

4. *Reference for implementers.* The producer(s) of a compiler or interpreter for a programming language must understand all aspects of the language in complete detail, as anyone who has ever implemented even a toy language will readily appreciate. If the language is not exactly and unambiguously defined, different implementers will understand it differently and will thus produce incompatible processors.[1]

5. *Proofs of implementations.* In order to prove the correctness of a program, its functional requirements must be rigorously formalized. A language implementation is a program whose functional requirements are given in part by the specifications of the language it implements. Therefore, formalization of these specifications is a necessary condition for establishing the correctness of an implementation.

6. *Automatic implementation.* The use of formal specification techniques opens up the possibility of automating or partially automating the process of constructing compilers or interpreters. This often involves the use of special programs that take the specifications of a language as input and produce as output processors or parts of processors for the language. A notably successful area of application of this idea has long been the automatic generation of syntactic analyzers from (the simpler kinds of) formal syntax specifications. In some formal definition methods, on the other hand, a set of language specifications already *is* an actual implementation or part of one. If the processor is too inefficient to be practical, there is still the problem of transforming or optimizing it into an efficient one.

7. *Improved language design.* "Good" language design, i.e., the design of programming languages that simultaneously possess all the qualities we would like to see, such as naturalness, conceptual clarity, power, and the multiple aspects of "usefulness," is exceedingly difficult and, in the eyes of many, yet to be achieved. Formal treatment of linguistic structure offers us a depth of insight into the fundamental nature of programming languages that is not possible otherwise. It can expose language irregularities not apparent from the surface, reveal underlying similarities between apparently different languages and differences between apparently similar languages, and isolate the reasons why certain combinations of facilities give rise to complex

---

[1] Even assuming that the implementer is not taking it upon himself or herself to implement a "better" variant of the language.

or inconsistent interactions, why the use of a certain feature in programs is difficult to prove correct, and so forth. The use of formal tools at the design stage will be an increasingly effective aid in providing better programming languages.

Formal definitions can thus affect many different people, including language designers, implementers, and users, in several different ways. We should bear in mind that it may well be impossible to devise a single methodology that simultaneously fulfills all these purposes. Perhaps that is not even desirable. It is a matter of opinion whether many of the present techniques fulfill *any* of the purposes in a completely satisfactory manner. It is clear nevertheless that most of the basic concepts involved in the approaches described in this book will survive as improved methods are developed.

Any kind of description or specification of a language must employ some *metalanguage*, which for our purposes is any language or notation used to describe programming languages. The metalanguage of an informal description is some natural language, possibly augmented by a few mathematical devices. A formal description requires a formal metalanguage. In this book, the language being defined will frequently be referred to as the *subject language*. (The term *object language* is more usual in other literature, but it has the disadvantage of also being a common term for the target language of a compiler.)

Much of the remainder of the book consists of informal explanations of formal metalanguages and examples of their use in defining programming languages. It is largely beyond our scope to discuss in detail how the definitions serve (or fail to serve) the potential applications listed above; in many cases further information on these aspects may be found in the literature referenced at the ends of various sections.

For Further Information

It would be impractical, and not very useful, to list all the literature sources containing discussions of the points raised so far, since such a list would include a majority of the books and articles in the bibliography, and more. The discussions most closely related to the one presented here are those contained in the introductory (pp. 192–94) and concluding (pp. 272–74) sections of the lengthy survey paper by Marcotty et al. (1976). In that article, the authors present a variety of complete, formal definitions of a miniature language called ASPLE.

2

formal syntax

The formalization of syntax is basically a simpler problem than the formalization of semantics. Historically, progress in the former has come earlier and more quickly than in the latter. Many languages, of which a notable early example is Algol 60, were originally defined by means of a formal syntactic description and an informal semantic description, the latter often including some aspects that could more properly be considered syntactic (i.e., the syntax is often only partially formalized). To date, formal syntactic specification has been considerably more successful than formal semantic specification in fulfilling the purposes and realizing the potential applications of formal language definition.

This chapter covers most of the more prominent methods for syntactic specification. The first of the metalanguages, BNF, will be familiar to most readers already, and it is convenient to introduce in that context the two miniature languages, arbitrarily named Pam and Eva, which will be used as examples throughout the book. Some simple and common variants and extensions of BNF are described in Sec. 2.2. Section 2.3 is concerned with attribute grammars and Sec. 2.4 with two-level grammars, both of which are significantly more powerful and comprehensive than the earlier formalisms.

2.1

BACKUS—NAUR FORM

2.1.1 The BNF Metalanguage

Backus-Naur form or *BNF* is the oldest formalism described in this book and is still very widely known and used. It combines great simplicity and naturalness with a fair degree of expressive power, and thus delivers considerable value for the effort required to understand it. Basically, it is a notation that one can use to specify a *generative grammar* which defines the set of all possible strings of symbols that constitute programs in the subject language together with their syntactic structure. BNF is thus closely related to certain aspects of natural linguistics and the theory of formal languages; in the terminology of those fields, the class of languages that can be defined in BNF is the class of *context-free* or *type 2 languages*, and the grammars expressible in BNF constitute the class of *context-free* or *type 2 grammars*.

A BNF grammar comprises a set of *production rules*. Each production rule has a left side and a right side separated by the metasymbol '::='. The left side consists of a *nonterminal* symbol, which is a string of one or more characters enclosed by '⟨' and '⟩'. A nonterminal is a name for a type of construct or syntactic category of the subject language. The symbol '::=' may be read as 'consists of' or 'is defined as'; i.e., a production rule is a definition for the nonterminal which forms its left side. There should be precisely one rule for each distinct nonterminal used in the grammar. The right side of a rule consists of one or more alternative specifications separated by occurrences of the metasymbol '|' (read as 'or'). Each alternative is a sequence of nonterminal and/or terminal symbols, where a *terminal* symbol is a token (character or indivisible group of characters) of the subject language.

For example, the production rule

⟨conditional statement⟩ ::= **if** ⟨comparison⟩ **then** ⟨series⟩ **fi** |

if ⟨comparison⟩ **then** ⟨series⟩ **else** ⟨series⟩ **fi**

states that a ⟨conditional statement⟩ consists either of the symbol **if** followed by a ⟨comparison⟩ followed by the symbol **then** followed by a ⟨series⟩ followed by the symbol **fi**, or of the symbol **if** followed by a ⟨comparison⟩ followed by the symbol **then** followed by a ⟨series⟩ followed by the symbol **else** followed by another ⟨series⟩ followed by the symbol **fi**. The nonterminals ⟨comparison⟩ and ⟨series⟩ must be defined by other rules; **if, then, else,** and **fi** are terminal symbols.

The rule for ⟨conditional statement⟩, together with the rules for the nonterminals it references and the rules for the nonterminals referenced in those rules, etc., determines the set of all strings of terminal symbols (*terminal strings*) that are particular examples of this type of construct. One of the grammar's nonterminal symbols, such as ⟨program⟩, is the "most general" or *distinguished* symbol in that it determines the whole subject language. The distinguished symbol is formally and uniquely identifiable if it does not appear in the right side of any production rule, and this can always be arranged by introducing one more rule, such as

⟨program⟩ ::= ⟨series⟩

where ⟨series⟩ would be the distinguished symbol were it not that it appears in the right sides of other rules. A grammar for a realistic programming language might contain hundreds of rules in all; for example, the definition of Algol 60 contains 117.

Any programming language permits the construction of an infinite number of possible programs. The use of *recursion* in the grammar is the device that enables an infinite number of terminal strings to be generated by a finite (and small) number of production rules. For example, the rule

⟨series⟩ ::= ⟨statement⟩ | ⟨series⟩ ; ⟨statement⟩

is recursive because the right side refers to the nonterminal being defined. According to the first alternative, a ⟨series⟩ may consist of a single ⟨statement⟩. Hence, according to the second alternative, it may also consist of two ⟨statement⟩s separated by a semicolon (a terminal). Hence, according to the second alternative again, it may also consist of three ⟨statement⟩s separated by (two) semicolons. By an inductive argument, one can see that it may in fact consist of any number of ⟨statement⟩s separated by semicolons. In this case, the rule

⟨series⟩ ::= ⟨statement⟩ | ⟨statement⟩ ; ⟨series⟩

would have done just as well. This rule is said to be *right-recursive* with respect to ⟨series⟩, whereas the first one is *left-recursive*.

The syntactic structure of a given terminal string as generated by a given grammar can be depicted as a *syntax tree* (sometimes called a *derivation tree* or *parse tree*). If our grammar includes the rules

⟨conditional statement⟩ ::= **if** ⟨comparison⟩ **then** ⟨series⟩ **fi** | . . .

⟨series⟩ ::= ⟨statement⟩ | ⟨series⟩ ; ⟨statement⟩

then Fig. 2.1 could be a portion of a syntax tree. In a tree for a complete program, all the leaf nodes are labeled with terminal symbols and all the other nodes are labeled with nonterminal symbols, the root being labeled with the

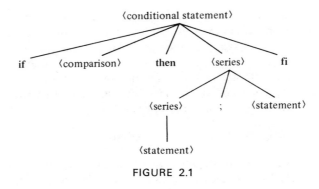

⟨conditional statement⟩

if   ⟨comparison⟩   then   ⟨series⟩   fi

⟨series⟩   ;   ⟨statement⟩

⟨statement⟩

FIGURE 2.1

grammar's distinguished symbol. Given a node with a nonterminal N, the immediate offspring of the node from left to right are labeled with the symbols that make up one of the alternative definitions in the production rule for N. Thus the structure in Fig. 2.1 would be part of a subtree beneath a node labeled with a nonterminal whose rule refers to ⟨conditional statement⟩. The terminal string obtained by scanning the leaves of the subtree from left to right would form a particular example of a ⟨conditional statement⟩, and the terminal string obtained by scanning the leaves of a complete tree would form a particular example of a ⟨program⟩.

Let us now consider a very simple class of arithmetic expressions constructed using the operators '+' and '*', parentheses, and the basic operands x, y, and z only. A first attempt to define the syntax of these expressions might result in the production rule

$$\langle expr \rangle ::= x \mid y \mid z \mid (\langle expr \rangle) \mid \langle expr \rangle + \langle expr \rangle \mid$$
$$\langle expr \rangle * \langle expr \rangle$$

Then the terminal string $(x + y) * z$ has the unique syntax tree shown in Fig. 2.2. But the string $x + y * z$ has two possible syntactic structures, as shown in Fig. 2.3. A string that has more than one syntax tree is said to be *ambiguous*, and a grammar that permits such a situation is also said to be ambiguous. Sometimes ambiguity is harmless, in that it does not affect the meaning of constructs. In this case, however, the first structure implies that multiplication of y and z should be the first operation performed while the second structure implies that addition of x and y should be the first operation performed, so that the overall result will generally be different in the two cases.

The general problem of deciding whether any given grammar is ambiguous is theoretically unsolvable, but in practice ambiguities can usually be avoided, especially if we restrict ourselves to certain subclasses of the context-

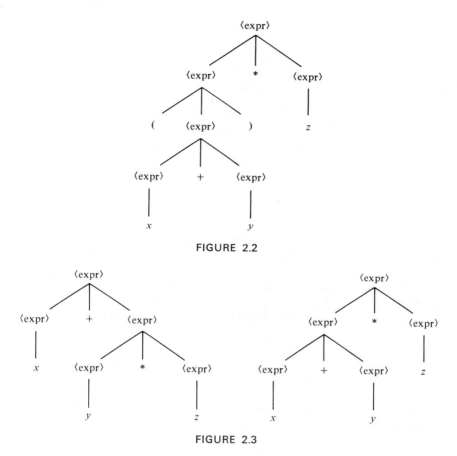

FIGURE 2.2

FIGURE 2.3

free grammars. One simple and useful rule is that a grammar will be ambiguous if it is both left- and right-recursive with respect to the same nonterminal, as is the case here. The ambiguity can be removed by introducing another nonterminal:

⟨expr⟩ ::= ⟨element⟩ | ⟨expr⟩ + ⟨element⟩ | ⟨expr⟩ * ⟨element⟩
⟨element⟩ ::= x | y | z | (⟨expr⟩)

Now $x + y * z$ has the unique structure shown in Fig. 2.4. The left-recursive rule for ⟨expr⟩ implies a left-to-right order of evaluation (apart from the effect of parentheses). The right-recursive rule

⟨expr⟩ ::= ⟨element⟩ | ⟨element⟩ + ⟨expr⟩ | ⟨element⟩ * ⟨expr⟩

would imply a right-to-left order.

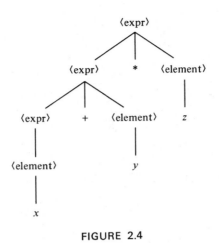

FIGURE 2.4

Note that the grammar still does not stipulate that multiplication should take precedence over addition, as is the case in most programming languages. This final refinement may be realized by incorporating a third nonterminal:

$$\langle expr \rangle ::= \langle term \rangle \mid \langle expr \rangle + \langle term \rangle$$
$$\langle term \rangle ::= \langle element \rangle \mid \langle term \rangle * \langle element \rangle$$
$$\langle element \rangle ::= x \mid y \mid z \mid (\langle expr \rangle)$$

Now the unique syntax tree for $x + y * z$ is that given in Fig. 2.5, whereas the tree for $y * z + x$ is the one shown in Fig. 2.6.

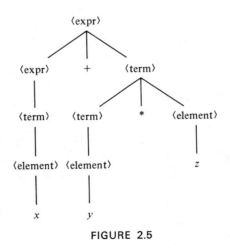

FIGURE 2.5

Examples of complete BNF grammars will now be given in conjunction with brief introductions to the two small, sample languages Pam and Eva.

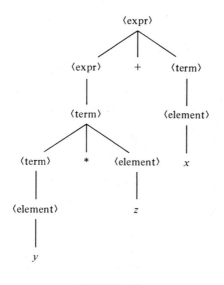

FIGURE 2.6

EXERCISES

1. Give a set of BNF production rules for subscripted variables of the form

⟨name⟩ (⟨subscript⟩ , . . . , ⟨subscript⟩)

as found in many commonly used programming languages.

2. A grammar that includes the production rules

⟨statement⟩ ::= ⟨conditional statement⟩ |
begin ⟨statement⟩ **end** |
. . .

⟨conditional statement⟩ ::= **if** ⟨comparison⟩ **then** ⟨statement⟩ |
if ⟨comparison⟩ **then** ⟨statement⟩ **else** ⟨statement⟩

gives rise to the so-called "dangling else" ambiguity. With the aid of syntax tree fragments,

(a) show how the ambiguity arises,
(b) explain how it can be eliminated by changing the grammar so that the symbol **then** is required to be followed by an ⟨unconditional statement⟩, which is any ⟨statement⟩ other than a ⟨conditional statement⟩, and
(c) explain how it can alternatively be eliminated by introducing a closing symbol such as **fi**.

2.1.2 The Language Pam

Pam is a very simple Algol-like language for specifying computations involving integer arithmetic only. Like its companion Eva, which is introduced in the next section, it is not a practical programming tool but is intended to serve as a vehicle for introducing and illustrating the various formal specification methods. Although it includes structured conditional and loop statements with arbitrary nesting permitted, it has no declarations or block structure; any two occurrences of the same identifier denote the same (scalar integer) variable.

A complete BNF grammar for Pam is given in Table 2.1. The syntax of the language should be quite clear from this grammar. Note that the operators '*' and '/' take precedence over '+' and '−', an (integer) ⟨constant⟩ consists of a string of one or more digits, and a ⟨variable⟩ begins with a letter which may be followed by any number of letters and/or digits.

Because of our experience with other languages, we can easily guess much of the intended semantics, although the grammar says nothing about this explicitly. For example, given a loop of the form

while C do S end

where C is a ⟨comparison⟩ and S is a ⟨series⟩, the intention is that S should be repeatedly executed, zero or more times, as long as C holds. In a loop of the form

to E do S end

the intended number of repetitions of S is fixed by the value of the ⟨expression⟩ E upon initiation. Another intention is that the value of a ⟨variable⟩ will be undefined unless and until it is given a value; any attempt to evaluate an undefined ⟨variable⟩ will be a semantic error.

The following is an example of a Pam program for calculating the factorials of n positive input values:

```
read n ;
to n do
    read x ;
    if x > 0 then
        y := 1 ; z := 1 ;
        while z <> x do
            z := z + 1 ;
            y := y * z
        end ;
        write y
    fi
end
```

TABLE 2.1   BNF Grammar for Pam

⟨program⟩ ::= ⟨series⟩

⟨series⟩ ::= ⟨statement⟩ | ⟨series⟩ ; ⟨statement⟩

⟨statement⟩ ::= ⟨input statement⟩ | ⟨output statement⟩ |
    ⟨assignment statement⟩ | ⟨conditional statement⟩ |
    ⟨definite loop⟩ | ⟨indefinite loop⟩

⟨input statement⟩ ::= **read** ⟨variable list⟩

⟨output statement⟩ ::= **write** ⟨variable list⟩

⟨variable list⟩ ::= ⟨variable⟩ | ⟨variable list⟩ , ⟨variable⟩

⟨assignment statement⟩ ::= ⟨variable⟩ := ⟨expression⟩

⟨conditional statement⟩ ::= **if** ⟨comparison⟩ **then** ⟨series⟩ **fi** |
    if ⟨comparison⟩ **then** ⟨series⟩ **else** ⟨series⟩ **fi**

⟨definite loop⟩ ::= **to** ⟨expression⟩ **do** ⟨series⟩ **end**

⟨indefinite loop⟩ ::= **while** ⟨comparison⟩ **do** ⟨series⟩ **end**

⟨comparison⟩ ::= ⟨expression⟩ ⟨relation⟩ ⟨expression⟩

⟨expression⟩ ::= ⟨term⟩ | ⟨expression⟩ ⟨weak operator⟩ ⟨term⟩

⟨term⟩ ::= ⟨element⟩ | ⟨term⟩ ⟨strong operator⟩ ⟨element⟩

⟨element⟩ ::= ⟨constant⟩ | ⟨variable⟩ | (⟨expression⟩)

⟨constant⟩ ::= ⟨digit⟩ | ⟨constant⟩ ⟨digit⟩

⟨variable⟩ ::= ⟨letter⟩ | ⟨variable⟩ ⟨letter⟩ | ⟨variable⟩ ⟨digit⟩

⟨relation⟩ ::= = | =< | < | > | >= | <>

⟨weak operator⟩ ::= + | −

⟨strong operator⟩ ::= * | /

⟨digit⟩ ::= 0 | 1 | 2 | 3 | 4 | 5 | 6 | 7 | 8 | 9

⟨letter⟩ ::= a | b | c | d | e | f | g | h | i | j | k | l | m |
    n | o | p | q | r | s | t | u | v | w | x | y | z

The grammar of Table 2.1 is a complete and exact syntactic description of Pam in the sense that it generates all valid Pam program texts and no terminal strings that are not valid program texts.

EXERCISES

1. Referring to Table 2.1, draw the complete syntax tree for a small Pam program.

2. Write a Pam program that reads a positive integer n and prints the smallest perfect number greater than n. [A perfect number is equal to the sum of its divisors, including 1; thus 6 ($= 1 + 2 + 3$) is a perfect number.] Be sure that your program is syntactically correct with respect to Table 2.1.

3. Rewrite the grammar in Table 2.1 using as few different nonterminals (and hence as few production rules) as possible.

4. Some languages, such as PL/I, employ the semicolon as a statement *terminator*, i.e., as the last symbol of every statement, instead of as a *separator* as in Pam and several actual Algol-like languages. Rewrite the grammar of Table 2.1 to define a dialect of Pam that uses semicolons as terminators.

2.1.3   The Language Eva

Eva incorporates the following significant concepts and features not present in Pam: identifiers of different types (**char**, **string**, and **proc**), a composite data structure (string values) and associated operations (**head**, **tail**, **cons**), declarations, block structure, recursive procedures, and parameter passing. The scale of the language is nevertheless quite small, as can be seen from the BNF grammar of Table 2.2.

Viewed strictly as a formal system for generating terminal strings, this grammar should present no difficulties. It may be noted that there are no explicit symbols such as semicolons for separating or terminating ⟨declaration⟩s or ⟨statement⟩s. An ⟨expression⟩ of the form "X", where X is a ⟨letter sequence⟩, is a ⟨char expression⟩ if the length of X is 1 and a ⟨string expression⟩ if the length of X is either 0 or greater than 1. (This does not imply that the value of a string variable cannot consist of one character; it is simply that such string values cannot be directly specified by constants in a program.) The constant **space** represents the blank character value. The conditional statement forms

$$\textbf{eq } E_1, E_2 : S$$

$$\textbf{neq } E_1, E_2 : S$$

where S is a ⟨statement⟩ and E_1 and E_2 are either both ⟨char expression⟩s or both ⟨string expression⟩s, would be more conventionally written as

$$\textbf{if } E_1 = E_2 \textbf{ then S fi}$$

$$\textbf{if } E_1 \neq E_2 \textbf{ then S fi}$$

A compound ⟨statement⟩ consists of a parenthesized ⟨statement sequence⟩; note that this is syntactically distinct from a ⟨block⟩, which is also a type of ⟨statement⟩, in that a ⟨block⟩ includes ⟨declaration⟩s and is enclosed by **begin** and **end**.

As for the intended semantics of the various constructs, the execution of a statement **input** N will cause the next character in the input data stream

TABLE 2.2 BNF Grammar for Eva

⟨program⟩ ::= ⟨block⟩

⟨block⟩ ::= **begin** ⟨declaration sequence⟩ ⟨statement sequence⟩ **end**

⟨declaration sequence⟩ ::= ⟨declaration⟩ |
    ⟨declaration sequence⟩ ⟨declaration⟩

⟨declaration⟩ ::= ⟨declarer⟩ ⟨name list⟩ | **proc** ⟨name⟩ = ⟨statement⟩ |
    proc ⟨name⟩ (⟨parameter list⟩) = ⟨statement⟩

⟨parameter list⟩ ::= ⟨declarer⟩ ⟨name list⟩ |
    ⟨parameter list⟩ , ⟨declarer⟩ ⟨name list⟩

⟨declarer⟩ ::= **char** | **string**

⟨name list⟩ ::= ⟨name⟩ | ⟨name list⟩ , ⟨name⟩

⟨statement sequence⟩ ::= ⟨statement⟩ | ⟨statement sequence⟩ ⟨statement⟩

⟨statement⟩ ::= **input** ⟨name⟩ | **output** ⟨char expression⟩ |
    call ⟨name⟩ | **call** ⟨name⟩ (⟨expression list⟩) |
    ⟨block⟩ | (⟨statement sequence⟩) |
    ⟨test⟩ ⟨pair⟩ : ⟨statement⟩ | **cons** ⟨char expression⟩ , ⟨name⟩

⟨test⟩ ::= **eq** | **neq**

⟨pair⟩ ::= ⟨char expression⟩ , ⟨char expression⟩ |
    ⟨string expression⟩ , ⟨string expression⟩

⟨expression list⟩ ::= ⟨expression⟩ | ⟨expression list⟩ , ⟨expression⟩

⟨expression⟩ ::= ⟨char expression⟩ | ⟨string expression⟩

⟨char expression⟩ ::= ⟨name⟩ | " ⟨letter⟩ " | **space** |
    head ⟨string expression⟩

⟨string expression⟩ ::= ⟨name⟩ | "" | " ⟨letter⟩ ⟨letter sequence⟩ " |
    tail ⟨string expression⟩

⟨name⟩ ::= ⟨letter sequence⟩

⟨letter sequence⟩ ::= ⟨letter⟩ | ⟨letter sequence⟩ ⟨letter⟩

⟨letter⟩ ::= a | b | c | d | e | f | g | h | i | j | k | l | m | n | o | p |
    q | r | s | t | u | v | w | x | y | z

to be associated with the ⟨name⟩ N, **output** E will cause the character that is the value of the ⟨char expression⟩ E to be appended to the output stream (e.g., printed), and **cons** E, N will cause the character that is the value of E to be prefixed to the string value of N, thus changing the value of N (in PL/I

terms, for example, it is equivalent to the assignment statement N = E | | N;).
A variable of type **string** has the null string as its initial value. The value of
head E is the first character in the non-null string value of E, and the value
of **tail** E is the string consisting of all but the first of the characters in the value
of E; if the value of E is the null string in these contexts, then we have a
semantic error. A **string** value consisting of one character is distinct from the
corresponding **char** value (cf. the distinction, in most common languages,
between an array with one element and a scalar value), and there are no
automatic type conversions from one to the other. The block and procedure
mechanisms are basically Algol-like (i.e., locally declared variables are created
on entry and deleted on exit), and parameters are passed by value.

Although Eva is nominally a language for character manipulation (letters
and blanks only), the primitive nature of its operations, the dearth of control
structures, and the lack of an **integer** data type prevent it from being useful as
a programming tool in this area except for a very narrow class of problems.

The following sample program outputs a copy of its input, which is
assumed to be terminated by the character z:

```
begin
    char ch
    proc copy = (
        input ch
        neq ch, "z": (
            output ch
            call copy ) )
    call copy
end
```

Note that recursion is the only means of achieving indefinite repetition of a
statement or group of statements.

The next program inputs data consisting of words separated by one or
more blanks and terminated by a dummy word zz, and outputs the words in
reverse order separated by single blanks:

```
begin
    char c
    proc printword (string word) = (
        neq tail word, "":
            call printword (tail word)
        output head word )
```

```
proc control = begin
    string w
    proc readword = (
        cons c, w
        input c
        neq c, space : call readword )
    call skipblanks
    call readword
    neq w, "zz": (
        call control
        output space
        call printword (w) ) end
    proc skipblanks = (
        input c
        eq c, space: call skipblanks )
    call control
end
```

The position of the procedure *skipblanks* illustrates the fact that a ⟨name⟩ may be used at a textually earlier point than its declaration. It is essential that *w* be local to the procedure *control*, since its value is set before and used after a recursive call. Since the procedure *readword* accesses and alters the value of *w*, its declaration is also placed inside *control*.

The grammar of Table 2.2 is an incomplete syntactic description of Eva in the sense that not all the terminal strings generated will be regarded as valid program texts. There is in fact no BNF grammar that generates all and only the legal Eva programs. Another way of saying this is that the set of Eva programs is not a context-free language and that Eva therefore has *context-sensitive* aspects. The latter may be informally indicated by a set of restrictions or *context conditions* as follows:

1. Each distinct ⟨name⟩ may be declared at most once in the ⟨declaration sequence⟩ of any ⟨block⟩ and listed at most once in any ⟨parameter list⟩.
2. A ⟨name⟩ contained in a ⟨statement⟩ S must either be declared in some ⟨block⟩ containing S or listed in the ⟨parameter list⟩ of some procedure containing S. If there is more than one such defining occurrence of the ⟨name⟩, it is the innermost one that applies in S.
3. The ⟨name⟩ in an **input** statement must be of type **char**.
4. The ⟨name⟩ in a **call** statement must be of type **proc**. If the procedure

so named has parameters, an equal number of ⟨expression⟩s must be present in the call, and the type (**char** or **string**) of each ⟨expression⟩ must match the type of the corresponding parameter.

5. The ⟨name⟩ in a **cons** statement must be of type **string**.
6. A ⟨name⟩ that forms a ⟨char expression⟩ must be of type **char**, and a ⟨name⟩ that forms a ⟨string expression⟩ must be of type **string**.

A terminal string that forms a ⟨program⟩ is a valid program only if it satisfies these context conditions.

As an illustration of the implications of condition (2), consider a program with the following outline:

```
begin
    proc p (char x)  =
            . . .                   (Region A—body of p)
    string a
    begin
        char a, b
            . . .                   (Region B—statements of inner block)
    end
            . . .                   (Region C—remaining statements of
                                     outer block)
    end
```

The inner block is acting as the first statement of the outer block. Any use of a and b in Region B refers to the locally declared variables, which are not accessible in any of the other regions. Similarly, any use of x in Region A refers to p's parameter, which is not accessible elsewhere. Since it is declared at the outer level, the scope of p is the whole program, i.e., it may be accessed (called) from Regions A, B, and C. The same would be true of the string variable a if there were not another a declared in the inner block; as it is, the outer a has a "hole" in its scope and can be accessed from Regions A and C only. Thus the expression **tail** a would be syntactically valid in Regions A and C but not in B. These scope rules are similar to those of many well-known, block-structured languages such as PL/I and Pascal.

EXERCISES

1. Refer to Table 2.2 and draw the complete syntax tree for a small Eva program.

2. Write an Eva program that inputs any string of letters and blanks terminated by a z and outputs the letters only in reverse order. Be sure that your program is

syntactically correct not only with respect to the grammar but also with respect to the context conditions.

3. Modify the grammar of Table 2.2 so that all the ⟨declaration⟩s in a ⟨block⟩ are no longer required to precede all the ⟨statement⟩s. An executable statement could then be immediately followed by a declaration, as in PL/I.

For Further Information

BNF is described in numerous books on the structure, description, and implementation of programming languages. Cleaveland and Uzgalis (1977, pp. 1–33) and Gries (1971, pp. 12–43), for example, provide good discussions of this metalanguage and its formal properties. The prime example of a BNF definition of the context-free aspects of a significant programming language is that of Algol 60 (Naur, 1963). Context-free grammars, when subjected to various restrictions, enable practical programs for the syntactic analysis of programming languages to be generated automatically. This important and successful application of formal specification is described by Gries (1971), by McKeeman et al (1970), and by the authors of several more recent books on compiler design.

2.2
VARIATIONS ON BNF

"Pure" BNF as described in the previous section is often rather verbose and awkward. In order to reduce the size and increase the clarity of grammars, it is common practice to augment the metalanguage with a few notational devices such as those described in this section. These devices do not provide a mathematically more powerful formalism; the expressible grammars are still the context-free grammars, and all languages definable in terms of them are also definable in pure BNF.

One of the most common extensions is the use of square brackets as metasymbols, indicating that the enclosed sequence of symbols is optional. This can reduce the number of nonterminal symbols and the number of alternatives in production rules; for example, the Pam ⟨conditional statement⟩ can now be defined as

⟨conditional statement⟩ ::= **if** ⟨comparison⟩ **then** ⟨series⟩ [**else** ⟨series⟩] **fi**

and the Eva ⟨declaration⟩ as

⟨declaration⟩ ::= ⟨declarer⟩ ⟨name list⟩ |
    proc ⟨name⟩ [(⟨parameter list⟩)] = ⟨statement⟩

Another very common extension is the use of braces as metasymbols, indicating that the enclosed sequence of symbols occurs any number of times (zero or more) in succession, thus providing a kind of "iterative" facility that can often be used in place of recursion. (This is analogous to the use of loops in programs instead of recursive procedures when the former are simpler and clearer.) For example,

$$\langle constant \rangle ::= \langle digit \rangle \mid \langle constant \rangle \langle digit \rangle$$

can be replaced by the nonrecursive rule

$$\langle constant \rangle ::= \langle digit \rangle \{ \langle digit \rangle \}$$

and

$$\langle series \rangle ::= \langle statement \rangle \mid \langle series \rangle ; \langle statement \rangle$$

can be replaced by

$$\langle series \rangle ::= \langle statement \rangle \{ ; \langle statement \rangle \}$$

Moreover, these rules can be eliminated completely if we are willing to replace all occurrences of $\langle constant \rangle$ and $\langle series \rangle$ in other rules by $\langle digit \rangle \{ \langle digit \rangle \}$ and $\langle statement \rangle \{ ; \langle statement \rangle \}$, respectively.

This extension suggests the use of a modified type of syntax tree in which there is no limit to the number of offspring of a node labeled with a nonterminal defined in an iterative rule. Pure BNF would imply tree fragments such as those shown in Fig. 2.7, whereas the corresponding tree fragments implied by the extended notation would be those of Fig. 2.8. Sometimes this is all the syntactic structure we are interested in. It could then be said that with pure BNF the structure is overspecified; it would still be overspecified, but in a different way, if right-recursion instead of left-recursion were used.

A grammar for Pam expressed in extended BNF is given in Table 2.3. Note that an $\langle expression \rangle$ is now characterized as a sequence of one or more $\langle term \rangle$s separated by $\langle weak operator \rangle$s, where a $\langle term \rangle$ is a sequence of one

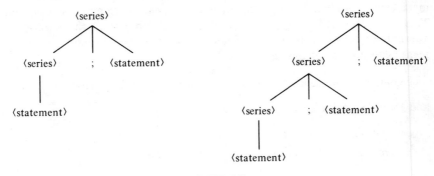

FIGURE 2.7

or more ⟨element⟩s separated by ⟨strong operator⟩s. The meta-expression

$$\{ \ \langle letter \rangle \mid \langle digit \rangle \ \}$$

denotes a sequence of zero or more ⟨letter⟩s and/or ⟨digit⟩s.

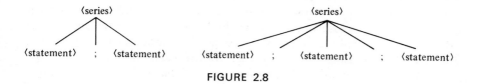

FIGURE 2.8

TABLE 2.3 Grammar for Pam Using Extended BNF

⟨program⟩ ::= ⟨series⟩

⟨series⟩ ::= ⟨statement⟩ { ; ⟨statement⟩ }

⟨statement⟩ ::= ⟨input statement⟩ | ⟨output statement⟩ |
     ⟨assignment statement⟩ | ⟨conditional statement⟩ |
     ⟨definite loop⟩ | ⟨indefinite loop⟩

⟨input statement⟩ ::= **read** ⟨variable⟩ { , ⟨variable⟩ }

⟨output statement⟩ ::= **write** ⟨variable⟩ { , ⟨variable⟩ }

⟨assignment statement⟩ ::= ⟨variable⟩ := ⟨expression⟩

⟨conditional statement⟩ ::= **if** ⟨comparison⟩ **then** ⟨series⟩ [**else** ⟨series⟩] **fi**

⟨definite loop⟩ ::= **to** ⟨expression⟩ **do** ⟨series⟩ **end**

⟨indefinite loop⟩ ::= **while** ⟨comparison⟩ **do** ⟨series⟩ **end**

⟨comparison⟩ ::= ⟨expression⟩ ⟨relation⟩ ⟨expression⟩

⟨expression⟩ ::= ⟨term⟩ { ⟨weak operator⟩ ⟨term⟩ }

⟨term⟩ ::= ⟨element⟩ { ⟨strong operator⟩ ⟨element⟩ }

⟨element⟩ ::= ⟨constant⟩ | ⟨variable⟩ | (⟨expression⟩)

⟨constant⟩ ::= ⟨digit⟩ { ⟨digit⟩ }

⟨variable⟩ ::= ⟨letter⟩ { ⟨letter ⟩ | ⟨digit⟩ }

⟨relation⟩ ::= = | =< | < | > | >= | <>

⟨weak operator⟩ ::= + | −

⟨strong operator⟩ ::= * | /

⟨digit⟩ ::= 0 | 1 | 2 | 3 | 4 | 5 | 6 | 7 | 8 | 9

⟨letter⟩ ::= a | b | c | d | e | f | g | h | i | j | k | l | m | n | o | p |
     q | r | s | t | u | v | w | x | y | z

A modified grammar for Eva is shown in Table 2.4. The BNF extensions have effectively compressed the production rules but cannot contribute to the specification of the context conditions.

Conflict between metalanguage and subject language is a potential source of difficulty for the types of grammar considered so far. If the subject language makes use of symbols such as '|', square brackets, or braces, which are also metasymbols, the production rules may be confusing or ambiguous. There is no standard way of resolving such difficulties; the possibilities include quoting the terminal symbols (assuming that the quotes cannot be terminal symbols themselves!) and using a special typeface for the metasymbols.

Many other notational variations on BNF have also been employed. For example, the notation {...}/ has been used to denote any number *n* of

TABLE 2.4 Grammar for Eva Using Extended BNF

⟨program⟩ ::= ⟨block⟩
⟨block⟩ ::= **begin** ⟨declaration⟩ { ⟨declaration⟩ } ⟨statement⟩ { ⟨statement⟩ } **end**
⟨declaration⟩ ::= ⟨declarer⟩ ⟨name list⟩ |

    proc ⟨name⟩ [(⟨parameter list⟩)] = ⟨statement⟩
⟨parameter list⟩ ::= ⟨declarer⟩ ⟨name list⟩ { , ⟨declarer⟩ ⟨name list⟩ }
⟨declarer⟩ ::= **char** | **string**
⟨name list⟩ ::= ⟨name⟩ { , ⟨name⟩ }

⟨statement⟩ ::= **input** ⟨name⟩ | **output** ⟨char expression⟩ |

    call ⟨name⟩ [(⟨expression⟩ { , ⟨expression⟩ })] |

    ⟨block⟩ | (⟨statement⟩ { ⟨statement⟩ }) |

    ⟨test⟩ ⟨pair⟩ : ⟨statement⟩ | **cons** ⟨char expression⟩ , ⟨name⟩
⟨test⟩ ::= **eq** | **neq**
⟨pair⟩ ::= ⟨char expression⟩ , ⟨char expression⟩ |

    ⟨string expression⟩ , ⟨string expression⟩

⟨expression⟩ ::= ⟨char expression⟩ | ⟨string expression⟩
⟨char expression⟩ ::= ⟨name⟩ | " ⟨letter⟩ " | **space** |

    head ⟨string expression⟩
⟨string expression⟩ ::= ⟨name⟩ | "" | " ⟨letter⟩ ⟨letter⟩ { ⟨letter⟩ } " |

    tail ⟨string expression⟩
⟨name⟩ ::= ⟨letter⟩ { ⟨letter⟩ }
⟨letter⟩ ::= a | b | c | d | e | f | g | h | i | j | k | l | m | n | o | p | q | r | s |

    t | u | v | w | x | y | z

occurrences of the enclosed sequence of symbols such that $i \leq n \leq j$. Then, if

$$\langle\text{alphanum}\rangle ::= \langle\text{letter}\rangle \mid \langle\text{digit}\rangle$$

the syntax of a Fortran identifier can be simply specified as

$$\langle\text{identifier}\rangle ::= \langle\text{letter}\rangle \{ \langle\text{alphanum}\rangle \}_0^5$$

instead of as

$\langle\text{identifier}\rangle ::= \langle\text{letter}\rangle \mid \langle\text{letter}\rangle \langle\text{alphanum}\rangle \mid$
  $\langle\text{letter}\rangle \langle\text{alphanum}\rangle \langle\text{alphanum}\rangle \mid$
  $\langle\text{letter}\rangle \langle\text{alphanum}\rangle \langle\text{alphanum}\rangle \langle\text{alphanum}\rangle \mid$
  $\langle\text{letter}\rangle \langle\text{alphanum}\rangle \langle\text{alphanum}\rangle \langle\text{alphanum}\rangle \langle\text{alphanum}\rangle \mid$
  $\langle\text{letter}\rangle \langle\text{alphanum}\rangle \langle\text{alphanum}\rangle \langle\text{alphanum}\rangle \langle\text{alphanum}\rangle \langle\text{alphanum}\rangle$

Some grammar writers dispense with the brackets '⟨' and '⟩' for nonterminals and distinguish between terminals and nonterminals in a different way, such as using all uppercase for the former and mostly lowercase for the latter with no internal blanks:

conditionalStatement := IF comparison THEN series [ELSE series] FI

Such variations present no difficulty as far as understanding is concerned, provided that the notational conventions are unambiguous and have been clearly explained.

For some subject languages, such as Cobol and PL/I, much greater conciseness of specification can be achieved by using a two-dimensional layout whereby alternatives may be listed vertically within a large pair of braces. Square brackets indicate optionality, and '. . .' (not braces) denotes arbitrary repetition of the preceding unit. For example, the following could be a specification for a simple Cobol-like ADD command:

add-sentence:

$$\text{ADD} \begin{Bmatrix} \text{constant} \\ \text{variable} \end{Bmatrix} \left[, \begin{Bmatrix} \text{constant} \\ \text{variable} \end{Bmatrix} \right] \cdots \begin{Bmatrix} \text{TO} \\ \text{GIVING} \end{Bmatrix} \text{variable}$$

An equivalent set of rules in pure BNF would be the following:

$\langle\text{add sentence}\rangle ::= \text{ADD} \langle\text{operand list}\rangle \langle\text{key}\rangle \langle\text{variable}\rangle$
$\langle\text{operand list}\rangle ::= \langle\text{operand}\rangle \mid \langle\text{operand list}\rangle , \langle\text{operand}\rangle$
$\langle\text{operand}\rangle ::= \langle\text{constant}\rangle \mid \langle\text{variable}\rangle$
$\langle\text{key}\rangle ::= \text{TO} \mid \text{GIVING}$

In a unit of the form [{---}], the braces may be omitted without ambiguity. The following defines the syntax of a PL/I loop specification:

specification:

$$\text{expression} \begin{bmatrix} \text{TO expression [BY expression]} \\ \text{BY expression [TO expression]} \end{bmatrix} \text{[WHILE (expression)]}$$

An equivalent set of pure BNF rules would be:

⟨specification⟩ ::= ⟨expression⟩ | ⟨expression⟩ ⟨rest⟩

⟨rest⟩ ::= ⟨to and by part⟩ | ⟨while part⟩ |

    ⟨to and by part⟩ ⟨while part⟩

⟨to and by part⟩ ::= ⟨to part⟩ | ⟨to part⟩ ⟨by part⟩ |

    ⟨by part⟩ | ⟨by part⟩ ⟨to part⟩

⟨to part⟩ ::= TO ⟨expression⟩

⟨by part⟩ ::= BY ⟨expression⟩

⟨while part⟩ ::= WHILE (⟨expression⟩)

EXERCISE

1. Translate each of the following into pure BNF:
   (a) ⟨Fortran DO statement⟩ ::=

   [⟨label⟩] DO ⟨label⟩ ⟨variable⟩ = ⟨initial⟩ ,
   ⟨limit⟩ [, ⟨increment⟩]

   (b) ⟨Pascal var decl⟩ ::= **var** ⟨var decl⟩ {; ⟨var decl⟩} ;
   ⟨var decl⟩ ::= ⟨identifier⟩ {, ⟨identifier⟩} : ⟨type⟩
   (c) PL/I block:

   [label :] ... BEGIN ; $\begin{Bmatrix} \text{declaration} \\ \text{command} \end{Bmatrix}$ ... END [label] ;

For Further Information

Pascal (Jensen and Wirth, 1974) is a well-known example of a language which was specified with the aid of BNF extended with braces as metasymbols. The two-dimensional notation is briefly described in the book by Cleaveland and Uzgalis (1977, pp. 35–38), as well as in many other places, and is given a formal treatment by Rochester (1966). Most manuals and other reference works on Cobol and PL/I employ this notation. Other variations on BNF are usually explained wherever they are used.

2.3

ATTRIBUTE GRAMMARS

2.3.1 Concepts and Characteristics

The specification technique described in this section may be used to formalize not only the context-free aspects of the syntax of a subject language but also the context-sensitive aspects. It is thus inherently more powerful than BNF or any of its variants described in the last section. A language specification constructed using this technique is called an *attribute grammar*. After introducing the basic tools and concepts, we shall illustrate the use of the approach by constructing an attribute grammar which constitutes a complete, formal definition of the syntax of Eva.

Basically, an attribute grammar is a context-free grammar augmented with certain formal devices ("attributes," "evaluation rules," and "conditions") that enable the non-context-free aspects to be specified by means of a powerful and elegant mechanism. In this book, we shall always employ the standard, unextended BNF notation for the context-free component of an attribute grammar.

With each distinct symbol of the context-free grammar, there is associated a finite set of *attributes*, which, notationally, are just names. (We adopt the convention that words with the first letter capitalized are attribute names.) With each distinct attribute, moreover, there is associated a domain of *values*. A given attribute may be associated with any number of grammatical symbols. We may regard each node of the syntax tree of a valid program as being labeled not only by a grammatical symbol but also by a set of attribute-value pairs, one for each attribute associated with the symbol, and possibly by a logical *condition* expressing a constraint that must be satisfied by the attribute values involved. The value associated with an attribute occurrence in the tree is determined by various *evaluation rules* associated with the grammar's production rules. Obviously, an example is needed to clarify these points.

Suppose that we are defining a machine-dependent dialect of PL/I for use on a computer with 32-bit words and that, as a consequence, an unsigned integer constant is to be considered syntactically invalid if its value exceeds $2^{31} - 1$ ($= 2,147,483,647$). While the set of *all* unsigned numerals is easily defined by the production rules

$$\langle numeral \rangle ::= \langle digit \rangle \mid \langle numeral \rangle \langle digit \rangle$$
$$\langle digit \rangle ::= 0 \mid 1 \mid 2 \mid 3 \mid 4 \mid 5 \mid 6 \mid 7 \mid 8 \mid 9$$

the set of numerals $\{0, 1, \ldots, 2147483646, 2147483647\}$ is difficult to define concisely in BNF or its variants (try it!). Instead, we associate an attribute

Val, corresponding to the domain of integers, with both of the symbols ⟨numeral⟩ and ⟨digit⟩ and write the following specifications:

> ⟨numeral⟩ ::= ⟨digit⟩
>   Val(⟨numeral⟩) ⟵ Val(⟨digit⟩)
> | ⟨numeral⟩₂ ⟨digit⟩
>   Val(⟨numeral⟩) ⟵ 10 × Val(⟨numeral⟩₂) + Val(⟨digit⟩)
>   Condition: Val(⟨numeral⟩) ≤ 2,147,483,647
>
> ⟨digit⟩ ::= 0
>   Val(⟨digit⟩) ⟵ 0
> | ...
>
>   ...
>
> | 9
>   Val(⟨digit⟩) ⟵ 9

The notation Val(S), where S is a grammatical symbol, may be read as 'the value of the attribute Val for this occurrence of S', and a line of the form

$$\text{Val}(S) \longleftarrow E$$

where E may be any integer-valued expression, is an evaluation rule that "assigns" a value to Val(S). Each alternative definition in a production rule has an associated set of evaluation rules and possibly a condition. Observe the layout conventions used—each evaluation rule or condition refers to the alternative above it. The only purpose of the subscript in the symbol ⟨numeral⟩₂ is to distinguish the two occurrences of ⟨numeral⟩ in the specifications.

To see how the rules work for a legal example, the basic form of the syntax tree for the terminal string 909 is that shown in Fig. 2.9. Note that we have written the attribute Val under each occurrence of a nonterminal symbol and the word Cond (for 'condition') at each fork corresponding to the second alternative of the first production rule (⟨numeral⟩ ::= ⟨numeral⟩₂ ⟨digit⟩). Now, using the evaluation rules associated with the production rules that were used to build the tree, we must fill in the attribute values and check that all the conditions are satisfied. We are allowed to do this in any order permitted by the evaluation rules. (The resulting attribute values should be the same regardless of the order of computation. If this is not the case, then the grammar is not well formed.) The evaluation rule

$$\text{Val}(\langle\text{numeral}\rangle) \longleftarrow 10 \times \text{Val}(\langle\text{numeral}\rangle_2) + \text{Val}(\langle\text{digit}\rangle)$$

implies that the Val value at the top node cannot be filled in until we know

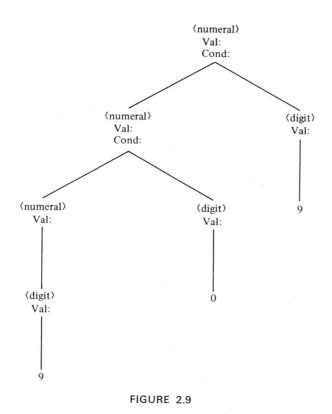

FIGURE 2.9

the values at its two offspring. Similarly, the values at the other two ⟨numeral⟩ nodes cannot be filled in until the values at their offspring are known. However, using the evaluation rules

$$\text{Val}(\langle\text{digit}\rangle) \leftarrow 0$$

and

$$\text{Val}(\langle\text{digit}\rangle) \leftarrow 9$$

the values at the three ⟨digit⟩ nodes can be filled (Fig. 2.10). Now, using the rule

$$\text{Val}(\langle\text{numeral}\rangle) \leftarrow \text{Val}(\langle\text{digit}\rangle)$$

we have Fig. 2.11. Next, the rule

$$\text{Val}(\langle\text{numeral}\rangle) \leftarrow 10 \times \text{Val}(\langle\text{numeral}\rangle_2) + \text{Val}(\langle\text{digit}\rangle)$$

is used, resulting in Fig. 2.12, and the condition $90 \leq 2{,}147{,}483{,}647$ is seen

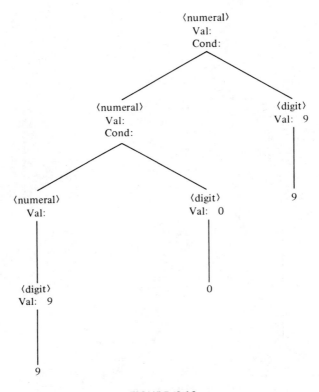

FIGURE 2.10

to be true. Repeating this process, the final tree is constructed as in Fig. 2.13. It should be clear that the tree for a numeral whose value exceeds 2,147,483,647 would contain a false condition, thus ruling out that string as one which is generated by the attribute grammar.

In this example, we have seen that the attribute value at each node in the tree is obtained from the values at the offspring of the node, so that, in a sense, we have information moving upward through the tree from the leaves to the root. Because of this, Val is said to be a *synthesized* attribute of ⟨numeral⟩ and of ⟨digit⟩. It is also possible for an attribute value at a node labeled by a symbol S to be obtained from the node's parent; the attribute is then said to be an *inherited* attribute of S. In general, a given grammatical symbol may have both synthesized and inherited attributes, and a given attribute may be synthesized with respect to one symbol and inherited with respect to another.

As a small example involving the use of an inherited attribute, consider the "Hollerith literals" of Fortran. These are essentially string constants,

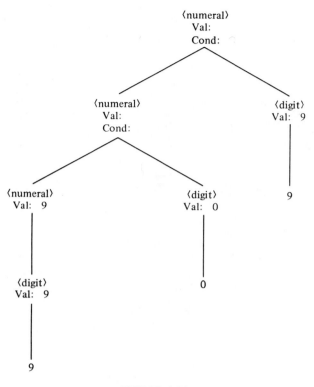

FIGURE 2.11

where the actual characters in the string are preceded by the letter H, which is itself preceded by an integer constant giving the length of the string. The following are some examples: 1HA, 6HSTRING, 15HA LONGER STRING. The number of characters following the H must be equal to the value of the integer constant preceding it. Clearly, the existence of an attribute grammar for this set of strings will demonstrate the superiority of this formalism over BNF.

We make use of two attributes, Val and Size, both corresponding to the domain of positive integer values. Val is a synthesized attribute of $\langle$numeral$\rangle$ and $\langle$digit$\rangle$, as in the previous example:

$\langle$numeral$\rangle$ ::= $\langle$digit$\rangle$

Val($\langle$numeral$\rangle$) $\longleftarrow$ Val($\langle$digit$\rangle$)

| $\langle$numeral$\rangle_2$ $\langle$digit$\rangle$

Val($\langle$numeral$\rangle$) $\longleftarrow$ 10 $\times$ Val($\langle$numeral$\rangle_2$) + Val($\langle$digit$\rangle$)

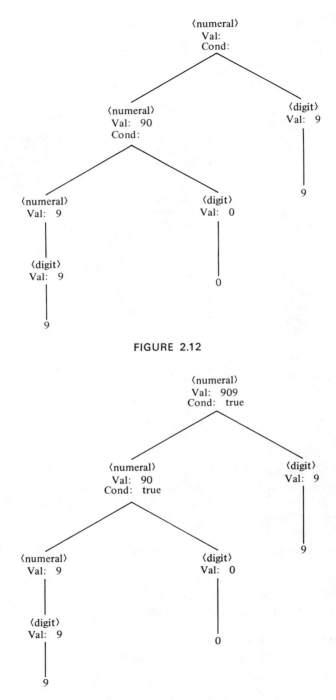

FIGURE 2.12

FIGURE 2.13

$\langle$digit$\rangle$ ::= 0

         Val($\langle$digit$\rangle$) $\leftarrow$ 0

   | ...

      ...

   | 9

         Val($\langle$digit$\rangle$) $\leftarrow$ 9

Size is an inherited attribute of the symbol $\langle$string$\rangle$, which is defined as follows:

         $\langle$string$\rangle$ ::= $\langle$char$\rangle$

            Condition: Size($\langle$string$\rangle$) = 1

        | $\langle$string$\rangle_2$ $\langle$char$\rangle$

            Size($\langle$string$\rangle_2$) $\leftarrow$ Size($\langle$string$\rangle$) $-$ 1

       $\langle$char$\rangle$ ::= $\langle$digit$\rangle$ | A | B | ...

(The symbol $\langle$char$\rangle$ has no synthesized or inherited attributes.) Now the following rules state that the size (> 0) inherited by the $\langle$string$\rangle$ following the H in a Hollerith literal is the value synthesized from the initial $\langle$numeral$\rangle$:

         $\langle$literal$\rangle$ ::= $\langle$numeral$\rangle$ H $\langle$string$\rangle$

         Size($\langle$string$\rangle$) $\leftarrow$ Val($\langle$numeral$\rangle$)

         Condition: Val($\langle$numeral$\rangle$) > 0

Figure 2.14 shows the complete tree for the literal 2HAB. The numbers preceding the attribute occurrences and conditions indicate the order in which the values were filled in. Observe how information moves up the $\langle$numeral$\rangle$ subtree and then down the $\langle$string$\rangle$ subtree. The illegal string 2HA is disallowed because a false condition arises, as shown in Fig. 2.15. Similarly, 1HAB is disallowed (Fig. 2.16).

Intuitively, a synthesized attribute at a node corresponds to information arising from the internal constituents of that construct, while an inherited attribute corresponds to information arising from the external context of the construct. Under each alternative of a production rule, there must be an evaluation rule for each *synthesized* attribute of the symbol on the *left* (the symbol being defined) and for each *inherited* attribute of *each* symbol on the *right* (each symbol in the alternative). This provides us with a useful aid for checking the completeness of complex attribute grammars.

There is no really "standard" metalanguage for attribute grammars that has been generally adopted by all grammar writers. Although the underlying mechanism would be the same, the previous examples could well have been specified using different conventions and notations, especially with

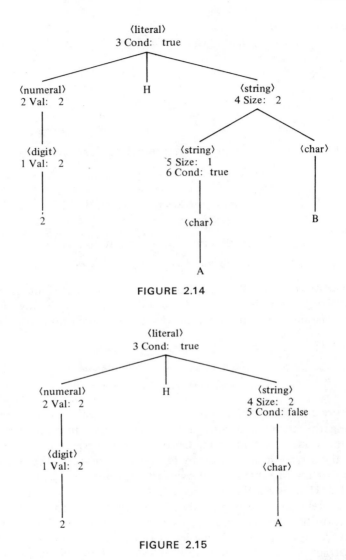

FIGURE 2.14

FIGURE 2.15

respect to the evaluation rules and conditions. More complicated grammars require additional notation, since it is generally necessary to deal with structured, nonnumeric domains of attribute values. For our purposes, we will make use of value domains that are *enumerations, sets, tuples,* or *sequences,* according to the following conventions:

1. The "constants" of an enumeration domain are arbitrarily chosen names enclosed in single quotes, e.g., 'full', 'empty'.

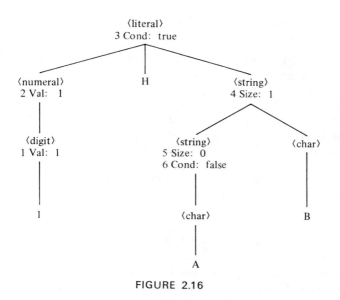

FIGURE 2.16

2. For sets, the evaluation rules will employ the usual notation, including the following symbols: { } (set brackets), ∪ (union), ∈ (membership).

3. Tuples belonging to a given domain consist of a fixed number of values, possibly of different types, in a certain order. The notation (..., ...) may be used to specify a tuple value in terms of its components. For example, (17, 'a') denotes an ordered pair where the first component is the integer 17 and the second component is the character 'a'. The primitive functions *field₁*, *field₂*, ... may be used to extract the components of a tuple.

4. A sequence is an ordered collection of any number of values of the same type. The notation ⟨..., ...⟩ denotes a sequence, and ⟨ ⟩ denotes the empty sequence. The following primitive functions apply to sequences:

   - *append*(s, v). The sequence obtained by adding the value v to the end of the sequence s.
   - *concat*(s₁, s₂, ..., sₙ). The sequence obtained by joining the sequences s₁, s₂, ..., sₙ in order.
   - *length*(s). The number of elements in the sequence s.
   - *first*(s). The first element of the sequence s.
   - *last*(s). The last element of the sequence s.

- *tail*(s). The sequence obtained by deleting the first element of the sequence s.
- *allbutlast*(s). The sequence obtained by deleting the last element of the sequence s.

The usual notations for arithmetic and logic will also be used freely. Sometimes it is desirable or necessary to make use of separately defined auxiliary functions in the evaluation rules; a self-explanatory notation similar to that commonly used in mathematical descriptions will be used to define such functions.

For the sake of uniformity, we further decree that the specification of a subject language by means of an attribute grammar will consist of four parts:

1. *Attributes and values* (a list of the attributes used and their corresponding value domains).
2. *Attributes associated with nonterminal symbols* (a table showing the sets of inherited and synthesized attributes associated with each nonterminal symbol of the grammar).
3. *Production and attribute evaluation rules* (the grammar itself, laid out according to the conventions introduced earlier).
4. *Definition of auxiliary evaluation functions.*

EXERCISES

1. Determine the set of terminal strings generated by the following attribute grammar, where Size is a synthesized attribute of $\langle x \text{ string} \rangle$ and an inherited attribute of $\langle y \text{ string} \rangle$ and $\langle z \text{ string} \rangle$:

$$\langle \text{string} \rangle ::= \langle x \text{ string} \rangle \; \langle y \text{ string} \rangle \; \langle z \text{ string} \rangle$$
$$\text{Size}(\langle y \text{ string} \rangle) \longleftarrow \text{Size}(\langle x \text{ string} \rangle)$$
$$\text{Size}(\langle z \text{ string} \rangle) \longleftarrow \text{Size}(\langle x \text{ string} \rangle)$$

$$\langle x \text{ string} \rangle ::= x$$
$$\text{Size}(\langle x \text{ string} \rangle) \longleftarrow 1$$
$$| \; \langle x \text{ string} \rangle_2 \; x$$
$$\text{Size}(\langle x \text{ string} \rangle) \longleftarrow \text{Size}(\langle x \text{ string} \rangle_2) + 1$$

$$\langle y \text{ string} \rangle ::= y$$
$$\text{Condition: Size}(\langle y \text{ string} \rangle) = 1$$
$$| \; \langle y \text{ string} \rangle_2 \; y$$
$$\text{Size}(\langle y \text{ string} \rangle_2) \longleftarrow \text{Size}(\langle y \text{ string} \rangle) - 1$$

$$\langle z \text{ string} \rangle ::= z$$
$$\text{Condition: Size}(\langle z \text{ string} \rangle) = 1$$
$$| \; \langle z \text{ string} \rangle_2 \; z$$
$$\text{Size}(\langle z \text{ string} \rangle_2) \longleftarrow \text{Size}(\langle z \text{ string} \rangle) - 1$$

2. Without changing the set of terminal strings generated, modify the grammar of Exercise 1 so that Size is used as a synthesized attribute only.

3. Construct an attribute grammar that generates the set of all integer constants corresponding to values of less than 2^{31} with any of the following forms:

⟨sequence of binary digits⟩ (2)
⟨sequence of octal digits⟩ (8)
⟨sequence of hexadecimal digits⟩ (16)

[For example, the constants 11010(2), 32(8), and 1A(16) all stand for the value 26.]

2.3.2 A Complete Syntactic Specification for Eva

To be complete, an attribute grammar for the syntax of Eva must include formal conditions corresponding to the various context-sensitive aspects, such as type matching, which were characterized informally in Sec. 2.1.3.

The main idea leading to the formalization of these context conditions is to make use of an attribute Nest, which is an inherited attribute of most of the nonterminal symbols in the grammar. A Nest value records the name and type information specified by just those declaration sequences and/or parameter lists that bear upon the construct with which it is associated. Specifically, it is a sequence of values corresponding to the attribute Decs, where a Decs value records the name and type information specified by a single ⟨declaration sequence⟩ or ⟨parameter list⟩.

To define these value domains precisely, we introduce the attribute Type with values 'char', 'string', and 'proc', and the attribute Tag with values that are sequences of letter values between 'a' and 'z'. Tag is a synthesized attribute of the symbol ⟨name⟩ and serves to record the actual characters in the name:

⟨name⟩ ::= ⟨letter sequence⟩

Tag(⟨name⟩) ⟵ Tag(⟨letter sequence⟩)

⟨letter sequence⟩ ::= ⟨letter⟩

Tag(⟨letter sequence⟩) ⟵ Tag(⟨letter⟩)

| ⟨letter sequence⟩₂ ⟨letter⟩

Tag(⟨letter sequence⟩) ⟵ *concat*(Tag(⟨letter sequence⟩₂), Tag(⟨letter⟩))

⟨letter⟩ ::= a

Tag(⟨letter⟩) ⟵ ⟨'a'⟩

| . . .

. . .

| z

Tag(⟨letter⟩) ⟵ ⟨'z'⟩

Now a Decs value is defined to be a set of triples of the form (Type, Tag, Params), where a Params value is a sequence of Type values. The Params field of a Decs triple will be a nonempty sequence of Type values only if the Type and Tag fields of the triple correspond to a procedure with parameters.

As a source of examples, consider the following Eva program:

> **begin**
>> **char** x
>> **proc** p = (
>>> **input** x
>>> **neq** x, "z": (**output** x **call** p))
>> **call** p
> **end**

The Nest value for the $\langle$block$\rangle$ that comprises the entire program will be the empty sequence, because there are no outer declarations affecting it. The Nest value for each principal construct inside the $\langle$block$\rangle$ will be the following list containing one Decs value:

$$\langle\{(\text{'char'}, \langle\text{'x'}\rangle, \langle\rangle), (\text{'proc'}, \langle\text{'p'}\rangle, \langle\rangle)\}\rangle$$

If the body of p were a $\langle$block$\rangle$ with a local string variable s, the Nest value for the constructs in p's body would be

$$\langle\{(\text{'char'}, \langle\text{'x'}\rangle, \langle\rangle), (\text{'proc'}, \langle\text{'p'}\rangle, \langle\rangle)\}, \{(\text{'string'}, \langle\text{'s'}\rangle, \langle\rangle)\}\rangle$$

Because a procedure body may make reference to names declared at a textually later point in the program, the correct specification of the evaluation rules for Nest requires a little ingenuity.

First, note that a $\langle$name list$\rangle$ may be part of either a $\langle$parameter list$\rangle$ or a $\langle$declaration$\rangle$. The symbol $\langle$name list$\rangle$ thus has Params as well as Decs as a synthesized attribute, but the Params value will be used subsequently only in the context of a $\langle$parameter list$\rangle$. The two attribute values are computed in parallel:

$\langle$name list$\rangle$ ::= $\langle$name$\rangle$

> Decs($\langle$name list$\rangle$) $\longleftarrow$ {(Type($\langle$name list$\rangle$), Tag($\langle$name$\rangle$), $\langle\rangle$)}
> Params($\langle$name list$\rangle$) $\longleftarrow$ $\langle$Type($\langle$name list$\rangle$)$\rangle$

| $\langle$name list$\rangle_2$, $\langle$name$\rangle$

> Decs($\langle$name list$\rangle$) $\longleftarrow$ Decs($\langle$name list$\rangle_2$) $\cup$
>> {(Type($\langle$name list$\rangle_2$), Tag($\langle$name$\rangle$), $\langle\rangle$)}
> Params($\langle$name list$\rangle$) $\longleftarrow$ *concat*(Params($\langle$name list$\rangle_2$),
>> $\langle$Type($\langle$name list$\rangle$)$\rangle$)

$$\text{Type}(\langle\text{name list}\rangle_2) \longleftarrow \text{Type}(\langle\text{name list}\rangle)$$

Condition: $\sim(\exists d \in \text{Decs}(\langle\text{name list}\rangle_2))(\text{Tag}(\langle\text{name}\rangle) = \textit{field}_2(d))$

The last line prevents duplicate names in the same $\langle\text{name list}\rangle$. (The symbol '$\sim$' means 'not' and '$\exists$' means 'there exists'.) Note that the Type values ('char' or 'string') used in constructing the Decs and Params values are inherited from the $\langle\text{name list}\rangle$. They are originally synthesized according to the rules

$$\langle\text{declarer}\rangle ::= \textbf{char}$$

$$\text{Type}(\langle\text{declarer}\rangle) \longleftarrow \text{'char'}$$

$$| \textbf{ string}$$

$$\text{Type}(\langle\text{declarer}\rangle) \longleftarrow \text{'string'}$$

and are "handed over" according to the following rules, which also complete the synthesis of the Params and Decs values associated with a $\langle\text{parameter list}\rangle$ and the Decs value associated with a $\langle\text{declaration}\rangle$:

$\langle\text{parameter list}\rangle ::= \langle\text{declarer}\rangle \langle\text{name list}\rangle$

Params($\langle\text{parameter list}\rangle$) $\longleftarrow$ Params($\langle\text{name list}\rangle$)

Decs($\langle\text{parameter list}\rangle$) $\longleftarrow$ Decs($\langle\text{name list}\rangle$)

Type($\langle\text{name list}\rangle$) $\longleftarrow$ Type($\langle\text{declarer}\rangle$)

$| \langle\text{parameter list}\rangle_2, \langle\text{declarer}\rangle \langle\text{name list}\rangle$

Params($\langle\text{parameter list}\rangle$) $\longleftarrow$ *concat*(Params($\langle\text{parameter list}\rangle_2$),

Params($\langle\text{name list}\rangle$))

Decs($\langle\text{parameter list}\rangle$) $\longleftarrow$ Decs($\langle\text{parameter list}\rangle_2$) $\cup$ Decs($\langle\text{name list}\rangle$)

Type($\langle\text{name list}\rangle$) $\longleftarrow$ Type($\langle\text{declarer}\rangle$)

$\langle\text{declaration}\rangle ::= \langle\text{declarer}\rangle \langle\text{name list}\rangle$

Decs($\langle\text{declaration}\rangle$) $\longleftarrow$ Decs($\langle\text{name list}\rangle$)

Type($\langle\text{name list}\rangle$) $\longleftarrow$ Type($\langle\text{declarer}\rangle$)

$| \textbf{proc} \langle\text{name}\rangle = \langle\text{statement}\rangle$

Decs($\langle\text{declaration}\rangle$) $\longleftarrow$ {('proc', Tag($\langle\text{name}\rangle$), $\langle\rangle$)}

Nest($\langle\text{statement}\rangle$) $\longleftarrow$ Nest($\langle\text{declaration}\rangle$)

$| \textbf{proc} \langle\text{name}\rangle (\langle\text{parameter list}\rangle) = \langle\text{statement}\rangle$

Decs($\langle\text{declaration}\rangle$) $\longleftarrow$ {('proc', Tag($\langle\text{name}\rangle$),

Params($\langle\text{parameter list}\rangle$))}

Nest($\langle\text{statement}\rangle$) $\longleftarrow$ *append*(Nest($\langle\text{declaration}\rangle$),

Decs($\langle\text{parameter list}\rangle$))

It can be seen that the Nest inherited by the body of a procedure with parameters is augmented with the Decs value corresponding to those parameters. The following rules complete the synthesis of the Decs value for a ⟨declaration sequence⟩, pass the relevant Nest value down to the individual declarations, and check that no name is declared more than once in the sequence:

⟨declaration sequence⟩ ::= ⟨declaration⟩

   Decs(⟨declaration sequence⟩) ⟵ Decs(⟨declaration⟩)

   Nest(⟨declaration⟩) ⟵ Nest(⟨declaration sequence⟩)

 | ⟨declaration sequence⟩$_2$ ⟨declaration⟩

   Decs(⟨declaration sequence⟩) ⟵ Decs(⟨declaration sequence⟩$_2$) ∪

                   Decs(⟨declaration⟩)

   Nest(⟨declaration sequence⟩$_2$) ⟵ Nest(⟨declaration sequence⟩)

   Nest(⟨declaration⟩) ⟵ Nest(⟨declaration sequence⟩)

   Condition: $(\forall d \in$ Decs(⟨declaration sequence⟩$_2$))$(\sim(\exists d' \in$

          Decs(⟨declaration⟩))$(field_2(d) = field_2(d')))$

(The symbol '$\forall$' means 'for all'.) Augmentation of the Nest external to a ⟨block⟩ with the Decs value synthesized in the ⟨block⟩ is achieved as follows:

  ⟨block⟩ ::= **begin** ⟨declaration sequence⟩ ⟨statement sequence⟩ **end**

    Decs(⟨block⟩) ⟵ Decs(⟨declaration sequence⟩)

    Nest(⟨declaration sequence⟩) ⟵ *append*(Nest(⟨block⟩),

             Decs(⟨declaration sequence⟩))

    Nest(⟨statement sequence⟩) ⟵ *append*(Nest(⟨block⟩),

             Decs(⟨declaration sequence⟩))

  ⟨program⟩ ::= ⟨block⟩

    Nest(⟨block⟩) ⟵ ⟨ ⟩

As an example of how all these rules interact, suppose that we have a program of the following form:

      begin

        proc *p* (**char** *a*) = . . .

        char *b*

        . . .

      end

In the partial tree shown in Fig. 2.17, the numbers preceding the attributes

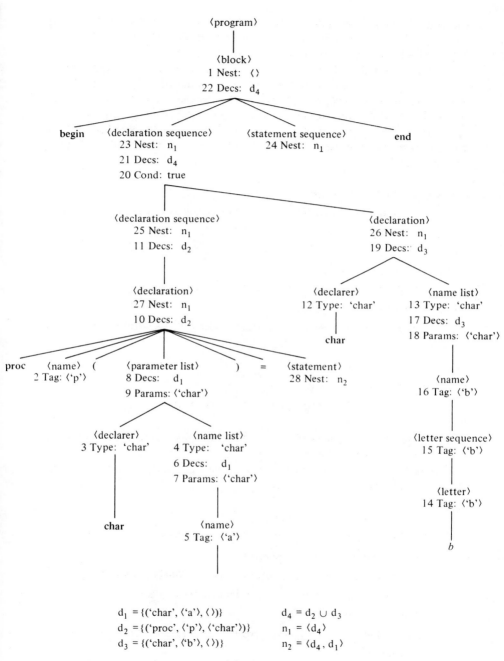

FIGURE 2.17

indicate the *relative* order in which the values were filled in. Observe how the Nest values can be inserted (in a downward direction) only after all the Decs values have been inserted (in an upward direction).

The part of the grammar dealing with statements and expressions is now relatively straightforward. Many of the evaluation rules simply serve to pass down the Nest value computed in the manner described above. Type checking of names is carried out with the aid of an auxiliary function *latesttype* which, in effect, searches the Nest value from back to front for an occurrence of a specified name. Thus two more context conditions are disposed of in the following rules:

$\langle$char expression$\rangle$ ::= $\langle$name$\rangle$

> Condition: *latesttype*(Tag($\langle$name$\rangle$), Nest($\langle$char expression$\rangle$)) = 'char'

> | " $\langle$letter$\rangle$ "

> | **space**

> | **head** $\langle$string expression$\rangle$

>> Nest($\langle$string expression$\rangle$) $\longleftarrow$ Nest($\langle$char expression$\rangle$)

$\langle$string expression$\rangle$ ::= $\langle$name$\rangle$

> Condition: *latesttype*(Tag($\langle$name$\rangle$), Nest($\langle$string expression$\rangle$)) = 'string'

> | " "

> | " $\langle$letter$\rangle$ $\langle$letter sequence$\rangle$ "

> | **tail** $\langle$string expression$\rangle_2$

>> Nest($\langle$string expression$\rangle_2$) $\longleftarrow$ Nest($\langle$string expression$\rangle$)

(No use is made of the Tag values synthesized for these occurrences of $\langle$letter$\rangle$ and $\langle$letter sequence$\rangle$.)

Apart from the treatment of procedure calls, the following rules should be readily understood:

$\langle$statement sequence$\rangle$ ::= $\langle$statement$\rangle$

> Nest($\langle$statement$\rangle$) $\longleftarrow$ Nest($\langle$statement sequence$\rangle$)

> | $\langle$statement sequence$\rangle_2$ $\langle$statement$\rangle$

>> Nest($\langle$statement sequence$\rangle_2$) $\longleftarrow$ Nest($\langle$statement sequence$\rangle$)

>> Nest($\langle$statement$\rangle$) $\longleftarrow$ Nest($\langle$statement sequence$\rangle$)

$\langle$statement$\rangle$ ::= **input** $\langle$name$\rangle$

> Condition: *latesttype*(Tag($\langle$name$\rangle$), Nest($\langle$statement$\rangle$)) = 'char'

> | **output** $\langle$char expression$\rangle$

>> Nest($\langle$char expression$\rangle$) $\longleftarrow$ Nest($\langle$statement$\rangle$)

| ⟨block⟩

    Nest(⟨block⟩) ⟵ Nest(⟨statement⟩)

| (⟨statement sequence⟩)

    Nest(⟨statement sequence⟩) ⟵ Nest(⟨statement⟩)

| ⟨test⟩ ⟨pair⟩ : ⟨statement⟩$_2$

    Nest(⟨pair⟩) ⟵ Nest(⟨statement⟩)

    Nest(⟨statement⟩$_2$) ⟵ Nest(⟨statement⟩)

| **cons** ⟨char expression⟩ , ⟨name⟩

    Nest(⟨char expression⟩) ⟵ Nest(⟨statement⟩)

    Condition: *latesttype*(Tag(⟨name⟩), Nest(⟨statement⟩)) = 'string'

| **call** ⟨name⟩

    Condition: *latesttype*(Tag(⟨name⟩), Nest(⟨statement⟩)) =

        'proc' $\wedge$ *parameters*(Tag(⟨name⟩), Nest(⟨statement⟩)) = ◇

| **call** ⟨name⟩ (⟨expression list⟩)

    Nest(⟨expression list⟩) ⟵ Nest(⟨statement⟩)

    Params(⟨expression list⟩) ⟵ *parameters*(Tag(⟨name⟩),

                               Nest(⟨statement⟩))

    Condition: *latesttype*(Tag(⟨name⟩), Nest(⟨statement⟩)) = 'proc'

⟨test⟩ ::= **eq**

    | **neq**

⟨pair⟩ ::= ⟨char expression⟩$_1$, ⟨char expression⟩$_2$

    Nest(⟨char expression⟩$_1$) ⟵ Nest(⟨pair⟩)

    Nest(⟨char expression⟩$_2$) ⟵ Nest(⟨pair⟩)

    | ⟨string expression⟩$_1$, ⟨string expression⟩$_2$

    Nest(⟨string expression⟩$_1$) ⟵ Nest(⟨pair⟩)

    Nest(⟨string expression⟩$_2$) ⟵ Nest(⟨pair⟩)

The auxiliary function *parameters* returns the Params value associated with a specified procedure name in the Nest. The argument list (⟨expression list⟩) of a call of a procedure with parameters inherits this value. In order that the type of each argument may be checked for compatibility with the type of the corresponding parameter, the symbol ⟨expression⟩ has Type as a synthesized attribute:

⟨expression⟩ ::= ⟨char expression⟩

    Type(⟨expression⟩) ⟵ 'char'

    Nest(⟨char expression⟩) ⟵ Nest(⟨expression⟩)

| ⟨string expression⟩

    Type(⟨expression⟩) ⟵ 'string'

    Nest(⟨string expression⟩) ⟵ Nest(⟨expression⟩)

⟨expression list⟩ ::= ⟨expression⟩

    Nest(⟨expression⟩) ⟵ Nest(⟨expression list⟩)

    Condition: $length$(Params(⟨expression list⟩)) = 1 $\land$ Type(⟨expression⟩)

                                     = $first$(Params(⟨expression list⟩))

| ⟨expression⟩ , ⟨expression list⟩$_2$

    Nest(⟨expression⟩) ⟵ Nest(⟨expression list⟩)

    Nest(⟨expression list⟩$_2$) ⟵ Nest(⟨expression list⟩)

    Params(⟨expression list⟩$_2$) ⟵ $tail$(Params(⟨expression list⟩))

    Condition: $length$(Params(⟨expression list⟩)) $\geq$ 1 $\land$ Type(⟨expression⟩)

                                       = $first$(Params(⟨expression list⟩))

These rules also require the number of arguments to be equal to the number of parameters.

The formal syntactic definition of Eva by means of an attribute grammar is now complete, and the specifications are summarized in Table 2.5.

TABLE 2.5 Attribute Grammar for the Syntax of Eva

Attributes and Values

Attribute	Values
Type	'char', 'string', 'proc'
Params	sequences of Type values
Tag	sequences of letters ('a', . . . , 'z')
Decs	sets of triples of the form (Type, Tag, Params)
Nest	sequences of Decs values

Attributes Associated with Nonterminal Symbols

Nonterminal	Inherited attributes	Synthesized attributes
⟨program⟩	—	—
⟨block⟩	Nest	Decs
⟨declaration sequence⟩	Nest	Decs
⟨declaration⟩	Nest	Decs
⟨parameter list⟩	—	Decs, Params
⟨declarer⟩	—	Type
⟨name list⟩	Type	Decs, Params

TABLE 2.5 (Continued)

⟨statement sequence⟩	Nest	—
⟨statement⟩	Nest	—
⟨pair⟩	Nest	—
⟨expression list⟩	Nest, Params	—
⟨expression⟩	Nest	Type
⟨char expression⟩	Nest	—
⟨string expression⟩	Nest	—
⟨name⟩	—	Tag
⟨letter sequence⟩	—	Tag
⟨letter⟩	—	Tag

Production and Attribute Evaluation Rules

⟨program⟩ ::= ⟨block⟩

   Nest(⟨block⟩) ⟵ ⟨ ⟩

⟨block⟩ ::= **begin** ⟨declaration sequence⟩ ⟨statement sequence⟩ **end**

   Decs(⟨block⟩) ⟵ Decs(⟨declaration sequence⟩)

   Nest(⟨declaration sequence⟩) ⟵ *append*(Nest(⟨block⟩),

$$Decs(⟨declaration\ sequence⟩))$$

   Nest(⟨statement sequence⟩) ⟵ *append*(Nest(⟨block⟩),

$$Decs(⟨declaration\ sequence⟩))$$

⟨declaration sequence⟩ ::= ⟨declaration⟩

   Decs(⟨declaration sequence⟩) ⟵ Decs(⟨declaration⟩)

   Nest(⟨declaration⟩) ⟵ Nest(⟨declaration sequence⟩)

   | ⟨declaration sequence⟩$_2$ ⟨declaration⟩

   Decs(⟨declaration sequence⟩) ⟵ Decs(⟨declaration sequence⟩$_2$) ∪

$$Decs(⟨declaration⟩)$$

   Nest(⟨declaration sequence⟩$_2$) ⟵ Nest(⟨declaration sequence⟩)

   Nest(⟨declaration⟩) ⟵ Nest(⟨declaration sequence⟩)

   Condition: (∀d ∈ Decs(⟨declaration sequence⟩$_2$))(∼(∃ d′ ∈

$$Decs(⟨declaration⟩))(field_2(d) = field_2(d')))$$

⟨declaration⟩ ::= ⟨declarer⟩ ⟨name list⟩

   Decs(⟨declaration⟩) ⟵ Decs(⟨name list⟩)

   Type(⟨name list⟩) ⟵ Type(⟨declarer⟩)

   | **proc** ⟨name⟩ = ⟨statement⟩

   Decs(⟨declaration⟩) ⟵ {('proc', Tag(⟨name⟩), ⟨ ⟩)}

   Nest(⟨statement⟩) ⟵ Nest(⟨declaration⟩)

   | **proc** ⟨name⟩ (⟨parameter list⟩) = ⟨statement⟩

   Decs(⟨declaration⟩) ⟵ {('proc', Tag(⟨name⟩), Params(⟨parameter list⟩))}

   Nest(⟨statement⟩) ⟵ *append*(Nest(⟨declaration⟩), Decs(⟨parameter list⟩))

TABLE 2.5 (Continued)

⟨parameter list⟩ ::= ⟨declarer⟩ ⟨name list⟩

        Params(⟨parameter list⟩) ⟵ Params(⟨name list⟩)

        Decs(⟨parameter list⟩) ⟵ Decs(⟨name list⟩)

        Type(⟨name list⟩) ⟵ Type(⟨declarer⟩)

  | ⟨parameter list⟩$_2$, ⟨declarer⟩ ⟨name list⟩

        Params(⟨parameter list⟩) ⟵ *concat* (Params(⟨parameter list⟩$_2$),

                                          Params(⟨name list⟩))

        Decs(⟨parameter list⟩) ⟵ Decs(⟨parameter list⟩$_2$) ∪ Decs(⟨name list⟩)

        Type(⟨name list⟩) ⟵ Type(⟨declarer⟩)

⟨declarer⟩ ::= **char**

        Type(⟨declarer⟩) ⟵ 'char'

  | **string**

        Type(⟨declarer⟩) ⟵ 'string'

⟨name list⟩ ::= ⟨name⟩

        Decs(⟨name list⟩) ⟵ {(Type(⟨name list⟩), Tag(⟨name⟩), ⟨⟩)}

        Params(⟨name list⟩) ⟵ ⟨Type(⟨name list⟩)⟩

  | ⟨name list⟩$_2$, ⟨name⟩

        Decs(⟨name list⟩) ⟵ Decs(⟨name list⟩$_2$) ∪ {(Type(⟨name list⟩$_2$),

                                    Tag(⟨name⟩), ⟨⟩)}

        Params(⟨name list⟩) ⟵ *concat* (Params(⟨name list⟩$_2$), ⟨Type(⟨name list⟩)⟩)

        Type(⟨name list⟩$_2$) ⟵ Type(⟨name list⟩)

        Condition: ∼(∃d ∈ Decs(⟨name list⟩$_2$))(Tag(⟨name⟩) = *field*$_2$(d))

⟨statement sequence⟩ ::= ⟨statement⟩

        Nest(⟨statement⟩) ⟵ Nest(⟨statement sequence⟩)

  | ⟨statement sequence⟩$_2$ ⟨statement⟩

        Nest(⟨statement sequence⟩$_2$) ⟵ Nest(⟨statement sequence⟩)

        Nest(⟨statement⟩) ⟵ Nest(⟨statement sequence⟩)

⟨statement⟩ ::= **input** ⟨name⟩

        Condition: *latesttype*(Tag(⟨name⟩), Nest(⟨statement⟩)) = 'char'

  | **output** ⟨char expression⟩

        Nest(⟨char expression⟩) ⟵ Nest(⟨statement⟩)

  | ⟨block⟩

        Nest(⟨block⟩) ⟵ Nest(⟨statement⟩)

  | (⟨statement sequence⟩)

        Nest(⟨statement sequence⟩) ⟵ Nest(⟨statement⟩)

TABLE 2.5 (Continued)

| ⟨test⟩ ⟨pair⟩ : ⟨statement⟩₂

      Nest(⟨pair⟩) ⟵ Nest(⟨statement⟩)

      Nest(⟨statement⟩₂) ⟵ Nest(⟨statement⟩)

| **cons** ⟨char expression⟩ , ⟨name⟩

      Nest(⟨char expression⟩) ⟵ Nest(⟨statement⟩)

      Condition: *latesttype*(Tag(⟨name⟩), Nest(⟨statement⟩)) = 'string'

| **call** ⟨name⟩

      Condition: *latesttype*(Tag(⟨name⟩), Nest(⟨statement⟩)) = 'proc'

          ∧ *parameters*(Tag(⟨name⟩), Nest(⟨statement⟩)) = ⟨⟩

| **call** ⟨name⟩ (⟨expression list⟩)

      Nest(⟨expression list⟩) ⟵ Nest(⟨statement⟩)

      Params(⟨expression list⟩) ⟵ *parameters*(Tag(⟨name⟩), Nest(⟨statement⟩))

      Condition: *latesttype*(Tag(⟨name⟩), Nest(⟨statement⟩)) = 'proc'

⟨test⟩ ::= **eq**

  | **neq**

⟨pair⟩ ::= ⟨char expression⟩₁ , ⟨char expression⟩₂

      Nest(⟨char expression⟩₁) ⟵ Nest(⟨pair⟩)

      Nest(⟨char expression⟩₂) ⟵ Nest(⟨pair⟩)

| ⟨string expression⟩₁ , ⟨string expression⟩₂

      Nest(⟨string expression⟩₁) ⟵ Nest(⟨pair⟩)

      Nest(⟨string expression⟩₂) ⟵ Nest(⟨pair⟩)

⟨expression list⟩ ::= ⟨expression⟩

      Nest(⟨expression⟩) ⟵ Nest(⟨expression list⟩)

      Condition: *length*(Params(⟨expression list⟩)) = 1 ∧ Type(⟨expression⟩)

          = *first*(Params(⟨expression list⟩))

| ⟨expression⟩ , ⟨expression list⟩₂

      Nest(⟨expression⟩) ⟵ Nest(⟨expression list⟩)

      Nest(⟨expression list⟩₂) ⟵ Nest(⟨expression list⟩)

      Params(⟨expression list⟩₂) ⟵ *tail*(Params(⟨expression list⟩))

      Condition: *length*(Params(⟨expression list⟩)) ≥ 1 ∧ Type(⟨expression⟩)

          = *first*(Params(⟨expression list⟩))

⟨expression⟩ ::= ⟨char expression⟩

      Nest(⟨char expression⟩) ⟵ Nest(⟨expression⟩)

      Type(⟨expression⟩) ⟵ 'char'

| ⟨string expression⟩

      Nest(⟨string expression⟩) ⟵ Nest(⟨expression⟩)

TABLE 2.5 (Continued)

$$Type(\langle expression \rangle) \longleftarrow \text{'string'}$$

$\langle char\ expression \rangle ::= \langle name \rangle$

          Condition: *latesttype*(Tag(\langle name \rangle), Nest(\langle char\ expression \rangle)) = 'char'

  | " $\langle letter \rangle$ "

  | **space**

  | **head** $\langle string\ expression \rangle$

          Nest(\langle string\ expression \rangle) \longleftarrow Nest(\langle char\ expression \rangle)

$\langle string\ expression \rangle ::= \langle name \rangle$

          Condition: *latesttype*(Tag(\langle name \rangle), Nest(\langle string\ expression \rangle)) = 'string'

  | " "

  | " $\langle letter \rangle$ $\langle letter\ sequence \rangle$ "

  | **tail** $\langle string\ expression \rangle_2$

          Nest(\langle string\ expression \rangle_2) \longleftarrow Nest(\langle string\ expression \rangle)

$\langle name \rangle ::= \langle letter\ sequence \rangle$

          Tag(\langle name \rangle) \longleftarrow Tag(\langle letter\ sequence \rangle)

$\langle letter\ sequence \rangle ::= \langle letter \rangle$

          Tag(\langle letter\ sequence \rangle) \longleftarrow Tag(\langle letter \rangle)

  | $\langle letter\ sequence \rangle_2 \langle letter \rangle$

          Tag(\langle letter\ sequence \rangle) \longleftarrow *concat*(Tag(\langle letter\ sequence \rangle_2), Tag(\langle letter \rangle))

$\langle letter \rangle ::= a$

          Tag(\langle letter \rangle) \longleftarrow \langle \text{'a'} \rangle

  | ...

      ...

  | z

          Tag(\langle letter \rangle) \longleftarrow \langle \text{'z'} \rangle

Definition of Auxiliary Evaluation Functions

latesttype (tag, nest) =

    'undefined', if nest = $\langle \rangle$;

    t, if ($\exists d \in$ *last*(nest))(d = (t, tag, p)) for some t, p;

    latesttype (tag, *allbutlast* (nest)), otherwise.

parameters (tag, nest) =

    $\langle$'undefined'$\rangle$, if nest = $\langle \rangle$;

    p, if ($\exists d \in$ *last*(nest))(d = (t, tag, p)) for some t, p;

    parameters (tag, *allbutlast* (nest)), otherwise.

EXERCISES

1. Referring to the grammar of Table 2.5, construct the complete, decorated syntax tree for the program

> **begin**
> **proc** p (**char** a, b) =
> **output** b
> **call** p ("x", "y")
> **end**

2. Replacement of the constant "y" by "yz" in the program of Exercise 1 introduces a violation of a context condition. Verify that the resulting erroneous program is not derivable from the grammar.

3. For some actual programming language with which you are familiar, identify the context condition(s) (or at least some of them) associated with the agreement of data types for the left and right sides of an assignment statement. Explain in general terms how the condition(s) might be formalized in an attribute grammar for the language.

For Further Information

The basic technique of augmenting context-free grammars with inherited and synthesized attributes is due to Knuth (1968), who also investigates its mathematical aspects. The attribute-grammar formalism and its application to the problem of compiler generation are further discussed by Lewis et al. (1974) and by Bochmann (1976). There is no sharp boundary between syntax and semantics as far as the linguistic properties definable by attribute grammars are concerned, and parts of these papers deal with the concept of "translational semantics" discussed in Sec. 3.2 of this book. Watt (1979) presents a complete definition of the syntax of Pascal using an extended version of the attribute-grammar formalism.

Ledgard's (1974, 1977) formalism of *production systems* is capable of defining the context-sensitive aspects of programming language syntax in a manner somewhat analogous to that of attribute grammars. Another powerful grammatical formalism which is closely related both to attribute grammars and to the two-level grammars described in the next section is that of *affix grammars* (Koster, 1971); Crowe (1972) and Watt (1977) discuss its application to compiler generation.

2.4

TWO-LEVEL GRAMMARS

We now turn to another formalism which is inherently much more powerful than BNF and which is capable of dealing with the context-sensitive as well as the context-free aspects of a subject language. We begin by describing a component of the formalism which is really just another variant of BNF, i.e., a metalanguage for context-free grammars only. This metalanguage is then extended to enable the specification of powerful *two-level grammars* or *W-grammars* of the kind used in the official definition of Algol 68.

2.4.1 Another Notation for Context-Free Grammars

In the terminology of this metalanguage, a *protonotion* is any sequence of lowercase letters, conventionally set in boldface type. Spaces may be freely inserted in a protonotion without changing it, so that the following are all the same protonotion:

> **something**
>
> **some thing**
>
> **so met hing**

A protonotion is said to be a *notion* of a particular grammar if there is a production rule that defines it, so that "notion" is basically a new word for nonterminal symbol. A protonotion ending in **symbol** corresponds to a (terminal) symbol of the subject language; in order to eliminate all possible conflicts between metalanguage and subject language, such protonotions are always used in rules, while the symbols themselves are listed in a separate *representation table*.

Four punctuation marks serve as metasymbols: the left and right sides of a rule are separated by a colon, alternative definitions are separated by semicolons, the protonotions within an alternative are separated by commas, and the entire rule is terminated by a period. Thus the Pam conditional statement could be defined by the rules

> **conditional statement: front part, fi symbol;**
>
> **front part, else symbol, series, fi symbol.**
>
> **front part: if symbol, comparison, then symbol, series.**

and the following entries in the representation table:

if symbol	**if**
then symbol	**then**
else symbol	**else**
fi symbol	**fi**

Table 2.6 contains a complete grammar for Pam using this formalism. We could easily translate the BNF grammar for Eva into this notation as

well, but to incorporate the context-sensitive aspects we need additional metalinguistic facilities, to which we now turn.

TABLE 2.6 Grammar for Pam in Two-Level Grammar Notation

Production Rules

program: series.
series: statement; series, semicolon symbol, statement.
statement: input statement; output statement; assignment statement;
    conditional statement; definite loop; indefinite loop.

input statement: read symbol, variable list.
output statement: write symbol, variable list.
variable list: variable; variable list, comma symbol, variable.
assignment statement: variable, becomes symbol, expression.
conditional statement: if symbol, comparison, then symbol, series,
    fi symbol; if symbol, comparison, then symbol, series, else symbol,
    series, fi symbol.
definite loop: to symbol, expression, do symbol, series, end symbol.
indefinite loop: while symbol, comparison, do symbol, series, end symbol.

comparison: expression, relation, expression.

expression: term; expression, weak operator, term.
term: element; term, strong operator, element.
element: constant; variable; lpar symbol, expression, rpar symbol.
constant: digit; constant, digit.
variable: letter; variable, letter; variable, digit.

relation: eq symbol; le symbol; lt symbol; gt symbol; ge symbol; ne symbol.

weak operator: plus symbol; minus symbol.
strong operator: star symbol; slash symbol.
digit: zero symbol; one symbol; two symbol; three symbol; four symbol;
    five symbol; six symbol; seven symbol; eight symbol; nine symbol.
letter: a symbol; b symbol; c symbol; d symbol; e symbol; f symbol;
    g symbol; h symbol; i symbol; j symbol; k symbol; l symbol; m symbol;
    n symbol; o symbol; p symbol; q symbol; r symbol; s symbol; t symbol;
    u symbol; v symbol; w symbol; x symbol; y symbol; z symbol.

Representation Table

read symbol	read	six symbol	6
write symbol	write	seven symbol	7
if symbol	if	eight symbol	8
then symbol	then	nine symbol	9
else symbol	else	a symbol	*a*
fi symbol	fi	b symbol	*b*
to symbol	to	c symbol	*c*

TABLE 2.6   (Continued)

while symbol	while	d symbol	d
do symbol	do	e symbol	e
end symbol	end	f symbol	f
semicolon symbol	;	g symbol	g
comma symbol	,	h symbol	h
becomes symbol	:=	i symbol	i
lpar symbol	(	j symbol	j
rpar symbol	)	k symbol	k
eq symbol	=	l symbol	l
le symbol	=<	m symbol	m
lt symbol	<	n symbol	n
gt symbol	>	o symbol	o
ge symbol	>=	p symbol	p
ne symbol	<>	q symbol	q
plus symbol	+	r symbol	r
minus symbol	−	s symbol	s
star symbol	*	t symbol	t
slash symbol	/	u symbol	u
zero symbol	0	v symbol	v
one symbol	1	w symbol	w
two symbol	2	x symbol	x
three symbol	3	y symbol	y
four symbol	4	z symbol	z
five symbol	5		

2.4.2   *Context-Sensitivity—Hyper-Rules and Metanotions*

A *hyper-rule* is a kind of abbreviation or abstraction of a number of different production rules that share a common pattern. For instance, the BNF grammar for Eva contains three production rules that we may now rewrite as

> declaration sequence: declaration; declaration sequence, declaration.
>
> statement sequence: statement; statement sequence, statement.
>
> letter sequence: letter; letter sequence, letter.

All these rules can be replaced by the hyper-rule

> **SEQITEM sequence: SEQITEM; SEQITEM sequence, SEQITEM.**

where the use of uppercase letters signifies that **SEQITEM** is a *metanotion* which stands for any of a number of protonotions. The latter are specified by a *metaproduction rule* (henceforth abbreviated to *metarule*) with the metanotion as its left side. This particular metanotion could be defined by the metarule

SEQITEM :: declaration; statement; letter.

(Note that the two sides of a metarule are separated by two colons instead of one.) The production rules represented by a given hyper-rule are obtained by *consistent substitution* of protonotions (specified by the metarules) for the contained metanotions: the same protonotion must be substituted for all occurrences of a given metanotion in the hyper-rule. Thus the hyper-rule given above represents the three desired production rules but not a rule such as

declaration sequence: statement; letter sequence, declaration.

where the substitution for **SEQITEM** has not been consistent. Two or more production rules for the same notion always collapse into one rule; thus the hyper-rule

thing: SEQITEM.

is in effect an abbreviation for

thing: declaration; statement; letter.

The right side of a metarule may also involve metanotions, possibly the metanotion being defined. By convention, metanotions are not broken up by spaces, and spaces (never commas) are used to separate metanotions and/or protonotions within each alternative definition in a metarule. The consistent substitution concept does not apply to metarules, whose interpretation is analogous to that of context-free production rules. The following metarules thus imply that **NOTION** stands for any sequence of lowercase letters, i.e., any protonotion:

NOTION :: ALPHA; NOTION ALPHA.

ALPHA :: a; b; c; d; e; f; g; h; i; j; k; l; m; n; o; p; q;
    r; s; t; u; v; w; x; y; z.

Then the hyper-rule

NOTION sequence: NOTION; NOTION sequence, NOTION.

stands for an infinite number of possible production rules, including the three represented by the rule for **SEQITEM sequence**. Similarly,

NOTION list: NOTION; NOTION list, comma symbol, NOTION.

is a very general hyper-rule standing for any number of production rules that define lists of things separated by commas.

It is usually convenient to define a metanotion standing for the empty protonotion:

EMPTY :: .

Then the following is a general hyper-rule which aids the demarcation of optional parts of constructs:

NOTION option: NOTION; EMPTY.

For example, **conditional statement** can now be defined by the rules

conditional statement: if symbol, comparison, then symbol,

series, else part option, fi symbol.

else part: else symbol, series.

Apart from the representation table, a two-level grammar consists of a set of metarules and a set of hyper-rules. Each hyper-rule stands for a number of production rules, possibly an infinite number, but only one if it involves no metanotions. For each metanotion used, there must be a metarule to specify what protonotions it stands for. The metarules may be thought of as a higher-level grammar that (with the aid of the hyper-rules) generates a grammar, where the generated grammar may involve an infinite number of notions and have an infinite number of production rules (or alternatives thereof). This, as we shall see, is basically the reason why two-level grammars are fundamentally more powerful than BNF and its variants, where we are restricted to a finite number of nonterminals and a finite number of rules.

Sometimes the requirement for consistent substitution of protonotions for metanotions appearing in a hyper-rule is inconvenient. Suppose that we wish to define a **mixed sequence** as a sequence of any combination of declarations, statements, and letters. The hyper-rule

mixed sequence: SEQITEM; mixed sequence, SEQITEM.

does not have the desired effect because of the consistent substitution requirement. But if we have the additional metarule

SEQITEM2 :: SEQITEM.

then the hyper-rule

mixed sequence: SEQITEM; mixed sequence, SEQITEM2.

is satisfactory, since there is no requirement for substitution of the same protonotion (**declaration, statement,** or **letter**) for both **SEQITEM** and **SEQITEM2**. This hyper-rule stands for nine different production rules in all. Because this technique is very common in two-level grammars, there is a metalinguistic convention that a metanotion ending in a digit character automatically stands for the same set of protonotions as the metanotion without the digit; there is no need to give an explicit metarule to equate them.

We may still represent syntactic structures in terms of syntax trees, labeling non-leaf nodes with notions and leaf nodes with protonotions ending in **symbol**. The use of an **EMPTY** alternative corresponds to an "invisible" subtree which has no leaves but simply "dies out" (Fig. 2.18).

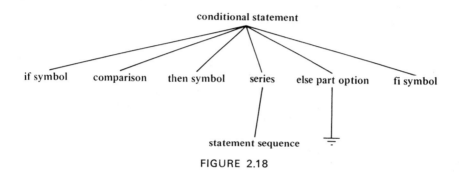

FIGURE 2.18

Metanotions and hyper-rules find their simplest applications in abbreviating context-free grammars in various ways. For example, the lengthy rule for **letter** in Table 2.6 can be shortened to

letter: ALPHA symbol.

provided that we add the metarule for **ALPHA** given above. General hyper-rules, such as those for **NOTION sequence**, **NOTION list**, and **NOTION option** given above, can be very useful in reducing the size of large grammars. As a further example, the metarule

NUMBER :: EMPTY; NUMBER i.

and the general hyper-rules

upto NUMBER i NOTION: upto NUMBER NOTION; NOTION,
upto NUMBER NOTION.
upto NOTION: EMPTY.

provide a convenient means of specifying zero or more occurrences of things up to a certain limit. For instance, given appropriate rules for **letter** and

alphanum, the syntax of Fortran identifiers can be specified as

identifier: letter, upto iiiii alphanum.

It may be verified that the structure of a three-character identifier can then be represented as in Fig. 2.19. Other structures are equally possible, but the ambiguity is of no consequence in this case.

The really significant property of two-level grammars as opposed to BNF and its variants is their ability to express the context-sensitive as well as the context-free aspects of a subject language. As a first illustration of this capability, suppose that we wish to give a syntactic specification of identifiers with the following peculiar restriction: each identifier must begin with a string of one or more x's, followed by a string of an equal number of y's, followed by a string of an equal number of z's; i.e., the (only) legal identifiers are

$$xyz, \ xxyyzz, \ xxxyyyzzz, \ xxxxyyyyzzzz, \ \dots$$

It is a well-known result of formal language theory that this set of strings cannot be defined by any context-free grammar, so that it is impossible to specify such identifiers in BNF or its variants (doubters are invited to try it!).

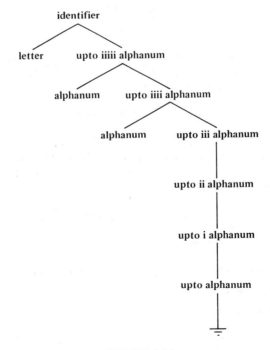

FIGURE 2.19

We shall make use of two metanotions, **LETTER** and **TALLY**, defined by the following metarules:

LETTER :: **letter x; letter y; letter z.**

TALLY :: **i; TALLY i.**

Note that **LETTER** stands for only three protonotions and acts as an abbreviation aid only, whereas **TALLY** stands for an infinite number of protonotions, each of which is a string of **i**'s. Now the following hyper-rules define the desired class of identifiers:

identifier: TALLY letter x, TALLY letter y, TALLY letter z.

TALLY i LETTER: TALLY LETTER, i LETTER.

i LETTER: LETTER symbol.

There are an infinite number of notions involved in these rules

(i letter x, ii letter x, iii letter x, ... , i letter y,

ii letter y, iii letter y, ... , i letter z, ii letter z,

iii letter z, ...)

and the second hyper-rule represents an infinite number of production rules, one for each of these notions. The first hyper-rule defines an infinite number of alternatives for **identifier**:

i letter x, i letter y, i letter z

ii letter x, ii letter y, ii letter z

iii letter x, iii letter y, iii letter z

. . .

Because of the consistent substitution requirement, only these alternatives are permitted. The third hyper-rule is merely an abbreviation for three production rules. If we substitute **i** for **TALLY**, we obtain the syntax tree for *xyz* using only the first and third hyper-rules (Fig. 2.20). Replacing **TALLY** by **ii** in the first rule and by **i** in the second rule leads to the tree for *xxyyzz* (Fig. 2.21). To verify his or her complete understanding of this miniature two-level grammar, the reader may wish to construct the tree for *xxxyyyzzz*.

More realistic instances of context sensitivity in a subject language can be rather difficult to capture in a two-level grammar. One very helpful device is the use of *predicates*—protonotions which are either notions that give rise to invisible subtrees only, in which case we say that the predicate "holds," or are not notions at all (i.e., they are "blind alleys" for which there are no

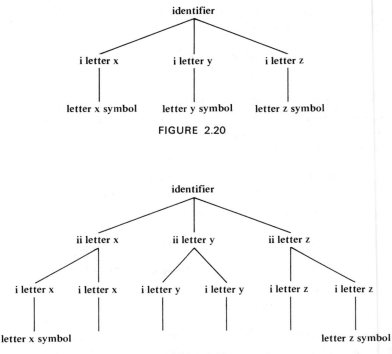

FIGURE 2.20

FIGURE 2.21

production rules). By convention, protonotions that act as predicates begin
with **where** or **unless**. As a simple example of their use, suppose that the subject
language has a (possibly infinite) number of different data types for variables
and expressions; that each type corresponds to a protonotion such as **int**,
real, or **char**, all of which are represented by the metanotion **TYPE**; and that
we wish to specify that the types of the left and right sides of an assignment
statement must be the same, except that an integer value may be assigned to
a real variable. This can be done as follows:

asmt: TYPE1 var, becomes symbol, TYPE2 expr,

where TYPE2 convertible to TYPE1.

where TYPE convertible to TYPE: EMPTY.

where int convertible to real: EMPTY.

These hyper-rules permit both of the structures (among others) shown in
Figs. 2.22 and 2.23. But we cannot have the structure in Fig. 2.24 because
where real convertible to int is a blind alley. This example does not really
illustrate the full power of predicates, since the same effect can be achieved

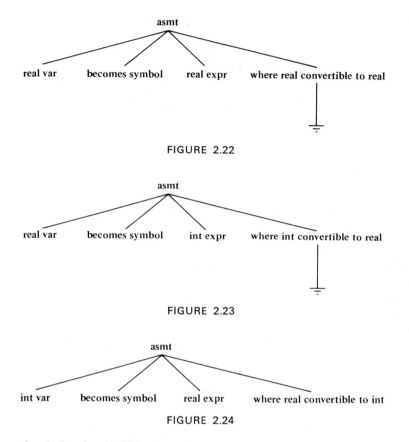

FIGURE 2.22

FIGURE 2.23

FIGURE 2.24

more simply by the single hyper-rule

> **asmt: TYPE var, becomes symbol, TYPE expr;**
>
> **real var, becomes symbol, int expr.**

In the two-level, context-sensitive grammar for Eva given in the next section, however, predicates play a significant role.

EXERCISES

1. List all the production rules represented by the following:

> **NUMERIC :: integer; real; complex.**
> **constant: NUMERIC numeral.**
> **NUMERIC expression: NUMERIC element;**
> **NUMERIC element, operator, NUMERIC expression.**

2. List all the production rules represented by the following:

> **EMPTY :: .**
> **TALLETY :: EMPTY; TALLETY i.**
> **integer constant: iiii digit.**
> **TALLETY i digit: digit, TALLETY digit; TALLETY digit.**

In informal terms, what may an **integer constant** consist of?

3. Write a two-level grammar that generates the set of all (26) strings of three letters which are all the same
(a) without using a predicate, and
(b) using a predicate.

2.4.3 Another Complete Syntactic Specification for Eva

The main problem now before us is the incorporation of the context conditions for Eva, stated informally in Sec. 2.1.3, into a formal, two-level grammar. The basic idea that will ultimately permit a full solution to this problem is to arrange for most of the grammar's notions to each begin with a protonotion represented by the metanotion **NEST**, which is defined by the following metarules:

> **NEST :: new; new DECS; NEST new DECS.**
>
> **DECS :: DEC; DECS DEC.**
>
> **DEC :: TYPE type TAG.**

Each **TAG** stands for a protonotion that acts as a metalinguistic analog of a name occurring in a program of the subject language:

> **TAG :: LETTER; TAG LETTER.**
>
> **LETTER :: letter ALPHA.**

(**ALPHA**, as well as **NOTION** and **EMPTY**, are as defined in the preceding section.) For example, **letter n letter u letter m** is a protonotion, derived from **TAG**, corresponding to the name *num*. The **TYPE** in each **TYPE type TAG** segment of a **NEST** stands for a protonotion corresponding to the data type of the name corresponding to the **TAG**:

> **TYPE :: VALTYPE; proc; proc with PARAMETERS.**
>
> **VALTYPE :: char; string.**
>
> **PARAMETERS :: PARAMETER; PARAMETERS PARAMETER.**
>
> **PARAMETER :: VALTYPE type TAG.**

Note that complete information on the parameters of a procedure, if any, is included in the protonotion corresponding to a procedure name. As examples of **TYPE type TAG** (i.e., **DEC**) protonotions, **char type letter c letter h** would correspond to the character variable *ch*, and **proc with string type letter s char type letter c letter c type letter s letter u letter b** would correspond to the procedure name *sub* declared as

proc sub (string s, char cc) = . . .

[When designing a two-level grammar, care must be taken to ensure that protonotions are derived from metanotions in an unambiguous manner. This is why the "meta-delimiter" **type** has been included in **TYPE type TAG**; the foregoing example of the latter would otherwise be ambiguous with respect to where the second-to-last **TAG** ended and the last one began. The use of **TAG**, as specified above, as opposed to **NOTION** also eliminates a potential source of ambiguity. Observe also that, if digit characters were permitted in Eva names, **TAG** would be defined more generally so as to include protonotions such as **letter c letter h digit seven** (for *ch7*).]

The significance of the protonotions arising from **NEST** is as follows: a notion of the form **NEST NOTION** (e.g., a notion of the form **NEST statement**) will characterize a syntactic unit of an Eva program if and only if the **NEST** protonotion ("nest" for short) records the name and type information specified by just those declaration sequences and/or parameter lists which bear upon that syntactic unit. The block that forms a complete program will just have the dummy nest **new**, since there are no outer declarations affecting it. The notion for each principal construct inside the main block will have a nest of the form **new new DECS**, where the **DECS** part records the information specified by the block's declarations. Notions for constructs inside a further inner block or body of a procedure with parameters will have a nest of the form **new new DECS1 new DECS2**, and so forth. For example, in the Eva program

begin
    char x
    proc p = (
        input x
        neq x, "z": (output x call p))
    call p
  end

each occurrence of **call** *p* is a **new new char type letter x proc type letter p statement**. If the body of *p* were a block with a local string variable *s*, the inner occurrence of **call** *p* would be a **new new char type letter x proc type letter p new string type letter s statement**.

In the case of the block and declaration constructs, this elaborate embellishment of the various syntactic notions is carried still further by suffixing a **DECS** protonotion corresponding to the new set of declarations involved. Where we would simply have the notion **block** in a context-free grammar, we will now be dealing with notions of the form **NEST block containing DECS**, where the **DECS** part records the information given by the declarations inside the block. For example, the "topmost" hyper-rule in the grammar is

program: new block containing DECS, where DECS consistent.

The predicate part **where DECS consistent** corresponds to the context condition which states that a name cannot be declared more than once at the same level in a program. The formalization of this condition requires a number of auxiliary hyper-rules. First, if the **DECS** is actually a single **DEC**, there is no problem:

where DEC consistent: EMPTY.

Otherwise, according to the metarules, the **DECS** must be of the form **DECS DEC**, which is the same as **DECS TYPE type TAG**. Since the type information is not relevant here, we merely stipulate that the final **TAG** must not appear earlier in the protonotion, as well as (recursively) requiring the earlier part to be itself consistent:

where DECS TYPE type TAG consistent:
where DECS consistent, where TAG not in DECS.

(Note that we are getting multiple branching of subtrees, all of which should turn out to be invisible.) The following rules reduce the problem to that of nonequality of **TAG**s:

where TAG not in DECS DEC:
where TAG not in DECS, where TAG not in DEC.
where TAG1 not in TYPE type TAG2: where TAG1 is not TAG2.

Nonequality of **TAG**s is a special case of nonequality of **NOTION**s. To deal with the latter, we need the additional metarule

NOTETY :: NOTION; EMPTY.

(The use of **-ETY** as a suffix in metanotions for which **EMPTY** is one of the alternatives is another useful convention. We shall also be making use of

DECSETY :: DECS; EMPTY.

in this definition of Eva.) A pair of **NOTION**s may be tested for inequality by repeatedly comparing pairs of corresponding letters until either a mismatch is found or it is discovered that the lengths are different. This is the basic idea behind the following hyper-rules:

where NOTETY1 ALPHA1 is not NOTETY2 ALPHA2:

    where NOTETY1 is not NOTETY2;

    where ALPHA1 precedes ALPHA2 in abcdefghijklmnopqrstuvwxyz;

    where ALPHA2 precedes ALPHA1 in abcdefghijklmnopqrstuvwxyz.

where NOTION is not EMPTY: EMPTY.

where EMPTY is not NOTION: EMPTY.

where ALPHA1 precedes ALPHA2 in NOTETY1 ALPHA1 NOTETY2 ALPHA2 NOTETY3: EMPTY.

As an example of the use of the last hyper-rule above, substitution of **h** for **ALPHA1**, **t** for **ALPHA2**, **abcdefg** for **NOTETY1**, **ijklmnopqrs** for **NOTETY2**, and **uvwxyz** for **NOTETY3** tells us that the predicate **where h precedes t in abcdefghijklmnopqrstuvwxyz** holds. The reader may verify that all such "reasonable" predicates hold, whereas all "unreasonable" ones like **where t precedes h in abcdefghijklmnopqrstuvwxyz** are blind alleys.

To see how these rules apply to the sample program given above, we take **DECS** to be **char type letter x proc type letter p** and are led inexorably to the structure shown in Fig. 2.25.

It remains to be seen just how the grammar forces a unique substitution for **DECS** for each Eva program. First, the hyper-rule for the block construct is

    NEST block containing DECS:

        begin symbol, NEST new DECS declaration sequence for DECS,

        NEST new DECS statement sequence, end symbol.

Observe how the nest for the inner constructs is augmented. Expanding the leftmost subtree in Fig. 2.25, we obtain Fig. 2.26. As for the declaration part, the hyper-rules

NEST declaration sequence for DECS DEC:

    NEST declaration sequence for DECS, NEST declaration of DEC.

NEST declaration sequence for DEC: NEST declaration of DEC.

NEST declaration of VALTYPE type TAG: VALTYPE symbol, TAG symbol.

NEST declaration of proc type TAG:

    proc symbol, TAG symbol, equals symbol, NEST statement.

are sufficient to allow us to derive the partial subtree of Fig. 2.27. (It should now be apparent that if our original choice of protonotion for **DECS** had been anything other than **char type letter x proc type letter p**, we could not have obtained the desired sequence of terminal symbols. Given any particular program, the grammar forces a unique substitution for each relevant metanotion.)

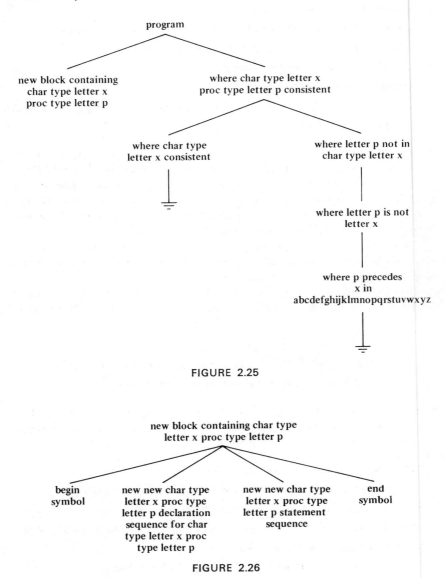

FIGURE 2.25

FIGURE 2.26

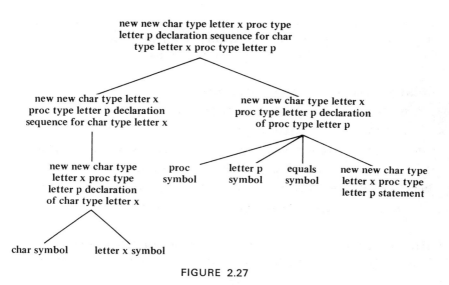

FIGURE 2.27

However, we have not taken account of the fact that character or string names may be grouped into lists, as in **char** *a, b, c*. One way of looking at this is to consider the commas as alternative symbols for the preceding declarer symbol, so that the situation can be salvaged by adding the rule

NEST new DECSETY1 VALTYPE type TAG1 VALTYPE type TAG2 DECSETY2

declaration of VALTYPE type TAG2: comma symbol, TAG2 symbol.

(In this rule, the last **DECS** in the nest has been decomposed in order to show that the name being declared must be of the same type as the preceding name in the declaration. The uniqueness of this decomposition is guaranteed by the "consistency" of the **DECS** as specified elsewhere.) We now have two alternative hyper-rules from which a production rule for the notion **char type letter a char type letter b declaration of char type letter b**, for example, can be derived. One of these rules defines the construct as consisting of a **char symbol** followed by a **letter b symbol**, and the other defines it as a **comma symbol** followed by a **letter b symbol**.

The following rules complete the specifications for declarations:

NEST declaration of proc with PARAMETERS type TAG:

  proc symbol, TAG symbol, lpar symbol,

  NEST new PARAMETERS definition part for PARAMETERS, rpar symbol,

  equals symbol,

  NEST new PARAMETERS statement, where PARAMETERS consistent.

(A procedure with parameters is analogous to an inner block. The fact that the protonotions represented by **PARAMETERS** are a subset of the protonotions represented by **DECS** has saved a considerable number of rules.)

NEST definition part for PARAMETERS PARAMETER:
    NEST definition part for PARAMETERS, comma symbol,
    NEST definition of PARAMETER.
NEST definition part for PARAMETER: NEST definition of PARAMETER.
NEST definition of VALTYPE type TAG: VALTYPE symbol, TAG symbol.
NEST new DECSETY1 VALTYPE type TAG1 VALTYPE type TAG2 DECSETY2
    definition of VALTYPE type TAG2: TAG2 symbol.

(Here the device used to account for groups of parameters of the same type is similar, but not identical, to the one used for declarations of groups of variables.)

Now we turn our attention to the statement part of a block:

    NEST statement sequence: NEST statement;
      NEST statement sequence, NEST statement.
    NEST statement:
      input symbol, char NEST name with TAG;
      output symbol, char NEST expression;
      call symbol, NEST call;
      NEST block containing DECS, where DECS consistent;
      lpar symbol, NEST statement sequence, rpar symbol;
      TEST symbol, VALTYPE NEST expression, comma symbol,
        VALTYPE NEST expression, colon symbol, NEST statement;
      cons symbol, char NEST expression, comma symbol,
        string NEST name with TAG.

Note that the nest in a notion for a name or expression is always preceded by a protonotion denoting the type of the name or expression. In addition, a notion for a name always ends with a **TAG**, which will subsequently be specified as the **TAG** corresponding to the name. Referring again to our sample program, the structure of the procedure body is that shown in Fig. 2.28. The metarule for **TEST** is simply

$$\textbf{TEST :: eq; neq.}$$

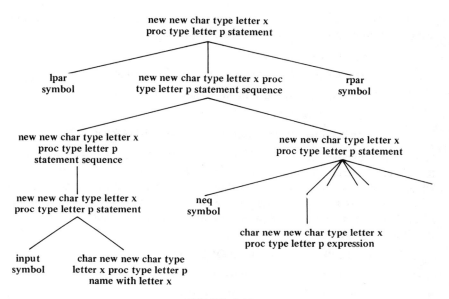

FIGURE 2.28

and the following hyper-rules complete the specifications for call statements:

> NEST call: proc NEST name with TAG;
>> proc with PARAMETERS NEST name with TAG, lpar symbol,
>>> NEST arglist for PARAMETERS, rpar symbol.
>
> NEST arglist for PARAMETERS PARAMETER:
>> NEST arglist for PARAMETERS, comma symbol,
>> NEST arglist for PARAMETER.
>
> NEST arglist for VALTYPE type TAG:
>> VALTYPE NEST expression.

It is now a straightforward matter to formulate the rules for expressions:

> char NEST expression: char NEST name with TAG;
>> quote symbol, letter, quote symbol; space symbol;
>> head symbol, string NEST expression.
>
> string NEST expression: string NEST name with TAG;
>> quote symbol, quote symbol;
>> quote symbol, letter, letter sequence, quote symbol;
>> tail symbol, string NEST expression.
>
> letter sequence: letter; letter sequence, letter.
>
> letter: LETTER symbol.

Finally, we come to the rules for names used as expressions and the all-important context condition that they must satisfy:

TYPE NEST name with TAG:

  TAG symbol, where TYPE type TAG found in NEST.

where TYPE type TAG found in NEST new DECS:

  where TYPE type TAG one of DECS;

  where TAG not in DECS, where TYPE type TAG found in NEST.

(The nest must be "searched" from back to front, since the name might have been declared at more than one level. The last rule excludes the case in which the innermost declaration of the name specifies a different type; recall that **where TAG not in DECS** has already been defined. There is no rule for **where TYPE type TAG found in new** because we want all such predicates to be blind alleys.)

  where TYPE type TAG one of DECS DEC:

  where TYPE type TAG one of DEC;

  where TYPE type TAG one of DECS.

  where TYPE type TAG one of TYPE type TAG: EMPTY.

Let us now expand one more subtree in our example, as shown in Fig. 2.29.

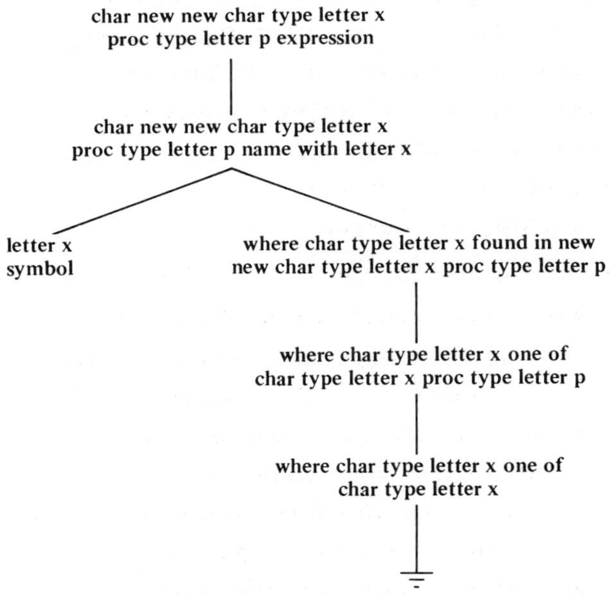

FIGURE 2.29

Thankfully, the grammar is now complete, and the rules are summarized in Table 2.7. The representations of symbols other than letters and names are also listed. The representations of name symbols, though infinite in number, are assumed to be constructed in the obvious manner; e.g., the representation for **letter c letter h symbol** is *ch*. It would not be difficult to modify the grammar so that each letter in a name would be a separate symbol.

The reader should now be convinced that all the context conditions stated in Sec. 2.1.3 have now been fully formalized. In essence, this has been achieved by having the grammar prescribe a tailor-made set of notions, complicated but finite in number, for each legal program. Each legal program has a unique syntax tree with **program** at the root, and no syntax tree can be derived for any illegal program.

TABLE 2.7 Two-Level Grammar for Eva

Metarules

ALPHA :: a; b; c; d; e; f; g; h; i; j; k; l; m; n; o; p; q; r; s; t; u; v; w; x; y; z.

DEC :: TYPE type TAG.

DECS :: DEC; DECS DEC.

DECSETY :: DECS; EMPTY.

EMPTY :: .

LETTER :: letter ALPHA.

NEST :: new; new DECS; NEST new DECS.

NOTETY :: NOTION; EMPTY.

NOTION :: ALPHA; NOTION ALPHA.

PARAMETER :: VALTYPE type TAG.

PARAMETERS :: PARAMETER; PARAMETERS PARAMETER.

TAG :: LETTER; TAG LETTER.

TEST :: eq; neq.

TYPE :: VALTYPE; proc; proc with PARAMETERS.

VALTYPE :: char; string.

Hyper-Rules

program: new block containing DECS, where DECS consistent.

NEST block containing DECS:

    begin symbol, NEST new DECS declaration sequence for DECS,

    NEST new DECS statement sequence, end symbol.

NEST declaration sequence for DECS DEC:

    NEST declaration sequence for DECS, NEST declaration of DEC.

TABLE 2.7   (Continued)

NEST declaration sequence for DEC: NEST declaration of DEC.

NEST declaration of VALTYPE type TAG: VALTYPE symbol, TAG symbol.

NEST new DECSETY1 VALTYPE type TAG1 VALTYPE type TAG2 DECSETY2

    declaration of VALTYPE type TAG2: comma symbol, TAG2 symbol.

NEST declaration of proc type TAG:

    proc symbol, TAG symbol, equals symbol, NEST statement.

NEST declaration of proc with PARAMETERS type TAG:

    proc symbol, TAG symbol, lpar symbol,

    NEST new PARAMETERS definition part for PARAMETERS, rpar symbol,

    equals symbol, NEST new PARAMETERS statement,

    where PARAMETERS consistent.

NEST definition part for PARAMETERS PARAMETER:

    NEST definition part for PARAMETERS, comma symbol,

    NEST definition of PARAMETER.

NEST definition part for PARAMETER: NEST definition of PARAMETER.

NEST definition of VALTYPE type TAG: VALTYPE symbol, TAG symbol.

NEST new DECSETY1 VALTYPE type TAG1 VALTYPE type TAG2 DECSETY2

    definition of VALTYPE type TAG2: TAG2 symbol.

NEST statement sequence: NEST statement;

    NEST statement sequence, NEST statement.

NEST statement:

    input symbol, char NEST name with TAG;

    output symbol, char NEST expression;

    call symbol, NEST call;

    NEST block containing DECS, where DECS consistent;

    lpar symbol, NEST statement sequence, rpar symbol;

    TEST symbol, VALTYPE NEST expression, comma symbol,

        VALTYPE NEST expression, colon symbol, NEST statement;

    cons symbol, char NEST expression, comma symbol,

        string NEST name with TAG.

NEST call: proc NEST name with TAG;

    proc with PARAMETERS NEST name with TAG, lpar symbol,

        NEST arglist for PARAMETERS, rpar symbol.

NEST arglist for PARAMETERS PARAMETER:

    NEST arglist for PARAMETERS, comma symbol,

    NEST arglist for PARAMETER.

TABLE 2.7 (Continued)

NEST arglist for VALTYPE type TAG:

    VALTYPE NEST expression.

char NEST expression: char NEST name with TAG;

    quote symbol, letter, quote symbol; space symbol;

    head symbol, string NEST expression.

string NEST expression: string NEST name with TAG;

    quote symbol, quote symbol;

    quote symbol, letter, letter sequence, quote symbol;

    tail symbol, string NEST expression.

letter sequence: letter; letter sequence, letter.

letter: LETTER symbol.

TYPE NEST name with TAG:

    TAG symbol, where TYPE type TAG found in NEST.

where TYPE type TAG found in NEST new DECS:

    where TYPE type TAG one of DECS;

    where TAG not in DECS, where TYPE type TAG found in NEST.

where TYPE type TAG one of DECS DEC:

    where TYPE type TAG one of DEC;

    where TYPE type TAG one of DECS.

where TYPE type TAG one of TYPE type TAG: EMPTY.

where DEC consistent: EMPTY.

where DECS TYPE type TAG consistent:

    where DECS consistent, where TAG not in DECS.

where TAG not in DECS DEC:

    where TAG not in DECS, where TAG not in DEC.

where TAG1 not in TYPE type TAG2: where TAG1 is not TAG2.

where NOTETY1 ALPHA1 is not NOTETY2 ALPHA2:

    where NOTETY1 is not NOTETY2;

    where ALPHA1 precedes ALPHA2 in abcdefghijklmnopqrstuvwxyz;

    where ALPHA2 precedes ALPHA1 in abcdefghijklmnopqrstuvwxyz.

where NOTION is not EMPTY: EMPTY.

where EMPTY is not NOTION: EMPTY.

where ALPHA1 precedes ALPHA2 in NOTETY1 ALPHA1 NOTETY2 ALPHA2

    NOTETY3: EMPTY.

TABLE 2.7 (Continued)

Representation Table

begin symbol	begin	output symbol	output
end symbol	end	call symbol	call
char symbol	char	eq symbol	eq
string symbol	string	neq symbol	neq
comma symbol	,	colon symbol	:
proc symbol	proc	cons symbol	cons
equals symbol	=	quote symbol	"
lpar symbol	(	space symbol	space
rpar symbol	)	head symbol	head
input symbol	input	tail symbol	tail

EXERCISES

1. Referring to the grammar of Table 2.7, construct the complete syntax tree for the program

> **begin**
> **proc** p (**char** a, b) $=$
> **output** b
> **call** p ("x", "y")
> **end**

2. Replacement of the constant "y" by "yz" in the program of Exercise 1 introduces a violation of a context condition. Verify that the resulting erroneous program is not derivable from the grammar.

3. For some actual programming language with which you are familiar, identify the static context conditions associated with subscripted variables such as $A(I)$ and $B(I,J+1)$. Explain in general terms how the conditions might be formalized in a two-level grammar for the language.

For Further Information

Cleaveland and Uzgalis (1977, pp. 45–129) present a very thorough and readable description of two-level grammars and their use in completely defining the syntax of programming languages. The prime example of a large-scale two-level grammar for a real programming language is that contained in the official definition of Algol 68 (van Wijngaarden et al., 1976). It incorporates *all* the static context conditions that should be checked by any good Algol 68 compiler, and some of these conditions are very complex and subtle.

3

from syntax to semantics

The concepts and techniques described in this chapter provide a convenient bridge for making the transition from the methods for formalizing syntax covered in Chap. 2 to the methods for formalizing semantics covered in Chap. 4. In particular, we shall see how two of the approaches already described—attribute grammars and two-level grammars—may be extended to include the specification not only of syntax but also of semantics, subject to the acceptance of certain interpretations of the phrase 'meaning of a program'. These approaches are covered in this transitional chapter because they basically involve taking a set of syntactic specifications similar to those seen earlier and "tacking on" a set of semantic specifications which are constructed using the same basic, formal tools as the syntactic specifications. In contrast, the approaches described in Chap. 4 are more directly aimed at semantics as the primary area of interest, with syntax playing an ancillary role. In order to lay the groundwork for all these approaches, it is necessary first to review and clarify our notion of the distinction between syntax and semantics and to introduce the concept of "abstract syntax" as an important interface between them.

SYNTAX, SEMANTICS, AND ABSTRACT SYNTAX

The terminological boundary between "syntax" and "semantics" is to some degree arbitrary, and different people have drawn the distinction in different ways. In this book, we have implicitly taken the position that all those aspects of a programming language which can "reasonably" be explained in terms of symbol sequences (program texts) alone belong to the realm of syntax, and that all other aspects of interest belong to the realms of semantics and pragmatics. The problem now is to clarify what we mean by "reasonably." One useful, but not foolproof, way of looking at the matter is to consider the problem of constructing a compiler for a given subject language. A program expressed in the subject language would be processed in two steps—translation (at "compile time") into machine language by the compiler followed by execution (at "runtime") of the machine code. A good compiler performs as much error checking as possible at compile time and arranges runtime checking only for those errors which cannot easily be detected at compile time. The point of view we are taking is that all linguistic aspects, other than code generation and optimization, which are normally handled by the processor at compile time are syntactic in nature and that all aspects normally handled at runtime are semantic in nature; in particular, errors detected at compile time are syntactic errors (i.e., the sequence of symbols input does not constitute a syntactically valid program of the subject language), and errors detected at runtime are semantic errors (i.e., the program is syntactically valid but semantically faulty).

Referring to our two illustrative languages, the various context conditions for Eva listed in Sec. 2.1.3 would normally all be handled at compile time. Therefore, we regard them as syntactic in nature and say that, for example,

$$\textbf{char } x$$
$$\textbf{string } x$$

is a syntactically invalid sequence of symbols comparable to the ill-formed Pam statement

$$\textbf{if } a + 1 \textbf{ then write } b \textbf{ fi}$$

On the other hand, we do not attempt to go beyond properties such as these and extend the realm of syntax to include such aspects as loop termination and (the non-occurrence of) division by zero. Although it may seem that, for example,

$$a := b \ / \ 0$$

could reasonably be excluded on purely syntactic grounds, it is not clear whether

$$\textbf{if } 2 = 2 \textbf{ then } a := 1 \textbf{ else } a := b \ / \ 0 \textbf{ fi}$$

should be disallowed (since the division can never take place), and the status of

$$\textbf{read } x \ ; \ y := 10 \ / \ x$$

can only be determined by taking the input data into account. The simplest course is to place all such matters, which generally entail some sort of modeling of an execution process, into the realm of semantics.

This informal notion of the syntactic/semantic boundary seems reasonably consistent with our intuitive knowledge about "form" versus "meaning" and is quite widely accepted. At the same time, however, much of the computing literature, especially that having to do with compilers, employs the term 'syntax' less liberally, so that aspects such as type checking and identification of occurrences of variables with their declarations are classified under 'semantics'. Sometimes a distinction is drawn between "static semantics," encompassing the non-context-free compile-time aspects, and "dynamic semantics," encompassing the runtime aspects. As far as the terminology of this book is concerned, syntax includes static semantics (but not code generation), and semantics is in large part dynamic semantics.

From this standpoint, we may say that a (syntactically valid) Pam program is semantically erroneous if its execution would necessarily give rise to any of the following:

1. Division by zero.
2. Nontermination (infinite looping).
3. Attempting to read past the end of the input file.
4. Evaluation of a variable that has not been given a value.

The "meaninglessness" of programs involving such errors is expressed with varying degrees of explicitness by different definitional techniques. It would also be possible, albeit awkward in some cases, for a formal specification to take into account the existence of implementation-dependent restrictions, such as a limit on the magnitude of integer values. The position taken in this book, however, is that such restrictions are properties of *implementations* rather than of *languages* themselves and thus need not be incorporated into our specifications.

The types of semantic error associated with Eva are as follows:

1. Nontermination (infinite recursion).
2. Attempting to read past the end of the input file.
3. Evaluation of a **char** variable that has not been given a value.
4. Application of **head** or **tail** to the null string.

All violations of context conditions are, according to our terminology, syntactic errors. Another common type of semantic error encountered with most realistic programming languages but not in Pam or Eva is that of an array subscript value being out of range.

Any semantic specification technique must in some sense associate "meaning" with the programs and constructs of a subject language. Programming language theorists have formulated various, differing concepts of what "meaning" is in this context, and this is one reason why there is a wide variety of approaches to semantic formalization. For example, in the "translational" approach described in Sec. 3.2, the meaning of a program is simply taken to be an equivalent program expressed in another, "primitive" language, while the "interpretive" method described in Sec. 3.3 specifies the meaning of a program basically by defining the (infinite) set of all pairs of the form (input file, output file) such that the program produces the output file from the input file.

In many approaches to formal semantics, it is inconvenient to employ syntactic specifications of the types considered so far as a basis for the description of meaning. Part of the reason for this is that program texts employ many notational devices that are devoid of semantic significance. For example, although the Pam statement form

$$\textbf{if } a = b \textbf{ then } \langle\text{statement}\rangle \textbf{ fi}$$

and the Eva statement form

$$\textbf{eq } a, b: \langle\text{statement}\rangle$$

are superficially quite different, they mean essentially the same thing. Thus, from a semantic point of view, the choice of such symbols as **if, then, fi**, ',', and ':' is arbitrary; as textual delimiters, their main function is merely to supply readability and to prevent syntactic ambiguities from arising. (The term 'syntactic sugar' is sometimes used to describe these and other semantically irrelevant aspects of languages.) Assuming that we know we are talking about a ⟨conditional statement⟩, the only constituents of the construct with semantic significance are its ⟨comparison⟩ and its ⟨statement⟩, irrespective of the textual details. A complete (and more precise) set of such statements identifying the semantically relevant structural features of a subject language constitute a description of the language's *abstract syntax*.

As an example, the following is a possible informal description of the abstract syntax of Pam:

- A series consists of a list of statements.
- A statement consists of *either* a read statement *or* a write statement

or an assignment statement *or* a conditional statement *or* a definite loop *or* an indefinite loop.

- A read statement consists of a list of variables.
- A write statement consists of a list of variables.
- An assignment statement consists of a variable *and* an expression.
- A conditional statement consists of *either* a comparison *and* a series *or* a comparison *and* a series *and* another series.
- A definite loop consists of an expression *and* a series.
- An indefinite loop consists of a comparison *and* a series.
- A comparison consists of an expression *and* a relation *and* another expression.
- An expression consists of *either* an infix expression *or* a variable *or* an integer.
- An infix expression consists of an expression *and* an operator *and* another expression.
- A variable consists of an (integer) address of a storage location.
- A relation consists of *either* 'eq' *or* 'gt' *or* 'le' *or* 'lt' *or* 'ge' *or* 'ne'.
- An operator consists of *either* 'plus' *or* 'minus' *or* 'times' *or* 'over'.

If these statements were expressed in a suitable formal metalanguage, they would represent a considerable simplification over the corresponding BNF (or equivalent) rules. Tree diagrams of program structure can now take a much simpler form also; for example, the abstract structure of

$$\text{read } k \ ; \ \textbf{while } k \ > \ 0 \ \textbf{do } k \ := \ k \ - \ 1 \ \textbf{end}$$

might be represented as in Fig. 3.1.

It is often useful to think of such an abstract structure, containing only the semantically relevant information about a program, as the "fundamental" form of the program and the textual version as a derived form, rather than vice versa. The textual form is then regarded merely as a linear encoding of the abstract form. This encoding is rendered correctly and unambiguously by the insertion of delimiter symbols; for example, the structure of Fig. 3.2 would be mapped into the textual expression $5 * (6 + 7)$, parentheses and operator precedence conventions being part of the "syntactic sugar" that we have eliminated from the abstract syntax.

The concept of abstract syntax is employed by most approaches to formal semantics in one form or another, either explicitly or implicitly. It is

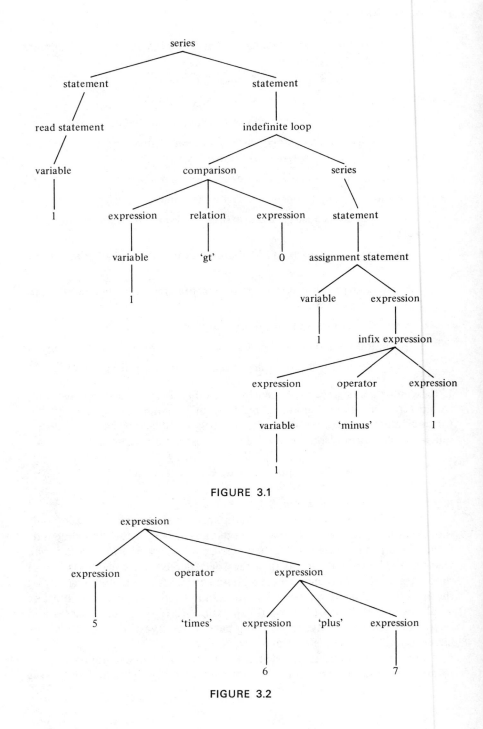

FIGURE 3.1

FIGURE 3.2

scarcely noticeable in the section that follows, but much of the rest of the book may be viewed as dealing with techniques for associating meaning with abstract program representations. Only the general idea of abstract syntax has been introduced here; each semantic formalism has its own conceptual refinements and notations.

EXERCISES

1. Give an informal but careful description of the abstract syntax of Eva.

2. Identify a small but usable subset of Fortran, Pascal, PL/I, or some other actual language, and give an informal but careful description of its abstract syntax.

3.2

TRANSLATIONAL SEMANTICS USING ATTRIBUTE GRAMMARS—A COMPLETE DEFINITION OF PAM

The definitional power of attribute grammars, which were introduced in Sec. 2.3, extends beyond the realm of syntax into the realm of semantics. In particular, the attribute grammar technique is well suited to the formal specification of a mapping from a subject language to some other language which, following the terminology associated with compilers, we may call an *object language*. The contention that such a mapping constitutes a complete semantic specification of the subject language rests upon the assumption that the object language either is itself defined independently or is "semantically primitive." In this section, we shall illustrate this "translational" approach to language definition by taking Pam as the subject language and a simple symbolic (assembly-like) machine language as the object language.

The machine-like object language corresponds to a very simple computer with one accumulator and a memory whose words are capable of holding integer values. There are 17 instruction types, with the following mnemonic operation codes:

LOAD	Load accumulator
STO	Store
ADD	Add
SUB	Subtract
MULT	Multiply
DIV	Divide
GET	Input a value
PUT	Output a value
J	Jump
JN	Jump on negative

JP	Jump on positive
JZ	Jump on zero
JNZ	Jump on negative or zero
JPZ	Jump on positive or zero
JNP	Jump on negative or positive
LAB	Label (no operation)
HALT	Halt execution

Each STO, GET, and PUT instruction includes one operand specifying a memory address. This may be either an address corresponding to a Pam variable, in which case the variable itself appears in the instruction, or an extra working-storage address ("temporary") represented by one of the symbols T1, T2, etc. Each LOAD, ADD, SUB, MULT, and DIV instruction includes one operand given either by a memory address or by an integer constant; the result of the operation is left in the accumulator. HALT and LAB have no operands, but the latter symbol is always preceded by a label of the form L1, L2, etc.; only LAB instructions may be so labeled. Each jump instruction includes one operand that is a label. Except in the case of a J instruction, whether the transfer of control actually occurs depends on the value currently in the accumulator.

As an example of a program expressed in this object language, the Pam program

> **read** x, y ;
>
> **while** $x <> 99$ **do**
>
> $\quad ans := (x + 1) - (y / 2)$;
>
> $\quad$ **write** *ans* ;
>
> $\quad$ **read** x, y
>
> **end**

could be translated as follows:

	GET	x		STO	T2
	GET	y		LOAD	T1
L1	LAB			SUB	T2
	LOAD	x		STO	ans
	SUB	99		PUT	ans
	JZ	L2		GET	x
	LOAD	x		GET	y
	ADD	1		J	L1
	STO	T1	L2	LAB	
	LOAD	y		HALT	
	DIV	2			

The basic strategy for constructing our attribute grammar is to associate with most of the nonterminal symbols a synthesized attribute Code, where a Code value represents a sequence of instructions such as that given above. The Code value for a given construct will represent the object-language translation of that construct, and the meaning of an entire ⟨program⟩ is therefore defined to be the Code value associated with the root of its syntax tree.

To make this precise, we introduce the attribute Num corresponding to sequences of digit characters and the attribute Tag corresponding to sequences of letter and/or digit characters. Num is a synthesized attribute of ⟨constant⟩ and Tag a synthesized attribute of ⟨variable⟩:

⟨constant⟩ ::= ⟨digit⟩

        Num(⟨constant⟩) ⟵ Num(⟨digit⟩)

  | ⟨constant⟩$_2$ ⟨digit⟩

        Num(⟨constant⟩) ⟵ *concat*(Num(⟨constant⟩$_2$), Num(⟨digit⟩))

⟨variable⟩ ::= ⟨letter⟩

        Tag(⟨variable⟩) ⟵ Tag(⟨letter⟩)

  | ⟨variable⟩$_2$ ⟨letter⟩

        Tag(⟨variable⟩) ⟵ *concat* (Tag(⟨variable⟩$_2$), Tag(⟨letter⟩))

  | ⟨variable⟩$_2$ ⟨digit⟩

        Tag(⟨variable⟩) ⟵ *concat* (Tag(⟨variable⟩$_2$), Num(⟨digit⟩))

⟨digit⟩ ::= 0

        Num(⟨digit⟩) ⟵ ⟨'0'⟩

  | . . .

    . . .

  | 9

        Num(⟨digit⟩) ⟵ ⟨'9'⟩

⟨letter⟩ ::= a

        Tag(⟨letter⟩) ⟵ ⟨'a'⟩

  | . . .

    . . .

  | z

        Tag(⟨letter⟩) ⟵ ⟨'z'⟩

We also introduce the attribute Opcode, with values 'LOAD', 'STO', 'ADD', 'SUB', 'MULT', 'DIV', 'GET', 'PUT', 'J', 'JN', 'JP', 'JZ', 'JNZ', 'JPZ', and 'JNP'. Then the values corresponding to Code are defined as sequences of values of the following forms:

> 'HALT'
> (Opcode, Num)
> (Opcode, Tag)
> (Tag, 'LAB')

The attribute grammar, which is shown in its entirety in Table 3.1, page 92, makes use of three further attributes, Temp, Labin, and Labout, all corresponding to nonnegative integer values. The attribute Temp serves to keep track of the number of temporaries (T1, T2, etc.) which are in use at any given point in a program and which therefore must not be reused by an embedded construct. A Temp value is inherited by each construct that may require the use of additional temporaries in its translation. For example, suppose that we have an ⟨expression⟩ of the form

$$\langle \text{expression} \rangle_2 \ - \ \langle \text{term} \rangle$$

If the ⟨term⟩ is just a variable or a constant, the code for the ⟨expression⟩ can simply take the form

> code for ⟨expression⟩₂
> SUB   ⟨term⟩

but if the ⟨term⟩ contains any operators, its code will contain instructions that alter the accumulator contents, so that the overall pattern of code should be something like

> code for ⟨expression⟩₂
> STO   T1
> code for ⟨term⟩
> STO   T2
> LOAD   T1
> SUB   T2

Now if the code for the ⟨term⟩ similarly requires the use of a pair of temporaries, these will obviously have to be different ones, say T3 and T4. To make this possible, we arrange for the ⟨term⟩ to inherit a Temp value that is greater by 2 than the Temp value for the original ⟨expression⟩.

At this point, we may examine the detailed specifications for expressions:

> ⟨expression⟩ ::= ⟨term⟩
>
>   Code(⟨expression⟩) ⟵ Code(⟨term⟩)
>
>   Temp(⟨term⟩) ⟵ Temp(⟨expression⟩)
>
> | ⟨expression⟩₂ ⟨weak operator⟩ ⟨term⟩
>
>   Code(⟨expression⟩) ⟵ *concat*(Code(⟨expression⟩₂),
>
>   *selectcode*(Code(⟨term⟩), Temp(⟨expression⟩),
>
>   Opcode(⟨weak operator⟩)))

$$\text{Temp}(\langle \text{expression} \rangle_2) \longleftarrow \text{Temp}(\langle \text{expression} \rangle)$$
$$\text{Temp}(\langle \text{term} \rangle) \longleftarrow \text{Temp}(\langle \text{expression} \rangle) + 2$$

Opcode is a synthesized attribute of $\langle \text{weak operator} \rangle$:

$$\langle \text{weak operator} \rangle ::= +$$
$$\text{Opcode}(\langle \text{weak operator} \rangle) \longleftarrow \text{`ADD'}$$
$$| -$$
$$\text{Opcode}(\langle \text{weak operator} \rangle) \longleftarrow \text{`SUB'}$$

If the $\langle \text{term} \rangle$ contains no operators, then, as will be seen shortly, Code ($\langle \text{term} \rangle$) will consist of a single LOAD instruction. In that case, the auxiliary function *selectcode* returns a single ADD or SUB instruction in place of the LOAD, but with the same operand. Otherwise, it returns the longer pattern of instructions involving the use of temporaries. The following rules are completely analogous to those given above:

$$\langle \text{term} \rangle ::= \langle \text{element} \rangle$$
$$\text{Code}(\langle \text{term} \rangle) \longleftarrow \text{Code}(\langle \text{element} \rangle)$$
$$\text{Temp}(\langle \text{element} \rangle) \longleftarrow \text{Temp}(\langle \text{term} \rangle)$$
$$| \ \langle \text{term} \rangle_2 \ \langle \text{strong operator} \rangle \ \langle \text{element} \rangle$$
$$\text{Code}(\langle \text{term} \rangle) \longleftarrow \textit{concat}(\text{Code}(\langle \text{term} \rangle_2), \textit{selectcode}(\text{Code}(\langle \text{element} \rangle),$$
$$\text{Temp}(\langle \text{term} \rangle), \text{Opcode}(\langle \text{strong operator} \rangle)))$$
$$\text{Temp}(\langle \text{term} \rangle_2) \longleftarrow \text{Temp}(\langle \text{term} \rangle)$$
$$\text{Temp}(\langle \text{element} \rangle) \longleftarrow \text{Temp}(\langle \text{term} \rangle) + 2$$
$$\langle \text{strong operator} \rangle ::= *$$
$$\text{Opcode}(\langle \text{strong operator} \rangle) \longleftarrow \text{`MULT'}$$
$$| \ /$$
$$\text{Opcode}(\langle \text{strong operator} \rangle) \longleftarrow \text{`DIV'}$$

The specifications for $\langle \text{element} \rangle$ are straightforward:

$$\langle \text{element} \rangle ::= \langle \text{constant} \rangle$$
$$\text{Code}(\langle \text{element} \rangle) \longleftarrow \langle (\text{`LOAD'}, \text{Num}(\langle \text{constant} \rangle))) \rangle$$
$$| \ \langle \text{variable} \rangle$$
$$\text{Code}(\langle \text{element} \rangle) \longleftarrow \langle (\text{`LOAD'}, \text{Tag}(\langle \text{variable} \rangle))) \rangle$$
$$| \ (\ \langle \text{expression} \rangle \ )$$
$$\text{Code}(\langle \text{element} \rangle) \longleftarrow \text{Code}(\langle \text{expression} \rangle)$$
$$\text{Temp}(\langle \text{expression} \rangle) \longleftarrow \text{Temp}(\langle \text{element} \rangle)$$

As a specific example of the operation of these rules, Fig. 3.3 shows the order in which the attribute values are filled in for $a + b * c$. Here we have assumed that the Temp value inherited by the top $\langle$expression$\rangle$ is 0. Evidently, we are not going out of our way to specify "optimized" code—a better translation of $a + b * c$ would be

$$
\begin{array}{ll}
\text{LOAD} & \text{b} \\
\text{MULT} & \text{c} \\
\text{ADD} & \text{a}
\end{array}
$$

It should be noted in passing that the same temporaries may be used for different purposes in disjoint constructs. For example, it may be verified that the expression $(x + y * z) + b * c$ is mapped into the code

$$
\begin{array}{llll}
\text{LOAD} & \text{x} & \text{STO} & \text{T1} \\
\text{STO} & \text{T1} & \text{LOAD} & \text{b} \\
\text{LOAD} & \text{y} & \text{MULT} & \text{c} \\
\text{MULT} & \text{z} & \text{STO} & \text{T2} \\
\text{STO} & \text{T2} & \text{LOAD} & \text{T1} \\
\text{LOAD} & \text{T1} & \text{ADD} & \text{T2} \\
\text{ADD} & \text{T2} & &
\end{array}
$$

whereas $a + (x + y * z)$ is mapped into

$$
\begin{array}{llll}
\text{LOAD} & \text{a} & \text{STO} & \text{T4} \\
\text{STO} & \text{T1} & \text{LOAD} & \text{T3} \\
\text{LOAD} & \text{x} & \text{ADD} & \text{T4} \\
\text{STO} & \text{T3} & \text{STO} & \text{T2} \\
\text{LOAD} & \text{y} & \text{LOAD} & \text{T1} \\
\text{MULT} & \text{z} & \text{ADD} & \text{T2}
\end{array}
$$

Turning now to the higher constructs of Pam, the attribute Labin, which is inherited by each construct whose code may contain one or more labels, serves to keep track of the number of labels generated so far. Each such construct also has a synthesized attribute Labout, whose value will be the Labin value plus the number of labels contained in the code for the construct. This scheme prevents the appearance of duplicate labels in the code.

At the beginning of a $\langle$program$\rangle$, no temporaries or labels have been used, and the code for the $\langle$program$\rangle$ is simply the code for the $\langle$series$\rangle$ of which it is composed followed by a HALT instruction:

$$
\begin{array}{l}
\langle\text{program}\rangle ::= \langle\text{series}\rangle \\
\quad \text{Code}(\langle\text{program}\rangle) \longleftarrow append(\text{Code}(\langle\text{series}\rangle), \text{'HALT'}) \\
\quad \text{Temp}(\langle\text{series}\rangle) \longleftarrow 0 \\
\quad \text{Labin}(\langle\text{series}\rangle) \longleftarrow 0
\end{array}
$$

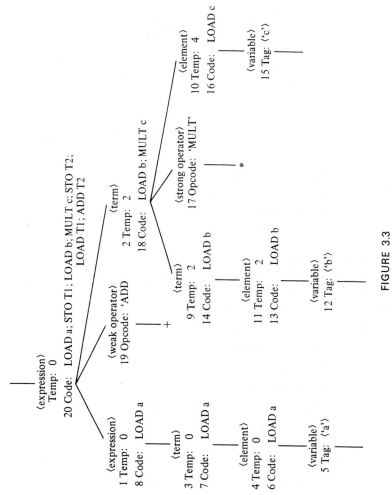

FIGURE 3.3

85

The situation where a ⟨series⟩ consists of a single ⟨statement⟩ is trivial:

$$⟨series⟩ ::= ⟨statement⟩$$

Code(⟨series⟩) ⟵ Code(⟨statement⟩)

Labout(⟨series⟩) ⟵ Labout(⟨statement⟩)

Temp(⟨statement⟩) ⟵ Temp(⟨series⟩)

Labin(⟨statement⟩) ⟵ Labin(⟨series⟩)

In the next part, note that a semicolon does not give rise to any code, and that the label count is "handed over" from one statement to the next by the last evaluation rule:

$$⟨series⟩ ::= ⟨series⟩_2 ; ⟨statement⟩$$

Code(⟨series⟩) ⟵ *concat*(Code(⟨series⟩$_2$), Code(⟨statement⟩))

Labout(⟨series⟩) ⟵ Labout(⟨statement⟩)

Temp(⟨series⟩$_2$) ⟵ Temp(⟨series⟩)

Labin(⟨series⟩$_2$) ⟵ Labin(⟨series⟩)

Temp(⟨statement⟩) ⟵ Temp(⟨series⟩)

Labin(⟨statement⟩) ⟵ Labout(⟨series⟩$_2$)

All types of ⟨statement⟩ synthesize code and a final label count (Labout); for input, output, and assignment statements, the latter is simply the inherited Labin value. Input and output statements do not inherit a Temp value because their code never involves the use of temporaries:

$$⟨statement⟩ ::= ⟨input statement⟩$$

Code(⟨statement⟩) ⟵ Code(⟨input statement⟩)

Labout(⟨statement⟩) ⟵ Labin(⟨statement⟩)

| ⟨output statement⟩

Code(⟨statement⟩) ⟵ Code(⟨output statement⟩)

Labout(⟨statement⟩) ⟵ Labin(⟨statement⟩)

| ⟨assignment statement⟩

Code(⟨statement⟩) ⟵ Code(⟨assignment statement⟩)

Labout(⟨statement⟩) ⟵ Labin(⟨statement⟩)

Temp(⟨assignment statement⟩) ⟵ Temp(⟨statement⟩)

| ⟨conditional statement⟩

Code(⟨statement⟩) ⟵ Code(⟨conditional statement⟩)

Labout(⟨statement⟩) ⟵ Labout(⟨conditional statement⟩)

Temp(⟨conditional statement⟩) ⟵ Temp(⟨statement⟩)

Labin(⟨conditional statement⟩) ⟵ Labin(⟨statement⟩)

| ⟨definite loop⟩

    Code(⟨statement⟩) ⟵ Code(⟨definite loop⟩)

    Labout(⟨statement⟩) ⟵ Labout(⟨definite loop⟩)

    Temp(⟨definite loop⟩) ⟵ Temp(⟨statement⟩)

    Labin(⟨definite loop⟩) ⟵ Labin(⟨statement⟩)

| ⟨indefinite loop⟩

    Code(⟨statement⟩) ⟵ Code(⟨indefinite loop⟩)

    Labout(⟨statement⟩) ⟵ Labout(⟨indefinite loop⟩)

    Temp(⟨indefinite loop⟩) ⟵ Temp(⟨statement⟩)

    Labin(⟨indefinite loop⟩) ⟵ Labin(⟨statement⟩)

Input and output statements synthesize an Opcode value of 'GET' and 'PUT', respectively, and pass it to the constituent ⟨variable list⟩, where a sequence of GET or PUT instructions is generated:

⟨input statement⟩ ::= **read** ⟨variable list⟩

    Code(⟨input statement⟩) ⟵ Code(⟨variable list⟩)

    Opcode(⟨variable list⟩) ⟵ 'GET'

⟨output statement⟩ ::= **write** ⟨variable list⟩

    Code(⟨output statement⟩) ⟵ Code(⟨variable list⟩)

    Opcode(⟨variable list⟩) ⟵ 'PUT'

⟨variable list⟩ ::= ⟨variable⟩

    Code(⟨variable list⟩) ⟵ ⟨(Opcode(⟨variable list⟩), Tag(⟨variable⟩)))⟩

| ⟨variable list⟩$_2$, ⟨variable⟩

    Code(⟨variable list⟩) ⟵ *append*(Code(⟨variable list⟩$_2$),

                (Opcode(⟨variable list⟩), Tag(⟨variable⟩)))

    Opcode(⟨variable list⟩$_2$) ⟵ Opcode(⟨variable list⟩)

In the code for an assignment statement, the variable at the beginning of the statement appears as the last operand:

⟨assignment statement⟩ ::= ⟨variable⟩ := ⟨expression⟩

    Code(⟨assignment statement⟩) ⟵ *append*(Code(⟨expression⟩),

                    ('STO', Tag(⟨variable⟩)))

    Temp(⟨expression⟩) ⟵ Temp(⟨assignment statement⟩)

For a ⟨conditional statement⟩ of the form

    if ⟨expression⟩$_1$ ⟨relation⟩ ⟨expression⟩$_2$ **then** ⟨series⟩ **fi**

a suitable pattern of code is

> code for $\langle expression \rangle_1$
> STO   Tn
> code for $\langle expression \rangle_2$
> SUB   Tn
> conditional jump to Lm
> code for $\langle series \rangle$
> Lm   LAB

where m is the numeral whose value is one more than the current label count, n is the numeral whose value is one more than the current temporary count, and the identity of the conditional jump instruction depends on the $\langle relation \rangle$. To handle the latter feature, $\langle relation \rangle$ has Opcode as a synthesized attribute:

> $\langle relation \rangle ::= \ =$
> > $\text{Opcode}(\langle relation \rangle) \longleftarrow$ 'JNP'
>
> $| \ =<$
> > $\text{Opcode}(\langle relation \rangle) \longleftarrow$ 'JN'
>
> $| \ <$
> > $\text{Opcode}(\langle relation \rangle) \longleftarrow$ 'JNZ'
>
> $| \ >$
> > $\text{Opcode}(\langle relation \rangle) \longleftarrow$ 'JPZ'
>
> $| \ >=$
> > $\text{Opcode}(\langle relation \rangle) \longleftarrow$ 'JP'
>
> $| \ <>$
> > $\text{Opcode}(\langle relation \rangle) \longleftarrow$ 'JZ'

Because it occurs in three different code patterns, the subpattern

> code for $\langle expression \rangle_1$
> STO   Tn
> code for $\langle expression \rangle_2$
> SUB   Tn
> conditional jump to Lm

is synthesized by $\langle comparison \rangle$, which inherits the value of m via Labin:

> $\langle comparison \rangle ::= \langle expression \rangle_1 \ \langle relation \rangle \ \langle expression \rangle_2$
> > $\text{Code}(\langle comparison \rangle) \longleftarrow concat($
> > $\text{Code}(\langle expression \rangle_1),$
> > $\langle$'STO', $temporary(\text{Temp}(\langle comparison \rangle) + 1))\rangle,$

$$\text{Code}(\langle\text{expression}\rangle_2),$$
$$\langle(\text{'SUB'}, \textit{temporary}(\text{Temp}(\langle\text{comparison}\rangle) + 1))\rangle,$$
$$\langle(\text{Opcode}(\langle\text{relation}\rangle), \textit{label}(\text{Labin}(\langle\text{comparison}\rangle)))\rangle\rangle)$$
$$\text{Temp}(\langle\text{expression}\rangle_1) \longleftarrow \text{Temp}(\langle\text{comparison}\rangle) + 1$$
$$\text{Temp}(\langle\text{expression}\rangle_2) \longleftarrow \text{Temp}(\langle\text{comparison}\rangle) + 1$$

Given a specified integer, the auxiliary functions *temporary* and *label* return Tag values of the form Tk and Lk, respectively, where k is the decimal representation of the integer. Now we may give the rules

$\langle\text{conditional statement}\rangle ::= \textbf{if } \langle\text{comparison}\rangle \textbf{ then } \langle\text{series}\rangle \textbf{ fi}$

$\quad\text{Code}(\langle\text{conditional statement}\rangle) \longleftarrow \textit{concat}(\text{Code}(\langle\text{comparison}\rangle),$
$\quad\quad\text{Code}(\langle\text{series}\rangle), \langle(\textit{label}(\text{Labin}(\langle\text{conditional statement}\rangle) + 1), \text{'LAB'})\rangle)$
$\quad\text{Labout}(\langle\text{conditional statement}\rangle) \longleftarrow \text{Labout}(\langle\text{series}\rangle)$
$\quad\text{Temp}(\langle\text{comparison}\rangle) \longleftarrow \text{Temp}(\langle\text{conditional statement}\rangle)$
$\quad\text{Labin}(\langle\text{comparison}\rangle) \longleftarrow \text{Labin}(\langle\text{conditional statement}\rangle) + 1$
$\quad\text{Temp}(\langle\text{series}\rangle) \longleftarrow \text{Temp}(\langle\text{conditional statement}\rangle)$
$\quad\text{Labin}(\langle\text{series}\rangle) \longleftarrow \text{Labin}(\langle\text{conditional statement}\rangle) + 1$

For a conditional statement of the form

$\quad\quad \textbf{if } \langle\text{expression}\rangle_1 \langle\text{relation}\rangle \langle\text{expression}\rangle_2 \textbf{ then } \langle\text{series}\rangle_1$
$\quad\quad \textbf{else } \langle\text{series}\rangle_2 \textbf{ fi}$

a suitable code pattern is

```
                code for ⟨expression⟩₁
                STO   Tn
                code for ⟨expression⟩₂
                SUB   Tn
                conditional jump to Lm
                code for ⟨series⟩₁
                J       Lm+1
        Lm      LAB
                code for ⟨series⟩₂
        Lm+1    LAB
```

Thus, taking into account the other necessary actions for attribute evaluation, we have

$\langle\text{conditional statement}\rangle ::= \textbf{if } \langle\text{comparison}\rangle \textbf{ then } \langle\text{series}\rangle_1$

$\quad \textbf{else } \langle\text{series}\rangle_2 \textbf{ fi}$

$\quad\quad\text{Code}(\langle\text{conditional statement}\rangle) \longleftarrow \textit{concat}($

$$Code(\langle comparison\rangle),$$

$$Code(\langle series\rangle_1),$$

$$\langle('J', \textit{label}(Labin(\langle conditional\ statement\rangle) + 2))\rangle,$$

$$\langle(\textit{label}(Labin(\langle conditional\ statement\rangle) + 1), 'LAB')\rangle,$$

$$Code(\langle series\rangle_2),$$

$$\langle(\textit{label}(Labin(\langle conditional\ statement\rangle) + 2), 'LAB')\rangle)$$

$$Labout(\langle conditional\ statement\rangle) \longleftarrow Labout(\langle series\rangle_2)$$

$$Temp(\langle comparison\rangle) \longleftarrow Temp(\langle conditional\ statement\rangle)$$

$$Labin(\langle comparison\rangle) \longleftarrow Labin(\langle conditional\ statement\rangle) + 1$$

$$Temp(\langle series\rangle_1) \longleftarrow Temp(\langle conditional\ statement\rangle)$$

$$Labin(\langle series\rangle_1) \longleftarrow Labin(\langle conditional\ statement\rangle) + 2$$

$$Temp(\langle series\rangle_2) \longleftarrow Temp(\langle conditional\ statement\rangle)$$

$$Labin(\langle series\rangle_2) \longleftarrow Labout(\langle series\rangle_1)$$

For a statement of the form

while $\langle expression\rangle_1$ $\langle relation\rangle$ $\langle expression\rangle_2$ **do** $\langle series\rangle$ **end**

the code pattern will be

```
Lm        LAB
          code for ⟨expression⟩₁
          STO   Tn
          code for ⟨expression⟩₂
          SUB   Tn
          conditional jump to Lm+1
          code for ⟨series⟩
          J     Lm
Lm+1      LAB
```

Hence we have

$$\langle indefinite\ loop\rangle ::= \textbf{while}\ \langle comparison\rangle\ \textbf{do}\ \langle series\rangle\ \textbf{end}$$

$$Code(\langle indefinite\ loop\rangle) \longleftarrow \textit{concat}($$

$$\langle(\textit{label}(Labin(\langle indefinite\ loop\rangle) + 1), 'LAB')\rangle,$$

$$Code(\langle comparison\rangle),$$

$$Code(\langle series\rangle),$$

$$\langle('J', \textit{label}(Labin(\langle indefinite\ loop\rangle) + 1))\rangle,$$

$$\langle(\textit{label}(Labin(\langle indefinite\ loop\rangle) + 2), 'LAB')\rangle)$$

$$Labout(\langle indefinite\ loop\rangle) \longleftarrow Labout(\langle series\rangle)$$

$$Temp(\langle comparison\rangle) \longleftarrow Temp(\langle indefinite\ loop\rangle)$$

$$\text{Labin}(\langle\text{comparison}\rangle) \longleftarrow \text{Labin}(\langle\text{indefinite loop}\rangle) + 2$$
$$\text{Temp}(\langle\text{series}\rangle) \longleftarrow \text{Temp}(\langle\text{indefinite loop}\rangle)$$
$$\text{Labin}(\langle\text{series}\rangle) \longleftarrow \text{Labin}(\langle\text{indefinite loop}\rangle) + 2$$

Finally, for a loop of the form

$$\textbf{to } \langle\text{expression}\rangle \textbf{ do } \langle\text{series}\rangle \textbf{ end}$$

a suitable code pattern is

```
           code for ⟨expression⟩
           STO     Tn
    Lm     LAB
           LOAD    Tn
           SUB     1
           JN      Lm+1
           STO     Tn
           code for ⟨series⟩
           J       Lm
    Lm+1   LAB
```

so that the following rules complete our definition of Pam:

$\langle\text{definite loop}\rangle ::= \textbf{to } \langle\text{expression}\rangle \textbf{ do } \langle\text{series}\rangle \textbf{ end}$

$\text{Code}(\langle\text{definite loop}\rangle) \longleftarrow concat($

$\quad\text{Code}(\langle\text{expression}\rangle),$

$\quad\langle(\text{`STO'}, temporary(\text{Temp}(\langle\text{definite loop}\rangle) + 1))\rangle,$

$\quad\langle(label(\text{Labin}(\langle\text{definite loop}\rangle) + 1), \text{`LAB'})\rangle,$

$\quad\langle(\text{`LOAD'}, temporary(\text{Temp}(\langle\text{definite loop}\rangle) + 1))\rangle,$

$\quad\langle(\text{`SUB'}, \langle\text{`1'}\rangle)\rangle,$

$\quad\langle(\text{`JN'}, label(\text{Labin}(\langle\text{definite loop}\rangle) + 2))\rangle,$

$\quad\langle(\text{`STO'}, temporary(\text{Temp}(\langle\text{definite loop}\rangle) + 1))\rangle,$

$\quad\text{Code}(\langle\text{series}\rangle),$

$\quad\langle(\text{`J'}, label(\text{Labin}(\langle\text{definite loop}\rangle) + 1))\rangle,$

$\quad\langle(label(\text{Labin}(\langle\text{definite loop}\rangle) + 2), \text{`LAB'})\rangle)$

$\text{Labout}(\langle\text{definite loop}\rangle) \longleftarrow \text{Labout}(\langle\text{series}\rangle)$

$\text{Temp}(\langle\text{expression}\rangle) \longleftarrow \text{Temp}(\langle\text{definite loop}\rangle) + 1$

$\text{Temp}(\langle\text{series}\rangle) \longleftarrow \text{Temp}(\langle\text{definite loop}\rangle) + 1$

$\text{Labin}(\langle\text{series}\rangle) \longleftarrow \text{Labin}(\langle\text{definite loop}\rangle) + 2$

The complete specifications are collected together in Table 3.1. It may be noted that, unlike the previous attribute grammar for the syntax of Eva, this grammar contains no conditions. If Pam had a non-context-free syntax, these would be present, along with extra attributes playing syntactic roles. The Eva grammar could be extended to include semantics using the general, translational approach taken in this section, but it would be necessary to employ a different object language.

TABLE 3.1   Attribute Grammar Mapping Pam into a Simple Symbolic Machine Language

Attributes and Values

Attribute	Values
Num	sequences of digits
Tag	sequences of letters and digits
Temp	non-negative integers
Labin	non-negative integers
Labout	non-negative integers
Opcode	'ADD', 'SUB', 'MULT', 'DIV', 'GET', 'PUT', 'JN', 'JP', 'JZ', 'JNZ', 'JPZ', 'JNP', 'J', 'LOAD', 'STO'
Code	sequences of values of the form 'HALT', (Opcode, Num), (Opcode, Tag), or (Tag, 'LAB')

Attributes Associated with Nonterminal Symbols

Nonterminal	Inherited attributes	Synthesized attributes
⟨program⟩	—	Code
⟨series⟩	Temp, Labin	Code, Labout
⟨statement⟩	Temp, Labin	Code, Labout
⟨input statement⟩	—	Code
⟨output statement⟩	—	Code
⟨variable list⟩	Opcode	Code
⟨assignment statement⟩	Temp	Code
⟨conditional statement⟩	Temp, Labin	Code, Labout
⟨definite loop⟩	Temp, Labin	Code, Labout
⟨indefinite loop⟩	Temp, Labin	Code, Labout
⟨comparison⟩	Temp, Labin	Code
⟨expression⟩	Temp	Code
⟨term⟩	Temp	Code
⟨element⟩	Temp	Code
⟨constant⟩	—	Num
⟨variable⟩	—	Tag
⟨relation⟩	—	Opcode
⟨weak operator⟩	—	Opcode
⟨strong operator⟩	—	Opcode
⟨digit⟩	—	Num
⟨letter⟩	—	Tag

TABLE 3.1 (Continued)

Production and Attribute Evaluation Rules

⟨program⟩ ::= ⟨series⟩

           Code(⟨program⟩) ⟵ *append*(Code(⟨series⟩), 'HALT')

           Temp(⟨series⟩) ⟵ 0

           Labin(⟨series⟩) ⟵ 0

⟨series⟩ ::= ⟨statement⟩

           Code(⟨series⟩) ⟵ Code(⟨statement⟩)

           Labout(⟨series⟩) ⟵ Labout(⟨statement⟩)

           Temp(⟨statement⟩) ⟵ Temp(⟨series⟩)

           Labin(⟨statement⟩) ⟵ Labin(⟨series⟩)

  | ⟨series⟩$_2$; ⟨statement⟩

           Code(⟨series⟩) ⟵ *concat*(Code(⟨series⟩$_2$), Code(⟨statement⟩))

           Labout(⟨series⟩) ⟵ Labout(⟨statement⟩)

           Temp(⟨series⟩$_2$) ⟵ Temp(⟨series⟩)

           Labin(⟨series⟩$_2$) ⟵ Labin(⟨series⟩)

           Temp(⟨statement⟩) ⟵ Temp(⟨series⟩)

           Labin(⟨statement⟩) ⟵ Labout(⟨series⟩$_2$)

⟨statement⟩ ::= ⟨input statement⟩

           Code(⟨statement⟩) ⟵ Code(⟨input statement⟩)

           Labout(⟨statement⟩) ⟵ Labin(⟨statement⟩)

  | ⟨output statement⟩

           Code(⟨statement⟩) ⟵ Code(⟨output statement⟩)

           Labout(⟨statement⟩) ⟵ Labin(⟨statement⟩)

  | ⟨assignment statement⟩

           Code(⟨statement⟩) ⟵ Code(⟨assignment statement⟩)

           Labout(⟨statement⟩) ⟵ Labin(⟨statement⟩)

           Temp(⟨assignment statement⟩) ⟵ Temp(⟨statement⟩)

  | ⟨conditional statement⟩

           Code(⟨statement⟩) ⟵ Code(⟨conditional statement⟩)

           Labout(⟨statement⟩) ⟵ Labout(⟨conditional statement⟩)

           Temp(⟨conditional statement⟩) ⟵ Temp(⟨statement⟩)

           Labin(⟨conditional statement⟩) ⟵ Labin(⟨statement⟩)

  | ⟨definite loop⟩

           Code(⟨statement⟩) ⟵ Code(⟨definite loop⟩)

           Labout(⟨statement⟩) ⟵ Labout(⟨definite loop⟩)

TABLE 3.1 (Continued)

Temp(⟨definite loop⟩) ⟵ Temp(⟨statement⟩)

Labin(⟨definite loop⟩) ⟵ Labin(⟨statement⟩)

| ⟨indefinite loop⟩

Code(⟨statement⟩) ⟵ Code(⟨indefinite loop⟩)

Labout(⟨statement⟩) ⟵ Labout(⟨indefinite loop⟩)

Temp(⟨indefinite loop⟩) ⟵ Temp(⟨statement⟩)

Labin(⟨indefinite loop⟩) ⟵ Labin(⟨statement⟩)

⟨input statement⟩ ::= **read** ⟨variable list⟩

Code(⟨input statement⟩) ⟵ Code(⟨variable list⟩)

Opcode(⟨variable list⟩) ⟵ 'GET'

⟨output statement⟩ ::= **write** ⟨variable list⟩

Code(⟨output statement⟩) ⟵ Code(⟨variable list⟩)

Opcode(⟨variable list⟩) ⟵ 'PUT'

⟨variable list⟩ ::= ⟨variable⟩

Code(⟨variable list⟩) ⟵ ⟨(Opcode(⟨variable list⟩), Tag(⟨variable⟩))⟩

| ⟨variable list⟩$_2$, ⟨variable⟩

Code(⟨variable list⟩) ⟵ *append*(Code(⟨variable list⟩$_2$),

(Opcode(⟨variable list⟩), Tag(⟨variable⟩)))

Opcode(⟨variable list⟩$_2$) ⟵ Opcode(⟨variable list⟩)

⟨assignment statement⟩ ::= ⟨variable⟩ := ⟨expression⟩

Code(⟨assignment statement⟩) ⟵ *append*(Code(⟨expression⟩),

('STO', Tag(⟨variable⟩)))

Temp(⟨expression⟩) ⟵ Temp(⟨assignment statement⟩)

⟨conditional statement⟩ ::= **if** ⟨comparison⟩ **then** ⟨series⟩ **fi**

Code(⟨conditional statement⟩) ⟵ *concat*(Code(⟨comparison⟩),

Code(⟨series⟩), ⟨(*label*(Labin(⟨conditional statement⟩) + 1), 'LAB')⟩)

Labout(⟨conditional statement⟩) ⟵ Labout(⟨series⟩)

Temp(⟨comparison⟩) ⟵ Temp(⟨conditional statement⟩)

Labin(⟨comparison⟩) ⟵ Labin(⟨conditional statement⟩) + 1

Temp(⟨series⟩) ⟵ Temp(⟨conditional statement⟩)

Labin(⟨series⟩) ⟵ Labin(⟨conditional statement⟩) + 1

| **if** ⟨comparison⟩ **then** ⟨series⟩$_1$ **else** ⟨series⟩$_2$ **fi**

Code(⟨conditional statement⟩) ⟵ *concat*(

Code(⟨comparison⟩),

Code(⟨series⟩$_1$),

TABLE 3.1 (Continued)

$\langle$('J', *label*(Labin($\langle$conditional statement$\rangle$) + 2))$\rangle$,

$\langle$(label(Labin($\langle$conditional statement$\rangle$) + 1), 'LAB')$\rangle$,

Code($\langle$series$\rangle_2$),

$\langle$(*label*(Labin($\langle$conditional statement$\rangle$) + 2), 'LAB')$\rangle$)

Labout($\langle$conditional statement$\rangle$) $\longleftarrow$ Labout($\langle$series$\rangle_2$)

Temp($\langle$comparison$\rangle$) $\longleftarrow$ Temp($\langle$conditional statement$\rangle$)

Labin($\langle$comparison$\rangle$) $\longleftarrow$ Labin($\langle$conditional statement$\rangle$) + 1

Temp($\langle$series$\rangle_1$) $\longleftarrow$ Temp($\langle$conditional statement$\rangle$)

Labin($\langle$series$\rangle_1$) $\longleftarrow$ Labin($\langle$conditional statement$\rangle$) + 2

Temp($\langle$series$\rangle_2$) $\longleftarrow$ Temp($\langle$conditional statement$\rangle$)

Labin($\langle$series$\rangle_2$) $\longleftarrow$ Labout($\langle$series$\rangle_1$)

$\langle$definite loop$\rangle$ ::= **to** $\langle$expression$\rangle$ **do** $\langle$series$\rangle$ **end**

Code($\langle$definite loop$\rangle$) $\longleftarrow$ *concat*(

Code($\langle$expression$\rangle$),

$\langle$('STO', *temporary*(Temp($\langle$definite loop$\rangle$) + 1))$\rangle$,

$\langle$(*label*(Labin($\langle$definite loop$\rangle$) + 1), 'LAB')$\rangle$,

$\langle$('LOAD', *temporary*(Temp($\langle$definite loop$\rangle$) + 1))$\rangle$,

$\langle$('SUB', $\langle$'1'$\rangle$)$\rangle$,

$\langle$('JN', *label*(Labin($\langle$definite loop$\rangle$) + 2))$\rangle$,

$\langle$('STO', *temporary*(Temp($\langle$definite loop$\rangle$) + 1))$\rangle$,

Code($\langle$series$\rangle$),

$\langle$('J', *label*(Labin($\langle$definite loop$\rangle$) + 1))$\rangle$,

$\langle$(*label*(Labin($\langle$definite loop$\rangle$) + 2), 'LAB')$\rangle$)

Labout($\langle$definite loop$\rangle$) $\longleftarrow$ Labout($\langle$series$\rangle$)

Temp($\langle$expression$\rangle$) $\longleftarrow$ Temp($\langle$definite loop$\rangle$) + 1

Temp($\langle$series$\rangle$) $\longleftarrow$ Temp($\langle$definite loop$\rangle$) + 1

Labin($\langle$series$\rangle$) $\longleftarrow$ Labin($\langle$definite loop$\rangle$) + 2

$\langle$indefinite loop$\rangle$ ::= **while** $\langle$comparison$\rangle$ **do** $\langle$series$\rangle$ **end**

Code($\langle$indefinite loop$\rangle$) $\longleftarrow$ *concat*(

$\langle$(*label*(Labin($\langle$indefinite loop$\rangle$) + 1), 'LAB')$\rangle$,

Code($\langle$comparison$\rangle$),

Code($\langle$series$\rangle$),

$\langle$('J', *label*(Labin($\langle$indefinite loop$\rangle$) + 1))$\rangle$,

$\langle$(*label*(Labin($\langle$indefinite loop$\rangle$) + 2), 'LAB')$\rangle$)

Labout($\langle$indefinite loop$\rangle$) $\longleftarrow$ Labout($\langle$series$\rangle$)

TABLE 3.1 (Continued)

Temp(⟨comparison⟩) ⟵ Temp(⟨indefinite loop⟩)

Labin(⟨comparison⟩) ⟵ Labin(⟨indefinite loop⟩) + 2

Temp(⟨series⟩) ⟵ Temp(⟨indefinite loop⟩)

Labin(⟨series⟩) ⟵ Labin(⟨indefinite loop⟩) + 2

⟨comparison⟩ ::= ⟨expression⟩$_1$ ⟨relation⟩ ⟨expression⟩$_2$

Code(⟨comparison⟩) ⟵ *concat*(

Code(⟨expression⟩$_1$),

⟨('STO', *temporary*(Temp(⟨comparison⟩) + 1))⟩,

Code(⟨expression⟩$_2$),

⟨('SUB', *temporary*(Temp(⟨comparison⟩) + 1))⟩,

⟨(Opcode(⟨relation⟩), *label*(Labin(⟨comparison⟩))))⟩)

Temp(⟨expression⟩$_1$) ⟵ Temp(⟨comparison⟩) + 1

Temp(⟨expression⟩$_2$) ⟵ Temp(⟨comparison⟩) + 1

⟨expression⟩ ::= ⟨term⟩

Code(⟨expression⟩) ⟵ Code(⟨term⟩)

Temp(⟨term⟩) ⟵ Temp(⟨expression⟩)

| ⟨expression⟩$_2$ ⟨weak operator⟩ ⟨term⟩

Code(⟨expression⟩) ⟵ *concat*(Code(⟨expression⟩$_2$),

selectcode(Code(⟨term⟩), Temp(⟨expression⟩),

Opcode(⟨weak operator⟩)))

Temp(⟨expression⟩$_2$) ⟵ Temp(⟨expression⟩)

Temp(⟨term⟩) ⟵ Temp(⟨expression⟩) + 2

⟨term⟩ ::= ⟨element⟩

Code(⟨term⟩) ⟵ Code(⟨element⟩)

Temp(⟨element⟩) ⟵ Temp(⟨term⟩)

| ⟨term⟩$_2$ ⟨strong operator⟩ ⟨element⟩

Code(⟨term⟩) ⟵ *concat*(Code(⟨term⟩$_2$),

selectcode(Code(⟨element⟩), Temp(⟨term⟩), Opcode(⟨strong operator⟩)))

Temp(⟨term⟩$_2$) ⟵ Temp(⟨term⟩)

Temp(⟨element⟩) ⟵ Temp(⟨term⟩) + 2

⟨element⟩ ::= ⟨constant⟩

Code(⟨element⟩) ⟵ ⟨('LOAD', Num(⟨constant⟩))⟩

| ⟨variable⟩

Code(⟨element⟩) ⟵ ⟨('LOAD', Tag(⟨variable⟩))⟩

| (⟨expression⟩)

TABLE 3.1 (Continued)

$$\text{Code}(\langle\text{element}\rangle) \longleftarrow \text{Code}(\langle\text{expression}\rangle)$$

$$\text{Temp}(\langle\text{expression}\rangle) \longleftarrow \text{Temp}(\langle\text{element}\rangle)$$

$\langle\text{constant}\rangle ::= \langle\text{digit}\rangle$

$$\text{Num}(\langle\text{constant}\rangle) \longleftarrow \text{Num}(\langle\text{digit}\rangle)$$

$\quad | \ \langle\text{constant}\rangle_2 \ \langle\text{digit}\rangle$

$$\text{Num}(\langle\text{constant}\rangle) \longleftarrow concat(\text{Num}(\langle\text{constant}\rangle_2), \text{Num}(\langle\text{digit}\rangle))$$

$\langle\text{variable}\rangle ::= \langle\text{letter}\rangle$

$$\text{Tag}(\langle\text{variable}\rangle) \longleftarrow \text{Tag}(\langle\text{letter}\rangle)$$

$\quad | \ \langle\text{variable}\rangle_2 \ \langle\text{letter}\rangle$

$$\text{Tag}(\langle\text{variable}\rangle) \longleftarrow concat(\text{Tag}(\langle\text{variable}\rangle_2), \text{Tag}(\langle\text{letter}\rangle))$$

$\quad | \ \langle\text{variable}\rangle_2 \ \langle\text{digit}\rangle$

$$\text{Tag}(\langle\text{variable}\rangle) \longleftarrow concat(\text{Tag}(\langle\text{variable}\rangle_2), \text{Num}(\langle\text{digit}\rangle))$$

$\langle\text{relation}\rangle ::= \ =$

$$\text{Opcode}(\langle\text{relation}\rangle) \longleftarrow \text{'JNP'}$$

$\quad | \ =<$

$$\text{Opcode}(\langle\text{relation}\rangle) \longleftarrow \text{'JN'}$$

$\quad | \ <$

$$\text{Opcode}(\langle\text{relation}\rangle) \longleftarrow \text{'JNZ'}$$

$\quad | \ >$

$$\text{Opcode}(\langle\text{relation}\rangle) \longleftarrow \text{'JPZ'}$$

$\quad | \ >=$

$$\text{Opcode}(\langle\text{relation}\rangle) \longleftarrow \text{'JP'}$$

$\quad | \ <>$

$$\text{Opcode}(\langle\text{relation}\rangle) \longleftarrow \text{'JZ'}$$

$\langle\text{weak operator}\rangle ::= \ +$

$$\text{Opcode}(\langle\text{weak operator}\rangle) \longleftarrow \text{'ADD'}$$

$\quad | \ -$

$$\text{Opcode}(\langle\text{weak operator}\rangle) \longleftarrow \text{'SUB'}$$

$\langle\text{strong operator}\rangle ::= \ *$

$$\text{Opcode}(\langle\text{strong operator}\rangle) \longleftarrow \text{'MULT'}$$

$\quad | \ /$

$$\text{Opcode}(\langle\text{strong operator}\rangle) \longleftarrow \text{'DIV'}$$

$\langle\text{digit}\rangle ::= \ 0$

$$\text{Num}(\langle\text{digit}\rangle) \longleftarrow \langle\text{'0'}\rangle$$

$\quad | \ \ldots$

TABLE 3.1 **(Continued)**

```
      . . .
   | 9
            Num(⟨digit⟩) ⟵ ⟨'9'⟩
⟨letter⟩ ::= a
            Tag(⟨letter⟩) ⟵ ⟨'a'⟩
   | . . .
      . . .
   | z
            Tag(⟨letter⟩) ⟵ ⟨'z'⟩
```

Definition of Auxiliary Evaluation Functions

label (int) =

   concat (⟨'L'⟩, *string* (int))

temporary (int) =

   concat (⟨'T'⟩, *string* (int))

string (n) =

   ⟨'0'⟩, if $n = 0$;

   . . .

   ⟨'9'⟩, if n = 9;

   concat (*string* (n ÷ 10), *string* (n mod 10)), otherwise.

selectcode (code, temp, opcode) =

   ⟨(opcode, *field₂* (*first* (code)))⟩, if *length* (code) = 1;

   concat (⟨('STO', *temporary* (temp + 1))⟩, code, ⟨('STO',
       temporary (temp + 2))⟩, ⟨('LOAD', *temporary* (temp + 1))⟩,
       ⟨(opcode, *temporary* (temp + 2))⟩), otherwise.

EXERCISES

1. Verify that the grammar of Table 3.1 maps the expressions

$$(x + y * z) + b * c$$
$$a + (x + y * z)$$

   into the code sequences given earlier in this section.

2. Construct the complete, decorated tree for the program

> **read** a ;
> **if** $a = 0$ **then read** b ; **write** b **else write** a **fi**

3. If you are familiar with reverse Polish (Polish postfix) notation, determine what modifications to the grammar of Table 3.1 would be required in order to define the semantics of Pam in terms of a suitable reverse Polish language.

For Further Information

The use of attribute grammars for defining translations is described in more general terms by Lewis et al. (1974), Bochmann (1976), Cohen and Harry (1979), and Kennedy and Ramanathan (1979). Marcotty et al. (1976) take a rather different approach to the specification of semantics using attribute grammars.

The concept of defining semantics translationally appears in a variety of approaches that do not involve attribute grammars. Feldman (1966), for example, describes a Formal Semantic Language, a metalanguage for describing abstract translators, and its application to the problem of compiler generation. Landin (1965) formalizes some of the semantics of Algol 60 by defining a mapping from that language into a modified form of λ-notation.

3.3
INTERPRETIVE SEMANTICS USING
TWO-LEVEL GRAMMARS

Using Pam and Eva as examples, this section examines an ingenious technique for formalizing semantics using the syntactic methods provided by two-level grammars. The philosophy on which this technique rests is that the "meaning" of a program should be described essentially in terms of the correspondence it defines between its input data and its output data and that a formal system therefore constitutes a complete semantic formalization if it generates triples consisting of (a) a syntactically valid program, (b) an input file, and (c) an output file such that the execution of the program with the input file produces the output file. Since input and output files are, like programs, basically sequences of characters, a program-input-output triple can be represented as a single character string of a form such as

$$\langle \text{program} \rangle \ \textbf{eof} \ \langle \text{input file} \rangle \ \textbf{eof} \ \langle \text{output file} \rangle \ \textbf{eof}$$

This suggests the possibility of constructing a grammar that generates all and only these sequences of symbols. In the case of Pam, for example, the grammar should imply a syntax tree for

$$\textbf{read} \ x, y \ ; \ \textbf{write} \ y \ \textbf{eof} \ -2. \ 7. \ 1. \ \textbf{eof} \ 7. \ \textbf{eof}$$

but not for

$$\textbf{read} \ x, y \ ; \ \textbf{write} \ y \ \textbf{eof} \ -2. \ 7. \ \textbf{eof} \ 3. \ \textbf{eof}$$

(because the program, although syntactically valid, does not produce the given output from the given input) and not for

read *x*, *y* ; **write** *x* **eof** 18. **eof** 18. **eof**

(because a semantic error—attempting to read past the end of the input file—is involved). Clearly, the construction of such a grammar is a tall order, especially when one considers all the implications of the possible presence of arithmetic expressions, conditional statements, and loop statements in programs. Remarkably enough, the formalism of two-level grammars is sufficiently powerful for this purpose, and the next part shows how the syntax and semantics of Pam can be fully specified using an extension of the grammatical techniques used in Sec. 2.3.3 for the syntactic definition of Eva.

3.3.1 A Complete Definition of Pam

To emphasize the fact that the strings generated by the grammar will include two "file" portions as well as a "program" portion, we will use **programme** as the distinguished symbol. The hyper-rule for **programme** will include a predicate part which has the effect of requiring the program to be one which will transform an "initial state" that includes the input file into a "final state" that includes the output file. Much of the grammar will be devoted to specifying transformations of states, so that a large portion of the syntax tree for a **programme** will consist of a complex, invisible subtree of semantic significance.

The various predicates involved in this semantic subtree include protonotions, subsumed by the metanotion **STATE**, which correspond to "states" existing at various instants during the execution of the program. Each state includes full information about the current values of variables, the unread portion of the input file, and the portion of the output file produced so far:

STATE :: state VARS FILE FILE.

VARS :: VAR; VARS VAR.

VARSETY :: VARS; EMPTY.

The **VARS** part of a state records all the different variables (in the form of **TAG**s) occurring in the program; in this respect, it is analogous to, but simpler than, a **NEST** protonotion of the kind used for Eva. A **VARS** protonotion, however, also records the numeric values of the variables:

VAR :: var TAG value VALUE.

VALUE :: undefined; NUMBER.

> NUMBER :: TALLETY; negative TALLY.
>
> TALLY :: i; TALLY i.
>
> TALLETY :: TALLY; EMPTY.

A positive value is represented by a protonotion consisting of the appropriate number of i's; for a negative value, the i's are prefixed by **negative**; zero is represented by the empty protonotion; a value is **undefined** if and only if, as of the current instant during execution, the variable has not been given a specific value. For the **FILE** parts of a state protonotion, we have the further metarules

> **FILE :: DATETY eof.**
>
> **DATA :: datum NUMBER; datum NUMBER DATA.**
>
> **DATETY :: DATA; EMPTY.**

Suppose that the Pam program makes use of the variables x and y only. Then the following protonotion denotes a state in which the current value of x is -11, y has not yet been given a value, the unread portion of the input file contains the values 0 and 7, and the only value output so far is -2:

> **state var letter x value negative iiiiiiiiii var letter y value**
>
> **undefined datum datum iiiiiii eof datum negative ii eof**

TAG, as well as several other general metanotions, is defined by the following metarules:

> **ALPHA :: a; b; c; d; e; f; g; h; i; j; k; l; m; n; o; p;**
>
> **q; r; s; t; u; v; w; x; y; z.**
>
> **BETA :: zero; one; two; three; four; five; six; seven; eight; nine.**
>
> **NOTION :: ALPHA; NOTION ALPHA.**
>
> **NOTETY :: NOTION; EMPTY.**
>
> **EMPTY :: .**
>
> **LETTER :: letter ALPHA.**
>
> **DIGIT :: digit BETA.**
>
> **LETGIT :: LETTER; DIGIT.**
>
> **TAG :: LETTER; TAG LETGIT.**

(The fact that Pam identifiers may include digits is reflected in the definition of **TAG**.)

In addition to **STATE** protonotions, the various predicates in the invisible semantic subtree contain protonotions which are abstract representations of parts of the Pam program. The metarules defining these protonotions may be viewed as a set of specifications for Pam's abstract syntax:

STMTS :: STMT; STMTS STMT.

STMTSETY :: STMTS; EMPTY.

STMT :: IO TAG var;

    asmt TAG lhs EXPR rhs;

    cond COMPARE ifpart STMTS thenpart STMTSETY elsepart;

    deflp EXPR limit STMTS body;

    indeflp COMPARE test STMTS body.

(Here the various short protonotions serve as "meta-delimiters"; for example, **cond** marks the beginning of a protonotion representing a conditional statement, and **thenpart** marks the end of the segment (derived from **STMTS**) representing the series following the word **then** in the lexical form of the statement. For a conditional statement with no **else** part, the **STMTSETY elsepart** segment of the protonotion will be just **elsepart**.)

COMPARE :: comp EXPR leftopd REL rel EXPR rightopd.

EXPR :: exp EXPR leftopd OP opr EXPR rightopd; TALLETY; TAG.

(A variable used as an expression is represented by the corresponding **TAG**, and a constant, which cannot be negative, is represented by the appropriate **TALLETY** protonotion.)

REL : eq; le; lt; gt; ge; ne.

OP :: WEAKOP; STRGOP.

IO :: input; output.

WEAKOP :: plus; minus.

STRGOP :: times; over.

As a complete example of the abstract representation of a program, the Pam program

        to 10 **do**

            read $x1$;

            if $x1 > 0$ **then**

                $x2 := x1 + x1 / 2$;

            write $x2$ **fi end**

would be represented by the following **STMTS** protonotion (laid out so as to facilitate comprehension):

> **deflp iiiiiiiii limit**
> > **input letter x digit one var**
> > **cond comp letter x digit one leftopd gt rel rightopd ifpart**
> > **asmt letter x digit two lhs**
> > > **exp letter x digit one leftopd plus opr exp letter x**
> > > > **digit one leftopd over opr ii rightopd rightopd rhs**
> > > **output letter x digit two var thenpart elsepart body**

At this point, all the necessary metarules have been given. Note, however, that we have not yet written any hyper-rules; i.e., we have not really defined anything yet as far as the generation of tree structures and terminal strings is concerned. This we are now ready to do.

The "topmost" hyper-rule is

> **programme: VARS1 STMTS series, eof symbol, FILE1 file, FILE2 file,**
> > **where STMTS transforms state VARS1 FILE1 eof into**
> > **state VARS2 FILE3 FILE2.**

Here **VARS1 STMTS series** corresponds to the Pam program part of the programme. In analogy to the **DECS** mechanism in the Eva grammar, subsequent rules will enforce appropriate substitutions for **VARS1** and **STMTS** for each program. For example, if the program is

> **read** *x*, *y* ; **write** *y*

it will turn out that **VARS1** must include **var letter x value undefined** and **var letter y value undefined** and that **STMTS** can only be **input letter x var input letter y var output letter y var**, so that the program is precisely describable as a **var letter x value undefined var letter y value undefined input letter x var input letter y var output letter y var series**. Similarly, the **FILE1** and **FILE2** protonotions will reflect the contents of the input and output files, respectively. The protonotions corresponding to **VARS1, STMTS, FILE1,** and **FILE2** are all carried over to the semantic predicate part **where STMTS transforms state VARS1 FILE1 eof into state VARS2 FILE3 FILE2**. Note that this predicate has the form **where STMTS transforms STATE1 into STATE2**, where the "initial" state **STATE1** (= **state VARS1 FILE1 eof**) has the complete **FILE1** as its input file and an empty output file, and the "final" state **STATE2** (= **state VARS2 FILE3 FILE2**) has **FILE2** as its output file; the **VARS2** segment will specify the final values of the variables, and the **FILE3** segment will describe any input data, if any, that are still unread upon completion of the program.

The syntax of the two file portions of a programme is specified as follows:

datum NUMBER FILE file: NUMBER constant, point symbol, FILE file.

eof file: eof symbol.

The rules for **TALLETY constant** will be given later as part of the syntax of Pam expressions. Negative constants, however, can occur only within files, and we define them by the rule

negative TALLY constant: minus symbol, TALLY constant.

For the program portion, here are two rules for **VARS STMTS series**:

VARS STMTS STMT series:

VARS STMTS series, semicolon symbol, VARS STMT statement.

VARS STMT series: VARS STMT statement.

VARS STMT statement has to be defined by a number of hyper-rules dealing with the various possibilities for **STMT**. For input and output statements, we have

VARS IO TAG var statement: IO symbol, VARS TAG variable.

(The representations for **input symbol** and **output symbol** are **read** and **write**, respectively.) Input/output statements containing more than one variable may be considered as abbreviations for sequences of separate statements; e.g., in the program

read *x*, *y* ; **write** *y*

read *x*, *y* is equivalent to

read *x* ; **read** *y*

The latter form is handled by the rules given already; for the abbreviated form, we add a third hyper-rule for **VARS STMTS series**:

VARS STMTSETY IO TAG1 var IO TAG2 var series:

VARS STMTSETY IO TAG1 var series, comma symbol, VARS TAG2 variable.

Thus both forms are described by the notion **var letter x value undefined var letter y value undefined input letter x var input letter y var series**, and the difference between the two can be seen by comparing the partial subtrees in Figs. 3.4 and 3.5 (where the protonotion **var letter x value undefined var letter y value undefined** has been elided throughout).

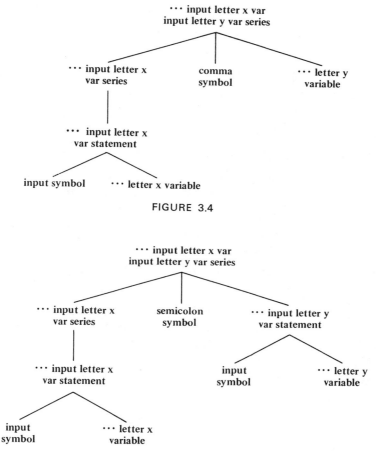

FIGURE 3.4

FIGURE 3.5

Variables are defined as follows:

VARS TAG variable: TAG token, where TAG occurs once in VARS.

LETTER token: LETTER symbol.

TAG LETGIT token: TAG token, LETGIT symbol.

The predicate part **where TAG occurs once in VARS** constrains the **VARS** protonotion to contain a single occurrence of the **TAG** protonotion, with value **undefined**:

where TAG occurs once in VARSETY1 var TAG value undefined VARSETY2:
    where TAG not in VARSETY1, where TAG not in VARSETY2.

The next three rules define **where TAG not in VARSETY**:

> **where TAG not in EMPTY: EMPTY.**
>
> **where TAG not in VARS VAR:**
>
> > **where TAG not in VARS, where TAG not in VAR.**
>
> **where TAG1 not in var TAG2 value VALUE: where TAG1 is not TAG2.**

Finally, nonequality of **TAG**s is a special case of nonequality of **NOTION**s, which is defined as follows:

where NOTETY1 ALPHA1 is not NOTETY2 ALPHA2:

> **where NOTETY1 is not NOTETY2;**
>
> **where ALPHA1 precedes ALPHA2 in abcdefghijklmnopqrstuvwxyz;**
>
> **where ALPHA2 precedes ALPHA1 in abcdefghijklmnopqrstuvwxyz.**

where NOTION is not EMPTY: EMPTY.

where EMPTY is not NOTION: EMPTY.

where ALPHA1 precedes ALPHA2 in NOTETY1 ALPHA1 NOTETY2 ALPHA2 NOTETY3: EMPTY.

The **VARS** protonotion is not prevented from having extra **VAR** parts corresponding to variables that do not appear in the Pam program, but this is of no significance. The ordering of the individual parts is not significant either. For simplicity, we assume that no extra parts are present and that the parts are ordered according to the first occurrences of the variables in the program.

We now have all the rules necessary for completing the tree for

read x, y ; **write** y

Much of the subtree for **read** x, y has already been shown, and so in Fig. 3.6 we focus on the structure of **write** y. It should be clear that, given the particular Pam program we are considering, the hyper-rules constrain the **STMTS** part of the top notion to be **input letter x var input letter y var output letter y var**. There will be a similar effect for all programs.

The rule for assignment statements is

> **VARS asmt TAG lhs EXPR rhs statement:**
>
> > **VARS TAG variable, becomes symbol, VARS EXPR expression.**

The two forms of conditional statement are specified by separate rules:

> **VARS cond COMPARE ifpart STMTS thenpart EMPTY elsepart statement:**
>
> > **if symbol, VARS COMPARE comparison, then symbol,**
> >
> > **VARS STMTS series, fi symbol.**

VARS cond COMPARE ifpart STMTS1 thenpart STMTS2 elsepart statement:
if symbol, VARS COMPARE comparison, then symbol,
VARS STMTS1 series, else symbol, VARS STMTS2 series, fi symbol.

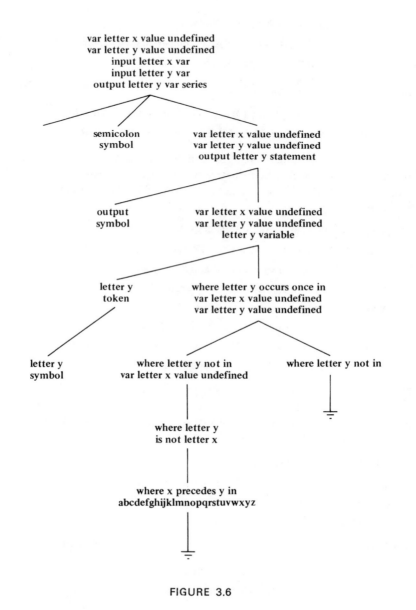

FIGURE 3.6

For loops we have

> **VARS deflp EXPR limit STMTS body statement:**
>> **to symbol, VARS EXPR expression, do symbol, VARS STMTS series,**
>> **end symbol.**
>
> **VARS indeflp COMPARE test STMTS body statement:**
>> **while symbol, VARS COMPARE comparison, do symbol,**
>> **VARS STMTS series, end symbol.**

and comparisons are defined by

> **VARS comp EXPR1 leftopd REL rel EXPR2 rightopd comparison:**
>> **VARS EXPR1 expression, REL symbol, VARS EXPR2 expression.**

The following hyper-rules for expressions ensure that the effects of operator precedence and parenthesization are properly reflected in the **EXPR** protonotions. There are two rules each for **VARS EXPR expression** and **VARS EXPR term**:

> **VARS EXPR expression: VARS EXPR term.**
>
> **VARS exp EXPR1 leftopd WEAKOP opr EXPR2 rightopd expression:**
>> **VARS EXPR1 expression, WEAKOP symbol, VARS EXPR2 term.**
>
> **VARS EXPR term: VARS EXPR element.**
>
> **VARS exp EXPR1 leftopd STRGOP opr EXPR2 rightopd term:**
>> **VARS EXPR1 term, STRGOP symbol, VARS EXPR2 element.**
>
> **VARS EXPR element: EXPR constant; VARS EXPR variable;**
>> **lpar symbol, VARS EXPR expression, rpar symbol.**

In the case of a variable, the **EXPR** protonotion must actually be a **TAG** protonotion, and **VARS TAG variable** has already been defined. In the case of a constant, the **EXPR** protonotion must actually be a **TALLETY**, and Pam programs employ the normal decimal notation:

> **TALLETY constant: TALLETY digit;**
>> **TALLETY2 constant, TALLETY3 digit, where TALLETY is TALLETY2**
>> **TALLETY2 TALLETY2 TALLETY2 TALLETY2 TALLETY2 TALLETY2**
>> **TALLETY2 TALLETY2 TALLETY2 TALLETY3.**

An example of a production rule derived from this hyper-rule would be

> **iiiiiiiiiii constant: iiiiiiiiiii digit;**
>> **i constant, ii digit, where iiiiiiiiiii is i i i i i i i i i i ii.**

The predicate part is simply defined by

> **where NOTETY is NOTETY: EMPTY.**

and only ten kinds of digit are defined:

> **EMPTY digit: digit zero symbol.**
> **i digit: digit one symbol.**
> **ii digit: digit two symbol.**
> **iii digit: digit three symbol.**
> **iiii digit: digit four symbol.**
> **iiiii digit: digit five symbol.**
> **iiiiii digit: digit six symbol.**
> **iiiiiii digit: digit seven symbol.**
> **iiiiiiii digit: digit eight symbol.**
> **iiiiiiiii digit: digit nine symbol.**

At last we are ready to give the hyper-rules which constitute the semantic specifications for Pam. By introducing suitable intermediate states, the first such rule has the effect of expressing the meaning of a series in terms of the meanings of its constituent statements:

> **where STMTS STMT transforms STATE1 into STATE3:**
> **where STMTS transforms STATE1 into STATE2,**
> **where STMT transforms STATE2 into STATE3.**

We shall also need the following trivial rule for the "empty series":

> **where EMPTY transforms STATE into STATE: EMPTY.**

Our next task is to define **where STMT transforms STATE1 into STATE2** for the various kinds of **STMT**. In the case of an input statement (**STMT = input TAG var**), a predicate of this form should hold if and only if the value associated with the **TAG** in the **VARS** part of **STATE2** is the first value in the input file part of **STATE1** and the input file part of **STATE2** does not include this first value:

where input TAG var transforms state VARSETY1 var TAG value
> **VALUE VARSETY2 datum NUMBER FILE1 FILE2 into state VARSETY1**
> **var TAG value NUMBER VARSETY2 FILE1 FILE2: EMPTY.**

The variable's original value (**VALUE**), the condition of the other variables

(**VARSETY1**, **VARSETY2**), and the contents of the output file (**FILE2**) are irrelevant. This rule does not allow the input file part of the first state to be empty; a program-input-output combination involving more input operations than data values is not a **programme** because a blind alley arises when we attempt to construct the semantic subtree.

In the case of an output statement (**STMT** = **output TAG var**), a "transforms" predicate should hold if and only if the output file part of the second state is the same as that of the first state except that the value associated with the **TAG** is appended at the end:

> **where output TAG var transforms state VARSETY1 var TAG value**
>
> **NUMBER VARSETY2 FILE1 DATETY eof into state**
>
> **VARSETY1 var TAG value NUMBER VARSETY2 FILE1**
>
> **DATETY datum NUMBER eof: EMPTY.**

This rule does not allow the value of the variable to be **undefined** as would be the case if, for example, the output statement were the first statement in a program.

Before going any further, we may observe the basic mechanism at work by constructing the complete semantic subtree for our sample programme

> **read** x, y ; **write** y **eof** -2. 7. **eof** 7. **eof**

According to the hyper-rule for **programme**, the top semantic predicate has the form **where STMTS transforms state VARS1 FILE1 eof into state VARS2 FILE3 FILE2**, and we have already seen that the hyper-rules for the program and file parts of the programme force **STMTS** to be **input letter x var input letter y var output letter y var**, **VARS1** to be **var letter x value undefined var letter y value undefined**, **FILE1** to be **datum negative ii datum iiiiiii eof**, and **FILE2** to be **datum iiiiiii eof**. Now, *if* we take **VARS2** to be **var letter x value negative ii var letter y value iiiiiii** and **FILE3** to be **eof**, the above hyper-rules give us the structure shown in Fig. 3.7. The reader is urged to study this example until convinced that any other substitutions for **VARS2** and **FILE3** would have led to a blind alley.

For an assignment statement (**STMT** = **asmt TAG lhs EXPR rhs**), the value associated with the **TAG** in the second state is the number yielded by "evaluating" the **EXPR** in the context of the first state:

> **where asmt TAG lhs EXPR rhs transforms state VARSETY1**
>
> **var TAG value VALUE VARSETY2 FILE1 FILE2 into state VARSETY1**
>
> **var TAG value NUMBER VARSETY2 FILE1 FILE2:**
>
> **where EXPR given state VARSETY1 var TAG value VALUE VARSETY2**
>
> **FILE1 FILE2 yields NUMBER.**

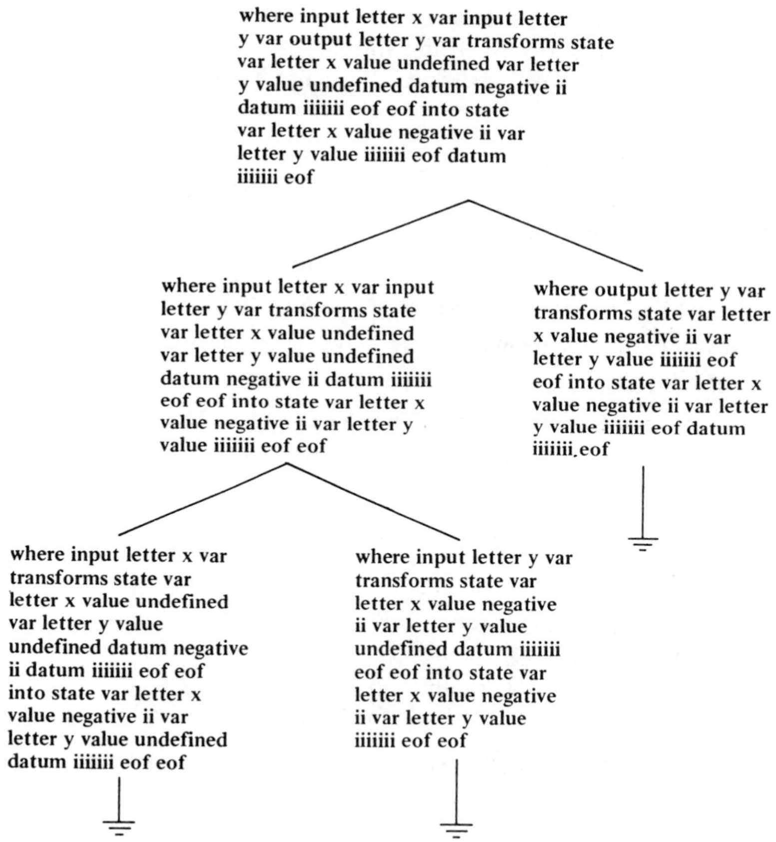

where input letter x var input letter
y var output letter y var transforms state
var letter x value undefined var letter
y value undefined datum negative ii
datum iiiiiii eof eof into state
var letter x value negative ii var
letter y value iiiiiii eof datum
iiiiiii eof

where input letter x var input
letter y var transforms state
var letter x value undefined
var letter y value undefined
datum negative ii datum iiiiiii
eof eof into state var letter x
value negative ii var letter y
value iiiiiii eof eof

where output letter y var
transforms state var letter
x value negative ii var
letter y value iiiiiii eof
eof into state var letter x
value negative ii var letter
y value iiiiiii eof datum
iiiiiii eof

where input letter x var
transforms state var
letter x value undefined
var letter y value
undefined datum negative
ii datum iiiiiii eof eof
into state var letter x
value negative ii var
letter y value undefined
datum iiiiiii eof eof

where input letter y var
transforms state var
letter x value negative
ii var letter y value
undefined datum iiiiiii
eof eof into state var
letter x value negative
ii var letter y value
iiiiiii eof eof

FIGURE 3.7

The right side of this rule is of the form **where EXPR given STATE yields NUMBER** and will be defined later.

The meaning of conditional statements is defined by

> **where cond COMPARE ifpart STMTS thenpart STMTSETY elsepart**
>> **transforms STATE1 into STATE2:**
>> **where COMPARE given STATE1 succeeds, where STMTS transforms**
>>> **STATE1 into STATE2;**
>> **where COMPARE given STATE1 fails, where STMTSETY transforms**
>>> **STATE1 into STATE2.**

This makes use of two further predicates still to be defined—**where COM-**

PARE given STATE succeeds and **where COMPARE given STATE fails**; in any given case, only one of them will hold.

A definite loop (**STMT = deflp EXPR limit STMTS body**) is semantically equivalent to a number of consecutive copies of **STMTS** given by the value of **EXPR** in the first state:

> **where deflp EXPR limit STMTS body transforms STATE1 into STATE2:**
>> **where NUMBER copies of STMTS transforms STATE1 into STATE2,**
>> **where EXPR given STATE1 yields NUMBER.**
>
> **where TALLY i copies of STMTS transforms STATE1 into STATE3:**
>> **where TALLY copies of STMTS transforms STATE1 into STATE2,**
>> **where STMTS transforms STATE2 into STATE3.**
>
> **where i copies of STMTS transforms STATE1 into STATE2:**
>> **where STMTS transforms STATE1 into STATE2.**
>
> **where EMPTY copies of STMTS transforms STATE into STATE: EMPTY.**
>
> **where negative TALLY copies of STMTS transforms STATE into STATE: EMPTY.**

The last rule states that a negative limit value is legal and gives rise to zero repetitions of the loop body.

The meaning of an indefinite loop is recursively defined in terms of a fictitious series consisting of the body followed by the entire loop statement:

> **where indeflp COMPARE test STMTS body transforms STATE1 into STATE2:**
>> **where COMPARE given STATE1 succeeds, where STMTS indeflp**
>>> **COMPARE test STMTS body transforms STATE1 into STATE2;**
>> **where COMPARE given STATE1 fails, where STATE1 is STATE2.**

For a large loop giving rise to a large number of repetitions, the semantic subtree will be very large. Programmes that result in infinite looping are ruled out by the fact that the subtree would have to be infinitely large.

The next task is to define the semantics of comparisons:

> **where comp EXPR1 leftopd REL rel EXPR2 rightopd given STATE succeeds:**
>> **where NUMBER1 REL NUMBER2,**
>> **where EXPR1 given STATE yields NUMBER1,**
>> **where EXPR2 given STATE yields NUMBER2.**
>
> **where comp EXPR1 leftopd REL rel EXPR2 rightopd given STATE fails:**
>> **where not NUMBER1 REL NUMBER2,**
>> **where EXPR1 given STATE yields NUMBER1,**
>> **where EXPR2 given STATE yields NUMBER2.**

The following rules specify just which predicates of the form **where NUMBER1 REL NUMBER2** hold. The definition of "equals" is trivial and, once "less than" has been defined by cases, the rest follow easily:

> **where NUMBER1 eq NUMBER2: where NUMBER1 is NUMBER2.**
>
> **where TALLETY lt TALLETY TALLY: EMPTY.**
>
> **where negative TALLY lt TALLETY: EMPTY.**
>
> **where negative TALLY1 lt negative TALLY2: where TALLY2 lt TALLY1.**
>
> **where NUMBER1 le NUMBER2:**
>
> > **where NUMBER1 lt NUMBER2; where NUMBER1 eq NUMBER2.**
>
> **where NUMBER1 gt NUMBER2: where NUMBER2 lt NUMBER1.**
>
> **where NUMBER1 ge NUMBER2: where NUMBER2 le NUMBER1.**
>
> **where NUMBER1 ne NUMBER2:**
>
> > **where NUMBER1 lt NUMBER2; where NUMBER2 lt NUMBER1.**

Now it is a simple matter to specify which predicates of the form **where not NUMBER1 REL NUMBER2** hold:

> **where not NUMBER1 eq NUMBER2: where NUMBER1 ne NUMBER2.**
>
> **where not NUMBER1 lt NUMBER2: where NUMBER1 ge NUMBER2.**
>
> **where not NUMBER1 le NUMBER2: where NUMBER1 gt NUMBER2.**
>
> **where not NUMBER1 gt NUMBER2: where NUMBER1 le NUMBER2.**
>
> **where not NUMBER1 ge NUMBER2: where NUMBER1 lt NUMBER2.**
>
> **where not NUMBER1 ne NUMBER2: where NUMBER1 eq NUMBER2.**

The final task is to define **where EXPR given STATE yields NUMBER** for the various kinds of **EXPR**. First, the value of a constant is known in advance and is independent of the state:

> **where TALLETY given STATE yields TALLETY: EMPTY.**

The value of a variable is recorded in the **VARS** part of the state:

> **where TAG given state VARSETY1 var TAG value NUMBER VARSETY2 yields NUMBER: EMPTY.**

(There is no provision for evaluation of a variable whose value is still **undefined**, so that the grammar excludes programmes giving rise to this situation.) The rule for expressions containing operators is

> **where exp EXPR1 leftopd OP opr EXPR2 rightopd given STATE yields NUMBER:**
>
> > **where NUMBER1 OP NUMBER2 equals NUMBER,**
> >
> > **where EXPR1 given STATE yields NUMBER1,**
> >
> > **where EXPR2 given STATE yields NUMBER2.**

The definition of **where NUMBER1 OP NUMBER2 equals NUMBER** is rather lengthy and amounts to a kind of axiomatization of integer arithmetic. We begin with addition of nonnegative numbers:

where TALLETY1 plus TALLETY2 equals TALLETY1 TALLETY2: EMPTY.

Use is made of this in the rule for addition of two negative numbers:

where negative TALLY1 plus negative TALLY2 equals negative TALLY3:
where TALLY1 plus TALLY2 equals TALLY3.

Addition of a negative and a nonnegative number is defined in terms of subtraction:

where TALLETY plus negative TALLY equals NUMBER:
where TALLETY minus TALLY equals NUMBER.
where negative TALLY plus TALLETY equals NUMBER:
where TALLETY minus TALLY equals NUMBER.

Subtraction of two nonnegative numbers is completely defined by the following pair of rules:

where TALLETY1 TALLETY2 minus TALLETY2 equals TALLETY1: EMPTY.
where TALLETY minus TALLETY TALLY equals negative TALLY: EMPTY.

This enables us to define subtraction of two negative numbers:

where negative TALLY1 minus negative TALLY2 equals NUMBER:
where TALLY2 minus TALLY1 equals NUMBER.

Subtractions involving one negative number and one nonnegative number are defined in terms of addition of two nonnegative numbers:

where TALLETY minus negative TALLY1 equals TALLY2:
where TALLETY plus TALLY1 equals TALLY2.
where negative TALLY1 minus TALLETY equals negative TALLY2:
where TALLY1 plus TALLETY equals TALLY2.

The number of rules for multiplication is slightly reduced by including the "commutative" rule

where NUMBER1 times NUMBER2 equals NUMBER3:
where NUMBER2 times NUMBER1 equals NUMBER3.

(This introduces an inconsequential ambiguity into the grammar.) Multiplication by zero and one are easy to define:

> **where EMPTY times NUMBER equals EMPTY: EMPTY.**
>
> **where i times NUMBER equals NUMBER: EMPTY.**

The remaining cases are reducible to multiplication by one:

> **where TALLY1 i times TALLY2 equals TALLY2 TALLY3:**
>
> **where TALLY1 times TALLY2 equals TALLY3.**
>
> **where negative TALLY1 times TALLY2 equals negative TALLY3:**
>
> **where TALLY1 times TALLY2 equals TALLY3.**
>
> **where negative TALLY1 times negative TALLY2 equals TALLY3:**
>
> **where TALLY1 times TALLY2 equals TALLY3.**

The rules for division will not provide for a denominator of zero, so that division by zero is yet another semantic error ruled out by the grammar. Apart from that, if the numerator is zero, so is the result:

> **where EMPTY over TALLY equals EMPTY: EMPTY.**
>
> **where EMPTY over negative TALLY equals EMPTY: EMPTY.**

For positive operands, the result is given by the number of times the numerator can be reduced by an amount equal to the denominator:

> **where TALLETY1 TALLY over TALLY equals TALLETY2 i:**
>
> **where TALLETY1 over TALLY equals TALLETY2.**
>
> **where TALLY1 over TALLY1 TALLY2 equals EMPTY: EMPTY.**

The analogous rules for division of a negative numerator by a positive denominator are

> **where negative TALLETY1 TALLY over TALLY equals negative**
>
> **TALLETY2 i: where TALLETY1 over TALLY equals TALLETY2.**
>
> **where negative TALLY1 over TALLY1 TALLY2 equals EMPTY: EMPTY.**

and these permit us to define division of a positive numerator by a negative denominator:

> **where TALLY1 over negative TALLY2 equals NUMBER:**
>
> **where negative TALLY1 over TALLY2 equals NUMBER.**

Finally, if both operands are negative, it is as if they were positive:

> **where negative TALLY1 over negative TALLY2 equals NUMBER:**
> **where TALLY1 over TALLY2 equals NUMBER.**

The definition is now complete in every detail, and all the rules of the grammar are collected in Table 3.2. The best way to verify one's understanding of the definition is to construct complete trees for small examples such as

> **read** k ; **while** $k > 0$ **do** $k := k - 1$ **end eof** 2. **eof eof**

It is also useful to consider some semantically illegal examples and check that the grammar excludes them.

> **TABLE 3.2 Two-Level Grammar Defining the Syntax and Semantics of Pam**

ALPHA :: a; b; c; d; e; f; g; h; i; j; k; l; m; n; o; p; q; r; s; t; u; v; w; x; y; z.

BETA :: zero; one; two; three; four; five; six; seven; eight; nine.

NOTION :: ALPHA; NOTION ALPHA.

NOTETY :: NOTION; EMPTY.

EMPTY :: .

LETTER :: letter ALPHA.

DIGIT :: digit BETA.

LETGIT :: LETTER; DIGIT.

TAG :: LETTER; TAG LETGIT.

STMTS :: STMT; STMTS STMT.

STMTSETY :: STMTS; EMPTY.

STMT :: IO TAG var;

> asmt TAG lhs EXPR rhs;
>
> cond COMPARE ifpart STMTS thenpart STMTSETY elsepart;
>
> deflp EXPR limit STMTS body;
>
> indeflp COMPARE test STMTS body.

COMPARE :: comp EXPR leftopd REL rel EXPR rightopd.

EXPR :: exp EXPR leftopd OP opr EXPR rightopd; TALLETY; TAG.

REL :: eq; le; lt; gt; ge; ne.

OP :: WEAKOP; STRGOP.

IO :: input; output.

TABLE 3.2 (Continued)

WEAKOP :: plus; minus.

STRGOP :: times; over.

STATE :: state VARS FILE FILE.

VARS :: VAR; VARS VAR.

VARSETY :: VARS; EMPTY.

VAR :: var TAG value VALUE.

VALUE :: undefined; NUMBER.

NUMBER :: TALLETY; negative TALLY.

TALLY :: i; TALLY i.

TALLETY :: TALLY; EMPTY.

FILE :: DATETY eof.

DATA :: datum NUMBER; datum NUMBER DATA.

DATETY :: DATA; EMPTY.

programme: VARS1 STMTS series, eof symbol, FILE1 file, FILE2 file,
    where STMTS transforms state VARS1 FILE1 eof into state VARS2
    FILE3 FILE2.

datum NUMBER FILE file: NUMBER constant, point symbol, FILE file.

eof file: eof symbol.

negative TALLY constant: minus symbol, TALLY constant.

VARS STMTS STMT series:
    VARS STMTS series, semicolon symbol, VARS STMT statement.

VARS STMT series: VARS STMT statement.

VARS STMTSETY IO TAG1 var IO TAG2 var series:
    VARS STMTSETY IO TAG1 var series, comma symbol, VARS TAG2 variable.

VARS IO TAG var statement: IO symbol, VARS TAG variable.

VARS asmt TAG lhs EXPR rhs statement:
    VARS TAG variable, becomes symbol, VARS EXPR expression.

VARS cond COMPARE ifpart STMTS thenpart EMPTY elsepart statement:
    if symbol, VARS COMPARE comparison, then symbol, VARS STMTS series,
    fi symbol.

VARS cond COMPARE ifpart STMTS1 thenpart STMTS2 elsepart statement:
    if symbol, VARS COMPARE comparison, then symbol, VARS STMTS1
    series, else symbol, VARS STMTS2 series, fi symbol.

VARS deflp EXPR limit STMTS body statement:

TABLE 3.2 (Continued)

to symbol, VARS EXPR expression, do symbol, VARS STMTS series,
end symbol.

VARS indeflp COMPARE test STMTS body statement:

while symbol, VARS COMPARE comparison, do symbol,
VARS STMTS series, end symbol.

VARS comp EXPR1 leftopd REL rel EXPR2 rightopd comparison:

VARS EXPR1 expression, REL symbol, VARS EXPR2 expression.

VARS EXPR expression: VARS EXPR term.

VARS exp EXPR1 leftopd WEAKOP opr EXPR2 rightopd expression:

VARS EXPR1 expression, WEAKOP symbol, VARS EXPR2 term.

VARS EXPR term: VARS EXPR element.

VARS exp EXPR1 leftopd STRGOP opr EXPR2 rightopd term:

VARS EXPR1 term, STRGOP symbol, VARS EXPR2 element.

VARS EXPR element: EXPR constant; VARS EXPR variable;

lpar symbol, VARS EXPR expression, rpar symbol.

TALLETY constant: TALLETY digit;

TALLETY2 constant, TALLETY3 digit, where TALLETY is TALLETY2
TALLETY2 TALLETY2 TALLETY2 TALLETY2 TALLETY2 TALLETY2
TALLETY2 TALLETY2 TALLETY2 TALLETY3.

EMPTY digit: digit zero symbol.

i digit: digit one symbol.

ii digit: digit two symbol.

iii digit: digit three symbol.

iiii digit: digit four symbol.

iiiii digit: digit five symbol.

iiiiii digit: digit six symbol.

iiiiiii digit: digit seven symbol.

iiiiiiii digit: digit eight symbol.

iiiiiiiii digit: digit nine symbol.

VARS TAG variable: TAG token, where TAG occurs once in VARS.

LETTER token: LETTER symbol.

TAG LETGIT token: TAG token, LETGIT symbol.

where NOTETY is NOTETY: EMPTY.

where TAG occurs once in VARSETY1 var TAG value undefined VARSETY2:

where TAG not in VARSETY1, where TAG not in VARSETY2.

TABLE 3.2 (Continued)

where TAG not in EMPTY: EMPTY.

where TAG not in VARS VAR:

    where TAG not in VARS, where TAG not in VAR.

where TAG1 not in var TAG2 value VALUE: where TAG1 is not TAG2.

where NOTETY1 ALPHA1 is not NOTETY2 ALPHA2:

    where NOTETY1 is not NOTETY2;

    where ALPHA1 precedes ALPHA2 in abcdefghijklmnopqrstuvwxyz;

    where ALPHA2 precedes ALPHA1 in abcdefghijklmnopqrstuvwxyz.

where NOTION is not EMPTY: EMPTY.

where EMPTY is not NOTION: EMPTY.

where ALPHA1 precedes ALPHA2 in NOTETY1 ALPHA1 NOTETY2 ALPHA2
    NOTETY3: EMPTY.

where STMTS STMT transforms STATE1 into STATE3:

    where STMTS transforms STATE1 into STATE2,

    where STMT transforms STATE2 into STATE3.

where EMPTY transforms STATE into STATE: EMPTY.

where input TAG var transforms state VARSETY1 var TAG value VALUE
    VARSETY2 datum NUMBER FILE1 FILE2 into state VARSETY1 var TAG
    value NUMBER VARSETY2 FILE1 FILE2: EMPTY.

where output TAG var transforms state VARSETY1 var TAG value NUMBER
    VARSETY2 FILE1 DATETY eof into state VARSETY1 var TAG value
    NUMBER VARSETY2 FILE1 DATETY datum NUMBER eof: EMPTY.

where asmt TAG lhs EXPR rhs transforms state VARSETY1
    var TAG value VALUE VARSETY2 FILE1 FILE2 into state VARSETY1
    var TAG value NUMBER VARSETY2 FILE1 FILE2:
    where EXPR given state VARSETY1 var TAG value VALUE VARSETY2
    FILE1 FILE2 yields NUMBER.

where cond COMPARE ifpart STMTS thenpart STMTSETY elsepart
    transforms STATE1 into STATE2:
    where COMPARE given STATE1 succeeds, where STMTS transforms
        STATE1 into STATE2;
    where COMPARE given STATE1 fails, where STMTSETY transforms
        STATE1 into STATE2.

where deflp EXPR limit STMTS body transforms STATE1
    into STATE2:

TABLE 3.2 (Continued)

where NUMBER copies of STMTS transforms STATE1 into STATE2,
    where EXPR given STATE1 yields NUMBER.
where TALLY i copies of STMTS transforms STATE1 into STATE3:
    where TALLY copies of STMTS transforms STATE1 into STATE2,
    where STMTS transforms STATE2 into STATE3.
where i copies of STMTS transforms STATE1 into STATE2:
    where STMTS transforms STATE1 into STATE2.
where EMPTY copies of STMTS transforms STATE into STATE: EMPTY.
where negative TALLY copies of STMTS transforms STATE into STATE: EMPTY.
where indeflp COMPARE test STMTS body transforms STATE1 into STATE2:
    where COMPARE given STATE1 succeeds, where STMTS indeflp COMPARE
        test STMTS body transforms STATE1 into STATE2;
    where COMPARE given STATE1 fails, where STATE1 is STATE2.

where comp EXPR1 leftopd REL rel EXPR2 rightopd given STATE succeeds:
    where NUMBER1 REL NUMBER2,
    where EXPR1 given STATE yields NUMBER1,
    where EXPR2 given STATE yields NUMBER2.
where NUMBER1 eq NUMBER2: where NUMBER1 is NUMBER2.
where TALLETY lt TALLETY TALLY: EMPTY.
where negative TALLY lt TALLETY: EMPTY.
where negative TALLY1 lt negative TALLY2: where TALLY2 lt TALLY1.
where NUMBER1 le NUMBER2:
    where NUMBER1 lt NUMBER2; where NUMBER1 eq NUMBER2.
where NUMBER1 gt NUMBER2: where NUMBER2 lt NUMBER1.
where NUMBER1 ge NUMBER2: where NUMBER2 le NUMBER1.
where NUMBER1 ne NUMBER2:
    where NUMBER1 lt NUMBER2; where NUMBER2 lt NUMBER1.
where comp EXPR1 leftopd REL rel EXPR2 rightopd given STATE fails:
    where not NUMBER1 REL NUMBER2,
    where EXPR1 given STATE yields NUMBER1,
    where EXPR2 given STATE yields NUMBER2.
where not NUMBER1 eq NUMBER2: where NUMBER1 ne NUMBER2.
where not NUMBER1 lt NUMBER2: where NUMBER1 ge NUMBER2.
where not NUMBER1 le NUMBER2: where NUMBER1 gt NUMBER2.
where not NUMBER1 gt NUMBER2: where NUMBER1 le NUMBER2.

TABLE 3.2 (Continued)

where not NUMBER1 ge NUMBER2: where NUMBER1 lt NUMBER2.

where not NUMBER1 ne NUMBER2: where NUMBER1 eq NUMBER2.

where TALLETY given STATE yields TALLETY: EMPTY.

where TAG given state VARSETY1 var TAG value NUMBER VARSETY2 yields
    NUMBER: EMPTY.

where exp EXPR1 leftopd OP opr EXPR2 rightopd given STATE yields NUMBER:
    where NUMBER1 OP NUMBER2 equals NUMBER,
    where EXPR1 given STATE yields NUMBER1,
    where EXPR2 given STATE yields NUMBER2.

where TALLETY1 plus TALLETY2 equals TALLETY1 TALLETY2: EMPTY.

where TALLETY plus negative TALLY equals NUMBER:
    where TALLETY minus TALLY equals NUMBER.

where negative TALLY plus TALLETY equals NUMBER:
    where TALLETY minus TALLY equals NUMBER.

where negative TALLY1 plus negative TALLY2 equals negative TALLY3:
    where TALLY1 plus TALLY2 equals TALLY3.

where TALLETY1 TALLETY2 minus TALLETY2 equals TALLETY1: EMPTY.

where TALLETY minus TALLETY TALLY equals negative TALLY: EMPTY.

where TALLETY minus negative TALLY1 equals TALLY2:
    where TALLETY plus TALLY1 equals TALLY2.

where negative TALLY1 minus TALLETY equals negative TALLY2:
    where TALLY1 plus TALLETY equals TALLY2.

where negative TALLY1 minus negative TALLY2 equals NUMBER:
    where TALLY2 minus TALLY1 equals NUMBER.

where NUMBER1 times NUMBER2 equals NUMBER3:
    where NUMBER2 times NUMBER1 equals NUMBER3.

where EMPTY times NUMBER equals EMPTY: EMPTY.

where i times NUMBER equals NUMBER: EMPTY.

where TALLY1 i times TALLY2 equals TALLY2 TALLY3:
    where TALLY1 times TALLY2 equals TALLY3.

where negative TALLY1 times TALLY2 equals negative TALLY3:
    where TALLY1 times TALLY2 equals TALLY3.

where negative TALLY1 times negative TALLY2 equals TALLY3:
    where TALLY1 times TALLY2 equals TALLY3.

where EMPTY over TALLY equals EMPTY: EMPTY.

121

TABLE 3.2 (Continued)

---

where EMPTY over negative TALLY equals EMPTY: EMPTY.

where TALLETY1 TALLY over TALLY equals TALLETY2 i:

    where TALLETY1 over TALLY equals TALLETY2.

where TALLY1 over TALLY1 TALLY2 equals EMPTY: EMPTY.

where negative TALLETY1 TALLY over TALLY equals negative TALLETY2 i:

    where TALLETY1 over TALLY equals TALLETY2.

where negative TALLY1 over TALLY1 TALLY2 equals EMPTY: EMPTY.

where TALLY1 over negative TALLY2 equals NUMBER:

    where negative TALLY1 over TALLY2 equals NUMBER.

where negative TALLY1 over negative TALLY2 equals NUMBER:

    where TALLY1 over TALLY2 equals NUMBER.

EXERCISES

1. If you have enough paper, construct the complete tree for

      read k ; **while** $k > 0$ **do** $k := k - 1$ **end eof** 2. **eof eof**

according to the grammar of Table 3.2.

2. Verify that

      read x, y ; **write** x **eof** 18. **eof** 18. **eof**

is not derivable from the grammar.

3.3.2   A Complete Definition of Eva

The two-level grammar (excluding symbol representations) for the syntax and semantics of Eva shown in Table 3.3, page 125, employs a combination of the devices used in the grammars for the complete syntax of Eva (Table 2.7) and the complete syntax and semantics of Pam (Table 3.2). Rather than discuss all the rules in detail, we shall concentrate most of our attention on the more difficult and significant aspects, such as the semantics of procedures and parameters. The rules in Table 3.3 have been numbered for convenience of reference.

The metarules (M1) through (M7) define the metanotions **ALPHA**, **NOTION**, **NOTETY**, **EMPTY**, **LETTER**, **LETTERS**, and **TAG** in the usual way. The 27 protonotions represented by **CHAR** (M8) correspond to the possible values of type **char**, so that **CHARSETY**, as defined by (M9) and (M10), represents the possible values of type **string**. As in the Pam definition, a **STATE** protonotion (M11) includes two file portions, but here the files consist of sequences of characters (M12) rather than of numbers. A state also contains a **NEST** protonotion as defined by (M13) through (M22). These rules are similar to those defining **NEST** in Table 2.7 (replacing **DECS** by **LAYER** and **DEC** by **ITEM**), except that, like the rules for **VARS** in Table 3.2, they enable values of the various names to be recorded. A protonotion representing a value [see (M22)] may be **undefined** (for **char** variables only), empty (for **string** variables), a single **CHAR** (for **char** or **string** variables), a sequence of two or more **CHAR**s (for **string** variables), or the abstract representation (**STMT**) of a procedure body (for procedure names). The rules (M23) through (M26) define the protonotions which act as abstract representations of parts of Eva programs; they are analogous to a subset of the metarules in Table 3.2. The reader who intends to study the present grammar in detail should thoroughly review all the metarules before going any further.

As in Table 3.2, the hyper-rules of Table 3.3 divide into two main groups, one [(H1) through (H52)] dealing with syntactic matters and the other [(H53) through (H74)] dealing with semantic matters. Many of the notions appearing in the visible (syntactic) part of a parse tree include first a **NEST** part to record the information specified by all declarations bearing on the construct and then a **STMTS** part which is the abstract representation of the construct. The "topmost" hyper-rule (H1) specifies that the nest for the block forming the entire program is empty (**new**) and that the abstract representation of the block is a protonotion of the form **blk LAYER1 decs STMTS body**, where the syntactic "consistency" of **LAYER1** is enforced by the rules (H44) through (H52) as in Table 2.7; the same **LAYER1**, when prefixed by **new new**, forms the nest portion of the initial state in the semantic "transforms" predicate, which expresses the effect of executing the body (**STMTS**) of the block. The treatment of files in (H1) through (H3) is entirely analogous to that in Table 3.2.

The hyper-rules for declarations are a slight extension of the corresponding rules in Table 2.7. Note that (H7) implies that the initial value of a character variable is undefined, while (H8) implies that the initial value of a string variable is the null string. Rules (H9), (H10), and (H16) permit redundant declarer symbols to be omitted.

Rules (H17) through (H27) for the syntax of statements are analogous to the statement rules of Table 3.2 and should not give rise to any difficulties in understanding. (H28) and (H29) constrain lists of arguments in calls to conform to the parameters of the procedure being called. Notions describing Eva expressions are of the form **VALTYPE NEST EXPR expression** or **VALTYPE NEST name with TAG**, and are defined by the rules (H30) through (H40). The matching of names with their declarations is handled by (H41) and subsequent rules.

The semantic rules beginning with (H53) are broadly similar to those in

Table 3.2, but the handling of the **NEST** portions of the **STATE** protonotions is more complicated. In the rules for **input** (H54), **call** (H56, H57), and **cons** (H62) statements, **NESTETY** denotes that part of the nest, if any, corresponding to declaration levels below the one (of the general form **new LAYETY1 ITEM LAYETY2**) containing the information (**ITEM**) about the name of interest. The predicate

where TAG not found in NESTETY

which guarantees that the name is not redeclared at one of the lower levels, is defined by (H73) and (H74), which in turn refer back to (H46) and (H47). In the rule for blocks (H58), **NEST1** contains the initial information about the nonlocal items, **LAYER1** the initial information about the local items (where all character values are undefined and all string values are null), **LAYER2** the final information about the local items, and **NEST2** the final information about the nonlocal items. The rule says in effect that the nest is augmented upon entry to a block and restored to its original size (although some values may be different) upon exit; the locally declared items only exist for the statements inside the block.

The rules for the semantics of procedure calls (H56, H57) are the most complex and the most interesting. The effect of executing a call of a procedure with no parameters is basically the same as the effect of executing the procedure's body [represented by **STMT** in (H56)], except that names declared at levels below that of the procedure declaration are not accessible while the body is being executed. For example, suppose that a program has the following outline:

begin

proc *p* =

. . .

string *a*

begin

char *a*

. . .

call *p*

. . .

end

. . .

end

The body of the procedure *p* can access the outer *a* (of type **string**) but not the inner one (of type **char**), whereas the reverse would be true if the body textually replaced the call statement. This phenomenon is dealt with by omitting the **NESTETY** portion of the nest in the initial and final states for the call statement from the predicate on the right side of (H56) describing the interpretation of the procedure body. We may think of the nest shrinking upon entry to a procedure and returning to its original size upon return to the point following the call. The procedure can change the value of variables declared at higher levels (described by **NEST1** initially and by **NEST2** finally), at the same level and before the procedure (**LAYETY1** initially, **LAYETY3** finally), and at the same level and after the procedure (**LAYETY2** initially, **LAYETY4** finally), as well as the input file (**FILE1** initially, **FILE3** finally) and the output file (**FILE2** initially, **FILE4** finally).

Rule (H57) for procedures with parameters is basically the same as (H56), with the added feature that the nest for the procedure body (which does not include the **NESTETY** part) is augmented with a layer (**LAYER1** initially, **LAYER2** finally) describing the parameters and their values. The values in **LAYER1** are obtained by evaluating the argument expressions in the context of the original nest applying to the call statement; this is specified by the last predicate in (H57) together with rules (H65) and (H66). As far as statements following the call are concerned, the **LAYER2** portion of the nest no longer exists (so that changes of parameter values carried out by the procedure body have no external effect) and the **NESTETY** portion has been restored.

The remaining semantic rules are quite straightforward. Note that (H60) and (H61) refer to (H63) and (H64). The latter, as well as several of the earlier rules, contain predicates of the form

where EXPR returns CHARSETY given NEST

for expression evaluation. This is defined by cases in (H67) through (H72). Observe that (H68) and (H71) evaluate a name by searching the nest from back to front, so that the most local variable with that name is accessed.

This discussion of the grammar in Table 3.3 has been very brief. The interested reader is invited to study the rules in detail and to work out the tree structures for some small examples.

TABLE 3.3 Two-Level Grammar Defining the Syntax and Semantics of Eva

---

(M1) **ALPHA** :: a; b; c; d; e; f; g; h; i; j; k; l; m; n; o; p; q; r; s; t; u; v; w; x; y; z.

(M2) **NOTION** :: ALPHA; NOTION ALPHA.

(M3) **NOTETY** :: NOTION; EMPTY.

(M4) **EMPTY** :: .

TABLE 3.3 (Continued)

(M5)   **LETTER :: letter ALPHA.**

(M6)   **LETTERS :: LETTER; LETTERS LETTER.**

(M7)   **TAG :: LETTER; TAG LETTER.**

(M8)   **CHAR :: LETTER; space.**

(M9)   **CHARS :: CHAR; CHARS CHAR.**

(M10) **CHARSETY :: CHARS; EMPTY.**

(M11) **STATE :: state NEST FILE FILE.**

(M12) **FILE :: CHARSETY eof.**

(M13) **NEST :: new; new LAYER; NEST new LAYER.**

(M14) **NESTETY :: NEST; EMPTY.**

(M15) **LAYER :: ITEM; LAYER ITEM.**

(M16) **LAYETY :: LAYER; EMPTY.**

(M17) **ITEM :: TYPE type TAG value VALUE.**

(M18) **TYPE :: VALTYPE; proc; proc with PARAMETERS.**

(M19) **VALTYPE :: char; string.**

(M20) **PARAMETER :: VALTYPE type TAG value VALUE.**

(M21) **PARAMETERS :: PARAMETER; PARAMETERS PARAMETER.**

(M22) **VALUE :: undefined; CHARSETY; STMT.**

(M23) **STMTS :: STMT; STMTS STMT.**

(M24) **STMT :: input TAG var;**

            output EXPR expr;

            call TAG procname;

            call TAG procname ARGUMENTS args;

            blk LAYER decs STMTS body;

            cmpdst STMTS body;

            eqtest EXPR leftopd EXPR rightopd STMT innerpart;

            neqtest EXPR leftopd EXPR rightopd STMT innerpart;

            cons EXPR char TAG var.

(M25) **ARGUMENTS :: EXPR; ARGUMENTS EXPR.**

(M26) **EXPR :: chvar TAG; chcon CHAR; hdexp EXPR expr; strvar TAG;**

            strcon CHARSETY; tlexp EXPR expr.

(H1)   **programme: new blk LAYER1 decs STMTS body block, eof symbol, FILE1 file,**

            FILE2 file, where LAYER1 consistent, where STMTS transforms state new new

            LAYER1 FILE1 eof into state new new LAYER2 FILE3 FILE2.

TABLE 3.3 (Continued)

(H2) CHAR FILE file: CHAR symbol, FILE file.

(H3) eof file: eof symbol.

(H4) NEST blk LAYER decs STMTS body block: begin symbol,
      NEST new LAYER declaration sequence for LAYER,
      NEST new LAYER STMTS statement sequence, end symbol.

(H5) NEST declaration sequence for LAYER ITEM: NEST declaration sequence for
      LAYER, NEST declaration of ITEM.

(H6) NEST declaration sequence for ITEM: NEST declaration of ITEM.

(H7) NEST declaration of char type TAG value undefined: char symbol, TAG symbol.

(H8) NEST declaration of string type TAG value EMPTY: string symbol, TAG symbol.

(H9) NEST new LAYETY1 char type TAG1 value undefined char type TAG2 value
      undefined LAYETY2 declaration of char type TAG2 value undefined:
      comma symbol, TAG2 symbol.

(H10) NEST new LAYETY1 string type TAG1 value EMPTY string type TAG2 value
      EMPTY LAYETY2 declaration of string type TAG2 value EMPTY:
      comma symbol, TAG2 symbol.

(H11) NEST declaration of proc type TAG value STMT:
      proc symbol, TAG symbol, equals symbol, NEST STMT statement.

(H12) NEST declaration of proc with PARAMETERS type TAG value STMT:
      proc symbol, TAG symbol, lpar symbol, NEST new PARAMETERS definition
      part for PARAMETERS, rpar symbol, equals symbol, NEST new
      PARAMETERS STMT statement, where PARAMETERS consistent.

(H13) NEST definition part for PARAMETERS PARAMETER:
      NEST definition part for PARAMETERS, comma symbol,
      NEST definition of PARAMETER.

(H14) NEST definition part for PARAMETER: NEST definition of PARAMETER.

(H15) NEST definition of VALTYPE type TAG value undefined:
      VALTYPE symbol, TAG symbol.

(H16) NEST new LAYETY1 VALTYPE type TAG1 value undefined VALTYPE type
      TAG2 value undefined LAYETY2 definition of VALTYPE type TAG2 value
      undefined:
      TAG2 symbol.

(H17) NEST STMTS STMT statement sequence:
      NEST STMTS statement sequence, NEST STMT statement.

(H18) NEST STMT statement sequence: NEST STMT statement.

TABLE 3.3 (Continued)

(H19)   NEST input TAG var statement: input symbol, char NEST name with TAG.

(H20)   NEST output EXPR expr statement: output symbol, char NEST EXPR expression.

(H21)   NEST call TAG procname statement: call symbol, proc NEST name with TAG.

(H22)   NEST call TAG procname ARGUMENTS args statement:
      call symbol, proc with PARAMETERS NEST name with TAG,
      lpar symbol, NEST ARGUMENTS arglist for PARAMETERS,
      rpar symbol.

(H23)   NEST blk LAYER decs STMTS body statement:
      NEST blk LAYER decs STMTS body block, where LAYER consistent.

(H24)   NEST cmpdst STMTS body statement:
      lpar symbol, NEST STMTS statement sequence, rpar symbol.

(H25)   NEST eqtest EXPR1 leftopd EXPR2 rightopd STMT innerpart statement:
      eq symbol, VALTYPE NEST EXPR1 expression, comma symbol,
      VALTYPE NEST EXPR2 expression, colon symbol,
      NEST STMT statement.

(H26)   NEST neqtest EXPR1 leftopd EXPR2 rightopd STMT innerpart statement:
      neq symbol, VALTYPE NEST EXPR1 expression, comma symbol,
      VALTYPE NEST EXPR2 expression, colon symbol,
      NEST STMT statement.

(H27)   NEST cons EXPR char TAG var statement:
      cons symbol, char NEST EXPR expression, comma symbol,
      string NEST name with TAG.

(H28)   NEST ARGUMENTS EXPR arglist for PARAMETERS PARAMETER:
      NEST ARGUMENTS arglist for PARAMETERS, comma symbol,
      NEST EXPR arglist for PARAMETER.

(H29)   NEST EXPR arglist for VALTYPE type TAG value undefined:
      VALTYPE NEST EXPR expression.

(H30)   char NEST chvar TAG expression: char NEST name with TAG.

(H31)   char NEST chcon LETTER expression:
      quote symbol, LETTER symbol, quote symbol.

(H32)   char NEST chcon space expression: space symbol.

(H33)   char NEST hdexp EXPR expr expression:
      head symbol, string NEST EXPR expression.

(H34)   string NEST strvar TAG expression: string NEST name with TAG.

(H35)   string NEST strcon EMPTY expression: quote symbol, quote symbol.

TABLE 3.3   (Continued)

(H36)   **string NEST strcon LETTERS LETTER expression:**
> **quote symbol, LETTERS sequence, LETTER symbol, quote symbol.**

(H37)   **LETTERS LETTER sequence: LETTERS sequence, LETTER symbol.**

(H38)   **LETTER sequence: LETTER symbol.**

(H39)   **string NEST tlexp EXPR expr expression:**
> **tail symbol, string NEST EXPR expression.**

(H40)   **TYPE NEST name with TAG:**
> **TAG symbol, where TYPE type TAG found in NEST.**

(H41)   **where TYPE type TAG found in NEST new LAYER:**
> **where TYPE type TAG one of LAYER;**
> **where TAG not in LAYER, where TYPE type TAG found in NEST.**

(H42)   **where TYPE type TAG one of LAYER ITEM:**
> **where TYPE type TAG one of ITEM;**
> **where TYPE type TAG one of LAYER.**

(H43)   **where TYPE type TAG one of TYPE type TAG value VALUE: EMPTY.**

(H44)   **where ITEM consistent: EMPTY.**

(H45)   **where LAYER TYPE type TAG value VALUE consistent:**
> **where LAYER consistent, where TAG not in LAYER.**

(H46)   **where TAG not in LAYER ITEM:**
> **where TAG not in LAYER, where TAG not in ITEM.**

(H47)   **where TAG1 not in TYPE type TAG2 value VALUE:**
> **where TAG1 is not TAG2.**

(H48)   **where NOTETY is NOTETY: EMPTY.**

(H49)   **where NOTETY1 ALPHA1 is not NOTETY2 ALPHA2:**
> **where NOTETY1 is not NOTETY2;**
> **where ALPHA1 precedes ALPHA2 in abcdefghijklmnopqrstuvwxyz;**
> **where ALPHA2 precedes ALPHA1 in abcdefghijklmnopqrstuvwxyz.**

(H50)   **where NOTION is not EMPTY: EMPTY.**

(H51)   **where EMPTY is not NOTION: EMPTY.**

(H52)   **where ALPHA1 precedes ALPHA2 in NOTETY1 ALPHA1 NOTETY2 ALPHA2 NOTETY3: EMPTY.**

(H53)   **where STMTS STMT transforms STATE1 into STATE3:**
> **where STMTS transforms STATE1 into STATE2,**
> **where STMT transforms STATE2 into STATE3.**

TABLE 3.3   (Continued)

(H54)   where input TAG var transforms state NEST new LAYETY1 char type TAG value
VALUE LAYETY2 NESTETY CHAR CHARSETY eof FILE into state
NEST new LAYETY1 char type TAG value CHAR LAYETY2 NESTETY
CHARSETY eof FILE:

where TAG not found in NESTETY.

(H55)   where output EXPR expr transforms state NEST FILE CHARSETY eof into state
NEST FILE CHARSETY CHAR eof:

where EXPR returns CHAR given NEST.

(H56)   where call TAG procname transforms state NEST1 new LAYETY1 proc type TAG
value STMT LAYETY2 NESTETY FILE1 FILE2 into state NEST2 new
LAYETY3 proc type TAG value STMT LAYETY4 NESTETY FILE3 FILE4:

where STMT transforms state NEST1 new LAYETY1 proc type TAG value
STMT LAYETY2 FILE1 FILE2 into state NEST2 new LAYETY3
proc type TAG value STMT LAYETY4 FILE3 FILE4,

where TAG not found in NESTETY.

(H57)   where call TAG procname ARGUMENTS args transforms state NEST1 new
LAYETY1 proc with PARAMETERS type TAG value STMT LAYETY2
NESTETY FILE1 FILE2 into state NEST2 new LAYETY3 proc with PAR-
AMETERS type TAG value STMT LAYETY4 NESTETY FILE3 FILE4:

where STMT transforms state NEST1 new LAYETY1 proc with
PARAMETERS type TAG value STMT LAYETY2 new LAYER1 FILE1
FILE2 into state NEST2 new LAYETY3 proc with PARAMETERS type
TAG value STMT LAYETY4 new LAYER2 FILE3 FILE4,

where TAG not found in NESTETY,

where NEST1 new LAYETY1 proc with PARAMETERS type TAG value
STMT LAYETY2 NESTETY implies LAYER1 derived from ARGU-
MENTS and PARAMETERS.

(H58)   where blk LAYER1 decs STMTS body transforms state NEST1 FILE1 FILE2
into state NEST2 FILE3 FILE4:

where STMTS transforms state NEST1 new LAYER1 FILE1 FILE2 into
state NEST2 new LAYER2 FILE3 FILE4.

(H59)   where cmpdst STMTS body transforms STATE1 into STATE2:

where STMTS transforms STATE1 into STATE2.

(H60)   where eqtest EXPR1 leftopd EXPR2 rightopd STMT innerpart transforms state
NEST FILE1 FILE2 into STATE:

TABLE 3.3 (Continued)

where EXPR1 equal to EXPR2 given NEST, where STMT transforms state NEST FILE1 FILE2 into STATE;

where EXPR1 not equal to EXPR2 given NEST, where state NEST FILE1 FILE2 is STATE.

(H61) where neqtest EXPR1 leftopd EXPR2 rightopd STMT innerpart transforms state NEST FILE1 FILE2 into STATE:

where EXPR1 not equal to EXPR2 given NEST, where STMT transforms state NEST FILE1 FILE2 into STATE;

where EXPR1 equal to EXPR2 given NEST, where state NEST FILE1 FILE2 is STATE.

(H62) where cons EXPR char TAG var transforms state NEST new LAYETY1 string type TAG value CHARSETY LAYETY2 NESTETY FILE1 FILE2 into state NEST new LAYETY1 string type TAG value CHAR CHARSETY LAYETY2 NESTETY FILE1 FILE2:

where EXPR returns CHAR given NEST new LAYETY1 string type TAG value CHARSETY LAYETY2 NESTETY,

where TAG not found in NESTETY.

(H63) where EXPR1 equal to EXPR2 given NEST:

where EXPR1 returns CHARSETY given NEST,

where EXPR2 returns CHARSETY given NEST.

(H64) where EXPR1 not equal to EXPR2 given NEST:

where EXPR1 returns CHARSETY1 given NEST,

where EXPR2 returns CHARSETY2 given NEST,

where CHARSETY1 is not CHARSETY2.

(H65) where NEST implies LAYER VALTYPE type TAG value CHARSETY derived from ARGUMENTS EXPR and PARAMETERS VALTYPE type TAG value undefined:

where EXPR returns CHARSETY given NEST,

where NEST implies LAYER derived from ARGUMENTS and PARAMETERS.

(H66) where NEST implies VALTYPE type TAG value CHARSETY derived from EXPR and VALTYPE type TAG value undefined:

where EXPR returns CHARSETY given NEST.

(H67) where chcon CHAR returns CHAR given NEST: EMPTY.

(H68) where chvar TAG returns CHAR given NESTETY1 new LAYETY1 char type TAG value CHAR LAYETY2 NESTETY2:

TABLE 3.3   (Continued)

---

        where TAG not found in NESTETY2.

(H69)   where hdexp EXPR expr returns CHAR given NEST:

        where EXPR returns CHAR CHARSETY given NEST.

(H70)   where strcon CHARSETY returns CHARSETY given NEST: EMPTY.

(H71)   where strvar TAG returns CHARSETY given NESTETY1 new LAYETY1 string

        type TAG value CHARSETY LAYETY2 NESTETY2:

        where TAG not found in NESTETY2.

(H72)   where tlexp EXPR expr returns CHARSETY given NEST:

        where EXPR returns CHAR CHARSETY given NEST.

(H73)   where TAG not found in NESTETY new LAYER:

        where TAG not found in NESTETY, where TAG not in LAYER.

(H74)   where TAG not found in EMPTY: EMPTY.

EXERCISE

1. If you still have enough paper, construct the complete tree for the following
programme according to the grammar of Table 3.3.

$$
\begin{array}{l}
\textbf{begin} \\
\quad \textbf{char } c \\
\quad \textbf{proc } p = (\\
\qquad \textbf{input } c \\
\qquad \textbf{neq } c, \text{``}z\text{''}: (\\
\qquad\qquad \textbf{output } c \\
\qquad\qquad \textbf{call } p\ )\ ) \\
\qquad \textbf{call } p \\
\textbf{end} \\
\textbf{eof} \\
abz \\
\textbf{eof} \\
ab \\
\textbf{eof}
\end{array}
$$

For Further Information

    The use of two-level grammars for the complete specification of dynamic
semantics in addition to syntax is described by Cleaveland and Uzgalis (1977, pp.
129–46) in the context of the miniature language ASPLE. Essentially the same
example is presented and discussed by Marcotty et al. (1976).

4

formal semantics

This chapter introduces particular versions of three important types of approach to the semantic formalization of programming languages. In contrast to the techniques illustrated in Chap. 3, these approaches tend to disregard questions of syntax and to focus attention directly on questions of semantics. In recognition of this, the actual examples of language definitions presented in this chapter will not be complete, syntactic/semantic specifications like those of Chap. 3, but will be definitions of semantics only, in much the same sense as the examples of Chap. 2 were definitions of syntax only. In each case study, we shall take as a starting point some suitable formulation of the abstract syntax of the subject language and assume that there will never be any attempt to use the semantic specifications for the analysis of syntactically invalid programs. Each set of semantic specifications could be extended to a complete definition of semantics *and* syntax by the addition of a suitable set of specifications defining the correspondence between the textual and abstract forms of programs and enforcing any necessary context conditions.

The three approaches, in order of increasing abstraction with respect to the concepts of 'meaning' underlying them, may be termed the *operational* approach, the *denotational* approach, and the *axiomatic* approach. In the operational approach, meaning is described in terms of such devices as abstract machines with discrete "states" and more-or-less explicit sequences of computational operations. In the denotational approach, the meaning of a construct is taken to be some abstract mathematical object, usually a function of some appropriate type; there is no explicit concept of a machine or computation sequence, but the notion of state is still present in an abstract form. In the axiomatic approach, meaning is explicated solely in terms of what formal statements can be made about the *effect* of executing programs; not only is there no explicit notion of machine or computation sequence in this case, but even the concept of state is implicit. As far as the different categories of people who stand to benefit from language formalization are concerned, the operational approach is most directly oriented toward language implementers, the denotational approach toward language designers, and the axiomatic approach toward language users.

The idea that an actual compiler or interpreter for a subject language can be regarded as the language's definitive specification may be seen as an extreme form of the operational approach. Some disadvantages of this "definition by processor" method are: (1) source listings of language processors are often very long and hard to read; (2) the run-an-example-to-see-what-happens technique of "referring to" a definition is unsatisfactory and inadequate; (3) practical compilers and interpreters have many aspects (such as error recovery and debugging aids) that have nothing to do with language definition; and (4) a processor must impose various machine-dependent limits and restrictions on the programs it will accept. Thus most operational definitions specify an abstract rather than a real processor for the subject language. As far as their semantic aspects are concerned, both of the definitional techniques described in Chap. 3 may be regarded as operational in nature, the first being further classified as compiler-oriented and the second as interpreter-oriented. A compiler-oriented, operational technique is one that emphasizes directly or indirectly, the specification of a process for translating the subject language into some other representation which is presumably simple to define and independent of the subject language. An interpreter-oriented technique, on the other hand, is largely concerned with modeling the process of executing subject-language programs (usually in abstract form); the specifications for any necessary translation of programs from textual to abstract form are deemphasized or omitted. The particular operational method—the Vienna Definition Language—described in this chapter is an interpreter-oriented method.

The denotational and axiomatic approaches are the objects of a great deal of ongoing research, and the development of metalanguages for writing language specifications is only one of the objectives, often not the primary one, of this research. Denotational semantics encompasses a sophisticated, mathematical theory of computation which provides the basis for a rigorous analysis of programs and programming languages as mathematical entities, and much of the work in axiomatic semantics is more concerned with the general problems of program verification and synthesis than with language specification (although these areas do overlap to some extent). It is beyond the scope of this book to attempt to do justice to these broad-ranging studies or the concerns of the people who have undertaken them. By restricting our attention to the problem of giving formal specifications for languages as simple as Pam and Eva, we shall be simplifying, glossing over, and omitting many important aspects of the theories, much more thorough treatments of which may be found elsewhere.

For Further Information

The case for the "definition by processor" notion is stated by Garwick (1966). Many brief overviews of the formal semantics area in general may be found in the literature; some of the more recent and comprehensive discussions are those offered by Brady (1977, pp. 218–23), Donahue (1976, pp. 5–21), Stoy (1977, pp. 1–25), Lucas (1978), and Anderson et al. (1978).

4.1
THE OPERATIONAL APPROACH—VIENNA DEFINITION LANGUAGE

An operational definition of the semantics of a programming language may consist of a formal system that models the *interpretation* of (usually abstract) programs, i.e., the process of performing the sequences of actions specified by the programs. The Vienna Definition Language, or VDL for short, is one of the oldest and best-known metalanguages for writing such definitions. The central aim in this approach is to define an *abstract machine* for interpreting abstract programs of the subject language. The machine interprets a program by passing through a sequence of discrete *states*, and to this extent its mode of operation is independent of the subject language. Actually, however, it is highly tailored to the subject language by virtue of the fact that the structure of its states and the allowable transitions from one state to another must be specifically defined. The allowable state transitions are defined by a set of *instruction definitions* written in a special notation; typically, the instruction definitions make up the bulk of a VDL language specification.

The next two sections introduce many of the concepts and notational devices of VDL and use them to specify the semantics of Pam. After that, a VDL definition of Eva will be given.

4.1.1 Notation for Objects and Abstract Syntax

In order to deal with "objects" as diverse as abstract programs and machine states in a uniform manner, VDL incorporates a quite general notation for describing and manipulating hierarchical structures. All such structures may be pictured (if desired) as trees with labeled edges and without left-right ordering.

An *elementary object* is an object with no internal structure of its own, so that it corresponds to a leaf node of a tree representing some structured object that contains it. Symbolically, we will usually denote an elementary object by a sequence of one or more uppercase letters or by some other character or sequence of characters enclosed in single quotes; MARK and '+' would be two examples. A structured object is denoted by a set of one or more pairs of the form $\langle s: a \rangle$, where s is a selector and a denotes another object (either elementary or structured). Selectors are usually just arbitrary names, and names in VDL are lowercase words possibly containing digits and internal hyphens. By convention, names used as selectors begin with 's-'. Pictorially, a set of n selector-object pairs may be represented as a tree with n branches, each of which is labeled with one of the selectors and leads to a subtree representing the object selected. For example, the object $\{\langle s\text{-part1} : A \rangle, \langle s\text{-part2} : B \rangle, \langle s\text{-part3} : C \rangle\}$ may be pictured as in Fig. 4.1, and $\{\langle s\text{-p1} : \{\langle s\text{-p2} : A \rangle\} \rangle, \langle s\text{-p3} : \{\langle s\text{-p4} : B \rangle, \langle s\text{-p5} : C \rangle\} \rangle\}$ as in Fig. 4.2. Since the elements of sets are not ordered, this last object could also be written as $\{\langle s\text{-p3} : \{\langle s\text{-p5} : C \rangle, \langle s\text{-p4} : B \rangle\} \rangle, \langle s\text{-p1} : \{\langle s\text{-p2} : A \rangle\} \rangle\}$ and drawn as shown in Fig. 4.3. The presence of the selectors makes left-right ordering unnecessary.

The *null object*, denoted by Ω, is a special elementary object which serves to indicate the "emptiness" of an object or absence of some component of

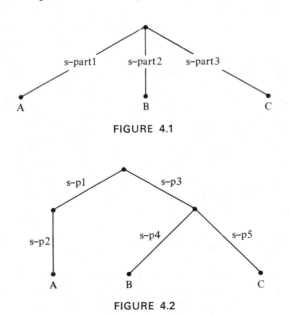

FIGURE 4.1

FIGURE 4.2

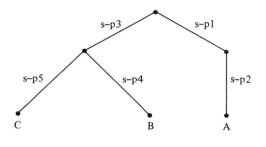

FIGURE 4.3

an object. For example, $\{\langle\text{s-p1} : A\rangle, \langle\text{s-p2} : \Omega\rangle\}$ is the same object as $\{\langle\text{s-p1} : A\rangle\}$; the null object and the name selecting it have no corresponding branch in the tree diagram:

A selector may be used as a function that takes an object as an argument and yields the corresponding component of the object; considering the object as a tree, the function yields the subtree below the branch labeled by the selector. If 't' denotes the structure shown in Fig. 4.3, then s-p3(t) yields Fig. 4.4, and s-p4(s-p3(t)) yields the elementary object B. Following the usual

FIGURE 4.4

notation for functional composition, the latter expression could be written as s-p4 ∘ s-p3(t). If the object does not have an immediate component corresponding to the selector, the null object results. For example, s-p6(t) = Ω and s-p2(t) = Ω. The selectors for the immediate components of any object must be all different (the selection functions would not be well-defined otherwise), but there is nothing wrong with an object such as that shown in Fig. 4.5. If 'q' denotes this object, then s-p1(q) = A, s-p1 ∘ s-p2(q) = B, and s-zz(q) = Ω.

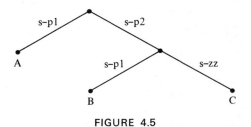

FIGURE 4.5

The *mutation operator* μ builds new objects which are modifications of old ones. An expression of the form $\mu(a; \langle s: b \rangle)$ yields the object obtained by replacing the s-component (the component selected by s) of the object a by the object b. For example, if 'q' denotes the object shown above, $\mu(q; \langle s\text{-}p2 : D \rangle)$ yields Fig. 4.6, and $\mu(q; \langle s\text{-}p1 : \{\langle s\text{-}p3 : E \rangle\} \rangle)$ yields Fig. 4.7.

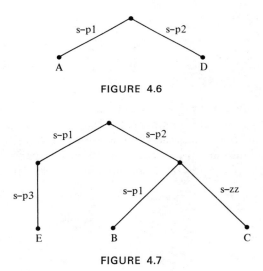

FIGURE 4.6

FIGURE 4.7

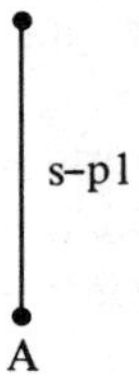

Note that $\mu(q; \langle s\text{-}p2 : \Omega \rangle)$ yields where the p2-component is absent. If the existing object does not have a component corresponding to the specified selector, the new object has an extra subtree; e.g., $\mu(q; \langle s\text{-}p4 : F\rangle)$ yields Fig. 4.8.

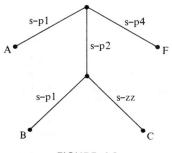

FIGURE 4.8

There is often a need for objects which are to be regarded as *lists* of other objects, such that there may be any number of objects in a list. The convention here is to use

$$\text{elem}(1), \text{elem}(2), \text{elem}(3), \ldots$$

as the selectors of the list components (elements). The "subscripts" in these selectors always start at 1 and run up to the number of elements. The list

$$f = \{\langle \text{elem}(1) : A\rangle, \langle \text{elem}(2) : B\rangle, \langle \text{elem}(3) : C\rangle\}$$

can be pictured as in Fig. 4.9, so that elem(2)(f), which means (elem(2))(f), yields B. The expression $\{\langle \text{elem}(1) : A\rangle, \langle \text{elem}(2) : B\rangle, \langle \text{elem}(3) : C\rangle\}$ may be abbreviated to $\langle A, B, C\rangle$.

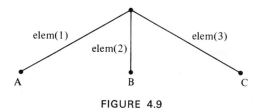

FIGURE 4.9

The standard function 'head' is equivalent to elem(1), so that head(f) yields A in this case. The function 'tail' produces the list consisting of all but the first element of the given list, so that tail(f) is $\langle B, C\rangle$ $(= \{\langle \text{elem}(1) : B\rangle,$ $\langle \text{elem}(2) : C\rangle\})$. The function 'length' gives the number of elements in a list, so that length(f) = 3. The concatenation operator for lists consists of a raised arc; for example, the expression f⌢tail(f) would yield ⟨A, B, C, B, C⟩ (= {⟨elem(1) : A⟩, ⟨elem(2) : B⟩, ⟨elem(3) : C⟩, ⟨elem(4) : B⟩, ⟨elem(5) : C⟩}). The expression f⌢head(f) is not valid because head(f) is not a list; however, ⟨head(f)⟩ denotes a list of one element, so that f⌢⟨head(f)⟩ yields ⟨A, B, C, A⟩. The empty list is denoted by ⟨⟩.

A *predicate* is a function that takes any object as an argument and yields one of the elementary objects T and F (for "true" and "false"). By convention, names used as predicates begin with 'is-'. Predicates that test for specific elementary objects are formed simply by appending the symbol for the object; thus we may write boolean expressions such as is-'+'(opr) and is-Ω(z). Other predicates, which test objects for membership in various classes, must be explicitly defined by means of equations.

An equation defining a predicate for a single class of structured objects must specify what selectors are involved and what kinds of object they select. For example, the equation

$$\text{is-triple} = (⟨\text{s-d1} : \text{is-abcd}⟩, ⟨\text{s-d2} : \text{is-abcd}⟩, ⟨\text{s-d3} : \text{is-abcd}⟩)$$

states that an object will satisfy the predicate 'is-triple' if and only if it consists of three components satisfying the predicate 'is-abcd' and selected by 's-d1', 's-d2', and 's-d3'. Similarly, the equation

$$\text{is-asmt-st} = (⟨\text{s-lhs} : \text{is-var}⟩, ⟨\text{s-rhs} : \text{is-expr}⟩)$$

states that an object will satisfy 'is-asmt-st' if and only if it consists of a component satisfying 'is-var' and selected by 's-lhs' and a component satisfying 'is-expr' and selected by 's-rhs'.

Predicates may also be defined as disjunctions of other predicates. For example, 'is-abcd' might be defined by

$$\text{is-abcd} = \text{is-A} \lor \text{is-B} \lor \text{is-C} \lor \text{is-D}$$

which states that an object will satisfy 'is-abcd' if and only if it satisfies one of the four predicates on the right. Similarly, 'is-expr' might be defined by

$$\text{is-expr} = \text{is-infix-expr} \lor \text{is-var} \lor \text{is-intg}$$

In general, a predicate used in the definition of another predicate can be replaced by its definition; e.g., the equation for 'is-asmt-st' could have been written as

$$\text{is-asmt-st} = (⟨\text{s-lhs} : \text{is-var}⟩, ⟨\text{s-rhs} : \text{is-infix-expr} \lor \text{is-var} \lor \text{is-intg}⟩)$$

By convention, predicates that test for lists end in '-list' and are not explicitly defined by equations. For example, the predicate 'is-expr-list' is satisfied by any list of objects that all satisfy 'is-expr'.

A VDL specification of the semantics of a programming language includes a set of predicate definitions describing the structure of a state ξ of the abstract machine. In the case of Pam, the machine states are relatively simple and only two equations are required:

$$\text{is-}\xi = (\langle \text{s-c} : \text{is-c} \rangle, \langle \text{s-stg} : \text{is-value-list} \rangle,$$
$$\langle \text{s-input} : \text{is-intg-list} \rangle, \langle \text{s-output} : \text{is-intg-list} \rangle)$$
$$\text{is-value} = \text{is-intg} \ \lor \ \text{is-UNDEFINED}$$

The component of a state selected by 's-c' and satisfying the predicate 'is-c' is a special object called a *control tree*, the nature of which will be described in the next section; all VDL abstract machines have such a control component, whatever subject language is being defined. The 'stg'-component of the machine is the "storage unit" for holding the values (integers) of Pam variables; given a state ξ, elem(i) ∘ s-stg(ξ) will be the current value of the ith distinct variable in a program. The predicate 'is-intg' is to be regarded as "primitive", with the understanding that it is satisfied (only) by all integers. The 'input'-component models an input file given to a program and the 'output'-component an output file produced by a program.

We also need a set of predicate definitions that describe the subject language's abstract syntax. For Pam, these abstract syntax "rules" may be formulated as follows:

is-series = is-st-list

is-st = is-read-st $\lor$ is-write-st $\lor$ is-asmt-st $\lor$ is-cond-st $\lor$
    is-def-loop $\lor$ is-indef-loop

is-read-st = ($\langle$s-r : is-var-list$\rangle$)

is-write-st = ($\langle$s-w : is-var-list$\rangle$)

is-asmt-st = ($\langle$s-lhs : is-var$\rangle$, $\langle$s-rhs : is-expr$\rangle$)

is-cond-st = ($\langle$s-ifpart : is-comp$\rangle$, $\langle$s-thenpart : is-series$\rangle$,
    $\langle$s-elsepart : is-series$\rangle$)

is-def-loop = ($\langle$s-limit : is-expr$\rangle$, $\langle$s-body : is-series$\rangle$)

is-indef-loop = ($\langle$s-test : is-comp$\rangle$, $\langle$s-body : is-series$\rangle$)

is-comp = ($\langle$s-left-opd : is-expr$\rangle$, $\langle$s-right-opd : is-expr$\rangle$,
    $\langle$s-rel : is-EQ $\lor$ is-GT $\lor$ is-LE $\lor$ is-LT $\lor$ is-GE $\lor$ is-NE$\rangle$)

is-expr = is-infix-expr $\lor$ is-var $\lor$ is-intg

is-infix-expr = ($\langle$s-left-opd : is-expr$\rangle$, $\langle$s-right-opd : is-expr$\rangle$,
    $\langle$s-opr : is-PLUS $\lor$ is-MINUS $\lor$ is-TIMES $\lor$ is-OVER$\rangle$)

is-var = ($\langle$s-addr : is-intg$\rangle$)

In its abstract form, a variable is basically an "address" of an element of the 'stg'-component of the machine; although we have used 'is-intg' in this last rule, such an address will always be positive and never zero or negative.

These abstract syntax rules are such that no object is ambiguous with respect to which predicates characterize its various components. This is the reason for the presence of the selectors 's-r', 's-w', and 's-addr'.

As a small example of an object satisfying 'is-series', it may be verified that the program

$$\textbf{read } k \; ; \; \textbf{while } k > 0 \textbf{ do } k := k - 1 \textbf{ end}$$

would be represented as in Fig. 4.10. (The variable k is represented by the "address" 1.)

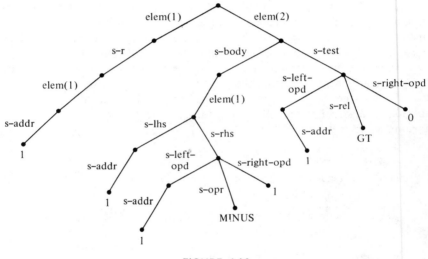

FIGURE 4.10

EXERCISES

1. Draw a tree diagram of a VDL object satisfying 'is-series' and corresponding to the Pam program

   $$\textbf{read } a \; ;$$

   $$\textbf{if } a = 0 \textbf{ then read } b \; ; \; \textbf{write } b \textbf{ else write } a \textbf{ fi}$$

2. Translate the abstract syntax description you wrote for Exercise 2 in Sec. 3.1 into a set of VDL predicate definitions, and draw a VDL tree diagram for a small but nontrivial sample construct.

4.1.2 Control Mechanism and Notation for Instruction Definitions—A Semantic Specification for Pam

The control part s-c(ξ) of a state may be thought of as a tree in which the edges are *not* labeled (even though there is no left–right ordering) and every node corresponds to an *instruction*. An instruction is analogous to a procedure call in a programming language in that it consists of an instruction name (conventionally set in boldface type) possibly followed by a parenthesized list of arguments separated by commas. For example, a control tree could have the form shown in Fig. 4.11.

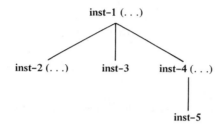

FIGURE 4.11

The names and significance of the various instruction types must be specified by a set of instruction definitions. An instruction definition is analogous to a procedure declaration in a programming language in that it consists of a "body" preceded by a "heading" which names the instruction and its formal parameters, if any. The notation for such headings is exemplified by the following forms:

$$\textbf{inst-1 } (a, b) =$$
$$\text{Body}_1$$
$$\textbf{inst-3 } =$$
$$\text{Body}_3$$

The body of an instruction definition is usually a conditional expression written in the form

$$\text{Condition}_1 \longrightarrow \text{Group}_1$$
$$\text{Condition}_2 \longrightarrow \text{Group}_2$$
$$\ldots$$
$$\text{Condition}_n \longrightarrow \text{Group}_n$$

and yielding one of the n "groups," viz., the group following the first true condition. [In other contexts, conditional expressions are written in the form $(c_1 \rightarrow e_1, c_2 \rightarrow e_2, \ldots, c_n \rightarrow e_n).$] The conditions are boolean expressions and generally involve predicates, but the last condition is often just T in order to ensure that the value of the conditional expression will always be defined. Each "group" is either a *self-replacing group* specifying a subtree of instructions to replace the one in the control tree being interpreted or a *value-returning group* specifying a value to be passed as an argument to one or more other instructions in the tree and/or mutate the state in certain ways. Sometimes the body of an instruction definition is just a single group.

A value-returning group consists of one or both of the following parts: a line of the form

PASS: Expression

specifying a value to be passed to other instructions, and a set of one or more lines of the form

Selector: Expression

each of which specifies that the (immediate) component of the state given by the selector is to be replaced by the object denoted by the expression. For example, the value-returning group

PASS: head ∘ s-input (ξ)

s-input: tail ∘ s-input (ξ)

specifies that the first element of the 'input'-component of the state is to be passed elsewhere and deleted from the 'input'-component.

A self-replacing group is an expression for a subtree of instructions, the structure of which is indicated by indention and punctuation. For example, the structure in Fig. 4.12 is represented by either of the following groups:

inst-5;		**inst-5**;		
	inst-4,		**inst-3**;	
	inst-3;			**inst-2**,
		inst-1,		**inst-1**
		inst-2	**inst-4**	

The disposition of a passed value is specified by prefixing a name to the instruction giving rise to the value and using that name in the argument lists of "higher" instructions. For example, a self-replacing group of the form

inst-2 ($\ldots$, a, $\ldots$);

a: **inst-1** ($\ldots$)

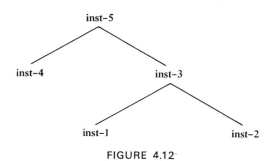

inst-5

inst-4   inst-3

inst-1   inst-2

FIGURE 4.12

specifies that one of the arguments of the **inst-2** is to be supplied as a result of the **inst-1**.

To see the point of all this, we must understand the basic operation cycle of a VDL abstract machine. Given a particular state, an instruction associated with a leaf of the control tree is chosen for execution—if there is more than one leaf instruction, any one of them may be chosen. The body of the corresponding instruction definition is evaluated, yielding either a self-replacing group or a value-returning group. In the case of a self-replacing group, the arguments of the instruction being executed are substituted for the formal parameters appearing in the group and the leaf instruction being executed is replaced by the subtree represented by the modified group. In the case of a value-returning group, the specified value-passing and/or state mutation actions are carried out and the leaf instruction being executed is deleted from the control tree. This whole cycle is repeated until the control tree is empty; in other words, an empty control tree signifies that the machine is in a final state. In the initial state, the control tree contains a single, standard instruction. For the definition of Pam, this initial instruction will always be

exec-series (t)

where 't' denotes the abstract program to be interpreted. As for the other parts of the initial state, the 'output'-component is empty, the 'input'-component is a list of zero or more integers, and all the values in the 'stg'-component are UNDEFINED.

The instruction **exec-series** is recursively defined as follows:

$$\textbf{exec-series} \text{ (ser)} =$$
$$\text{is-}\lozenge\text{(ser)} \longrightarrow \textbf{null}$$
$$\text{T} \longrightarrow \textbf{exec-series} \text{ (tail (ser))};$$
$$\textbf{exec-stmt} \text{ (head (ser))}$$

Intuitively, this means that the execution of a series consists of the execution of its first statement followed by the execution of the subseries starting with the second statement. It is assumed here that 'ser' satisfies the predicate 'is-series', so that head(ser) satisfies 'is-st' and tail(ser) satisfies 'is-series'. Since the formulation of the instruction definitions is strongly influenced by the predicate definitions for the abstract machine and the abstract syntax of the subject language, these definitions are repeated in Table 4.1, pp. 152–55, together with the instruction definitions to facilitate understanding of the latter.

The parameterless instruction **null** is in effect a dummy instruction that does nothing but delete itself from the control tree. It may be defined as follows:

$$\textbf{null} = \text{PASS}: \Omega$$

Suppose now that 't' denotes the abstract form (pictured earlier) of the program

$$\textbf{read } k \; ; \; \textbf{while } k > 0 \textbf{ do } k := k - 1 \textbf{ end}$$

For purposes of abbreviation, we shall sometimes write an expression for a segment of the abstract program in the form [P], where P is the normal textual form of the segment; for example, [k > 0] is short for

$$\{\langle\text{s-left-opd} : \{\langle\text{s-addr} : 1\rangle\}\rangle, \; \langle\text{s-rel} : \text{GT}\rangle, \; \langle\text{s-right-opd} : 0\rangle\}$$

and satisfies 'is-comp'. As stated above, the control part of the initial state is the single-node subtree

$$\bullet \quad \textbf{exec-series } (t)$$

The definition of **exec-series** implies that in the next state this will be expanded to

$$\begin{array}{l} \bullet \quad \textbf{exec-series } ([\textbf{while } k > 0 \textbf{ do } k := k - 1 \textbf{ end}]) \\ \bullet \quad \textbf{exec-stmt } ([\textbf{read } k]) \end{array}$$

The instruction **exec-stmt** is defined as follows:

$$\begin{array}{l} \textbf{exec-stmt } (\text{stmt}) = \\ \quad \text{is-read-st } (\text{stmt}) \longrightarrow \textbf{read } (\text{s-r } (\text{stmt})) \\ \quad \text{is-write-st } (\text{stmt}) \longrightarrow \textbf{write } (\text{s-w } (\text{stmt})) \\ \quad \text{is-asmt-st } (\text{stmt}) \longrightarrow \\ \qquad \textbf{store } (\text{s-addr} \circ \text{s-lhs } (\text{stmt}), \text{val}); \\ \qquad \text{val}: \textbf{eval-expr } (\text{s-rhs } (\text{stmt})) \end{array}$$

is-cond-st (stmt) $\longrightarrow$

    choose (c, s-thenpart (stmt), s-elsepart (stmt));

        c: **eval-comp** (s-ifpart (stmt))

is-def-loop (stmt) $\longrightarrow$

    repeat-series (s-body (stmt), r);

        r: **eval-expr** (s-limit (stmt))

is-indef-loop (stmt) $\longrightarrow$

    choose (c, s-body (stmt)$\frown\langle$stmt$\rangle$, $\Diamond$);

        c: **eval-comp** (s-test (stmt))

Here, 'stmt' is assumed to satisfy 'is-st', which is a disjunction of the six predicates used in the body of the instruction definition. Since [**read** k] satisfies 'is-read-st', the third state in our example will contain

    exec-series ([**while** $k > 0$ **do** $k := k - 1$ **end**])

    read ([k])

    The VDL instruction **read** takes a parameter satisfying 'is-var-list' and is defined as

    read (vars) $=$

        is-$\Diamond$ (vars) $\longrightarrow$ **null**

        T $\longrightarrow$ **read** (tail (vars));

                store (s-addr $\circ$ head (vars), val);

                    val: **input-val**

so that in state 4 we have

    exec-series ([**while** $k > 0$ **do** $k := k - 1$ **end**])

    read ($\langle\rangle$)

    store (1, val)

    val: **input-val**

The definitions of **store** and **input-val** are as follows:

    store (loc, val) $=$

        s-stg: μ(s-stg(ξ); $\langle$elem (loc) : val$\rangle$)

    input-val $=$

        is-$\Diamond$ $\circ$ s-input (ξ) $\longrightarrow$ **error**

        T $\longrightarrow$ PASS: head $\circ$ s-input (ξ)

                s-input: tail $\circ$ s-input (ξ)

(The instruction **error** is undefined and indicates that the program being interpreted is semantically invalid.) If the 'input'-component consists of the value 2 through state 4, in state 5 it will be empty and the control tree will be

    exec-series ([while $k > 0$ do $k := k - 1$ end])
    read ($\Diamond$)
    store (1, 2)

In state 6, it will be the case that elem(1) ∘ s-stg(ξ) = 2 and the control tree will be

    exec-series ([while $k > 0$ do $k := k - 1$ end])
    read ($\Diamond$)

The control trees in the next four states are as follows:

    exec-series ([while $k > 0$ do $k := k - 1$ end])
    null
    exec-series ([while $k > 0$ do $k := k - 1$ end])
    exec-series ($\Diamond$)
    exec-stmt ([while $k > 0$ do $k := k - 1$ end])
    exec-series ($\Diamond$)
    choose (c, [$k := k - 1$; while $k > 0$ do $k := k - 1$ end], $\Diamond$)
    c: **eval-comp** ([$k > 0$])

The instruction **eval-comp** takes a parameter satisfying 'is-comp' and is defined as

$$\textbf{eval-comp (comp)} =$$
$$\textbf{compare} (a, b, \text{s-rel (comp)});$$
$$a: \textbf{eval-expr} (\text{s-left-opd (comp)}),$$
$$b: \textbf{eval-expr} (\text{s-right-opd (comp)})$$

Thus the control part of state 11 is

    exec-series ($\Diamond$)
    choose (c, [$k := k - 1$; while $k > 0$ do $k := k - 1$ end], $\Diamond$)
    c: **compare** (a, b, GT)
    a: **eval-expr** ([k])   b: **eval-expr** (0)

Eval-expr takes a parameter satisfying 'is-expr' and is defined as

> **eval-expr** (expr) =
> > is-intg (expr) $\longrightarrow$ PASS: expr
> > is-var (expr) $\longrightarrow$ **eval-var** (expr)
> > is-infix-expr (expr) $\longrightarrow$
> > > **calculate** (a, b, s-opr (expr));
> > > > a: **eval-expr** (s-left-opd (expr)),
> > > > b: **eval-expr** (s-right-opd (expr))

where **eval-var** is defined as

> **eval-var** (var) =
> > is-UNDEFINED (elem (s-addr (expr)) (s-stg (ζ)) $\longrightarrow$ **error**
> > T $\longrightarrow$ PASS: elem (s-addr (expr)) (s-stg (ζ))

It does not matter which of the two current leaf instructions is processed first. Taking the one on the right, we have

> • **exec-series** ($\Diamond$)
> • **choose** (c, [$k := k - 1$;
> > **while** $k > 0$ **do** $k := k - 1$ **end**], $\Diamond$)
> • c: **compare** (a, 0, GT)
> • a: **eval-expr** ([k])

as the control part of state 12. Then in state 13 we have

> • **exec-series** ($\Diamond$)
> • **choose** (c, [$k := k - 1$;
> > **while** $k > 0$ **do** $k := k - 1$ **end**], $\Diamond$)
> • c: **compare** (a, 0, GT)
> • a: **eval-var** ([k])

and in state 14 we have

> • **exec-series** ($\Diamond$)
> • **choose** (c, [$k := k - 1$;
> > **while** $k > 0$ **do** $k := k - 1$ **end**], $\Diamond$)
> • c: **compare** (2, 0, GT)

The result of a **compare** instruction, denoted by 'c' in the diagram, is a boolean value:

$$
\begin{aligned}
\textbf{compare} \ &(\text{val-1, val-2, rel}) \ = \\
&\text{is-EQ (rel)} \ \wedge \ (\text{val-1} \ = \ \text{val-2}) \ \vee \\
&\quad \text{is-GT (rel)} \ \wedge \ (\text{val-1} \ > \ \text{val-2}) \ \vee \\
&\quad \text{is-LE (rel)} \ \wedge \ (\text{val-1} \ \le \ \text{val-2}) \ \vee \\
&\quad \text{is-LT (rel)} \ \wedge \ (\text{val-1} \ < \ \text{val-2}) \ \vee \\
&\quad \text{is-GE (rel)} \ \wedge \ (\text{val-1} \ \ge \ \text{val-2}) \ \vee \\
&\quad \text{is-NE (rel)} \ \wedge \ (\text{val-1} \ \ne \ \text{val-2}) \ \longrightarrow \ \text{PASS: T} \\
&\text{T} \ \longrightarrow \ \text{PASS: F}
\end{aligned}
$$

(Note that the metalanguage includes relations such as $>$ and $\ge$.) In this case, T is passed, resulting in

> ● **exec-series** $(\langle\rangle)$
> ● **choose** (T, $[k := k - 1$;
>   **while** $k > 0$ **do** $k := k - 1$ **end**], $\langle\rangle$)

as the control part of state 15. Given that **choose** is defined by

$$
\begin{aligned}
\textbf{choose} \ &(\text{flag, ser-1, ser-2}) \ = \\
&\text{flag} \ \longrightarrow \ \textbf{exec-series} \ (\text{ser-1}) \\
&\text{T} \ \longrightarrow \ \textbf{exec-series} \ (\text{ser-2})
\end{aligned}
$$

the control trees in the next four states are as follows:

> ● **exec-series** $(\langle\rangle)$
> ● **exec-series** $([k := k - 1$;
>   **while** $k > 0$ **do** $k := k - 1$ **end**])
> ● **exec-series** $(\langle\rangle)$
> ● **exec-series** $([\textbf{while} \ k > 0 \ \textbf{do} \ k := k - 1 \ \textbf{end}])$
> ● **exec-stmt** $([k := k - 1])$

> ● **exec-series** $(\langle\rangle)$
> ● **exec-series** $([\textbf{while} \ k > 0 \ \textbf{do} \ k := k - 1 \ \textbf{end}])$
> ● **store** (1, val)
> ● val: **eval-expr** $([k - 1])$

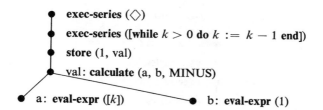

This is similar to the situation in state 11; regardless of which leaf instruction is executed first, the control tree three steps later (state 22) will be

> • exec-series ($\Diamond$)
> • exec-series ([**while** $k > 0$ **do** $k := k - 1$ **end**])
> • store (1, val)
> • val: **calculate** (2, 1, MINUS)

The result of a **calculate** instruction ('val' in the foregoing diagram) is an integer:

> calculate (val-1, val-2, opr) =
>> is-PLUS (opr) $\longrightarrow$ PASS: val-1 $+$ val-2
>> is-MINUS (opr) $\longrightarrow$ PASS: val-1 $-$ val-2
>> is-TIMES (opr) $\longrightarrow$ PASS: val-1 $\times$ val-2
>> is-OVER (opr) $\longrightarrow$ PASS: val-1 $\div$ val-2

(Note that the metalanguage includes the arithmetic operators.) In this case, the value 1 is passed so that, in state 24, we will have 1 as the value of k [i.e., elem(1) $\circ$ s-stg(ξ)] and

> • exec-series ($\Diamond$)
> • exec-series ([**while** $k > 0$ **do** $k := k - 1$ **end**])

as the control tree. Comparing the latter with the tree of state 8, it should be clear that the next 16 steps will be analogous to the last 16, so that in state 40 the value of k will be 0 and the control tree will be

> • exec-series ($\Diamond$)
> • exec-series ($\Diamond$)
> • exec-series ([**while** $k > 0$ **do** $k := k - 1$ **end**])

This time around, the **eval-comp** instruction executed two steps later will pass the value F, and in state 47 the control tree will be

> • exec-series ($\langle \diamond \rangle$)
> • exec-series ($\langle \diamond \rangle$)
> • exec-series ($\langle \diamond \rangle$)
> • exec-series ($\langle \diamond \rangle$)

It may be easily verified that this tree quickly collapses and that a final state is reached after a total of 55 steps.

In working out this particular example, no use was made of the instructions **repeat-series**, **write**, and **output-val**. The definitions of these instructions are included in Table 4.1.

TABLE 4.1   VDL Definition of the Semantics of Pam

Abstract Machine

is-ξ = ($\langle$s-c : is-c$\rangle$, $\langle$s-stg : is-value-list$\rangle$,

$\quad$ $\langle$s-input : is-intg-list$\rangle$, $\langle$s-output : is-intg-list$\rangle$)

is-value = is-intg $\vee$ is-UNDEFINED

Abstract Syntax

is-series = is-st-list

is-st = is-read-st $\vee$ is-write-st $\vee$ is-asmt-st $\vee$ is-cond-st $\vee$

$\quad$ is-def-loop $\vee$ is-indef-loop

is-read-st = ($\langle$s-r : is-var-list$\rangle$)

is-write-st = ($\langle$s-w : is-var-list$\rangle$)

is-asmt-st = ($\langle$s-lhs : is-var$\rangle$, $\langle$s-rhs : is-expr$\rangle$)

is-cond-st = ($\langle$s-ifpart : is-comp$\rangle$, $\langle$s-thenpart : is-series$\rangle$,

$\quad$ $\langle$s-elsepart : is-series$\rangle$)

is-def-loop = ($\langle$s-limit : is-expr$\rangle$, $\langle$s-body : is-series$\rangle$)

is-indef-loop = ($\langle$s-test : is-comp$\rangle$, $\langle$s-body : is-series$\rangle$)

is-comp = ($\langle$s-left-opd : is-expr$\rangle$, $\langle$s-right-opd : is-expr$\rangle$,

$\quad$ $\langle$s-rel : is-EQ $\vee$ is-GT $\vee$ is-LE $\vee$ is-LT $\vee$ is-GE $\vee$ is-NE$\rangle$)

is-expr = is-infix-expr $\vee$ is-var $\vee$ is-intg

is-infix-expr = ($\langle$s-left-opd : is-expr$\rangle$, $\langle$s-right-opd : is-expr$\rangle$,

$\quad$ $\langle$s-opr : is-PLUS $\vee$ is-MINUS $\vee$ is-TIMES $\vee$ is-OVER$\rangle$)

is-var = ($\langle$s-addr : is-intg$\rangle$)

TABLE 4.1 (Continued)

Instruction Definitions

exec-series (ser) =

    is-$\langle\rangle$ (ser) $\longrightarrow$ **null**

    T $\longrightarrow$ **exec-series** (tail (ser));

                exec-stmt (head (ser))

exec-stmt (stmt) =

    is-read-st (stmt) $\longrightarrow$ **read** (s-r (stmt))

    is-write-st (stmt) $\longrightarrow$ **write** (s-w (stmt))

    is-asmt-st (stmt) $\longrightarrow$

        store (s-addr $\circ$ s-lhs (stmt), val);

            val: **eval-expr** (s-rhs (stmt))

    is-cond-st (stmt) $\longrightarrow$

        choose (c, s-thenpart (stmt), s-elsepart (stmt));

            c: **eval-comp** (s-ifpart (stmt))

    is-def-loop (stmt) $\longrightarrow$

      repeat-series (s-body (stmt), r);

          r: **eval-expr** (s-limit (stmt))

    is-indef-loop (stmt) $\longrightarrow$

      choose (c, s-body (stmt)$\frown\langle$stmt$\rangle$, $\langle\rangle$);

         c: **eval-comp** (s-test (stmt))

repeat-series (ser, n) =

    n $\leq$ 0 $\longrightarrow$ **null**

    T $\longrightarrow$ **repeat-series** (ser, n $-$ 1);

             exec-series (ser)

choose (flag, ser-1, ser-2) =

    flag $\longrightarrow$ **exec-series** (ser-1)

    T $\longrightarrow$ **exec-series** (ser-2)

eval-comp (comp) =

    compare (a, b, s-rel (comp));

        a: **eval-expr** (s-left-opd (comp)),

        b: **eval-expr** (s-right-opd (comp))

TABLE 4.1 (Continued)

compare (val-1, val-2, rel) =

    is-EQ (rel) $\wedge$ (val-1 = val-2) $\vee$

        is-GT (rel) $\wedge$ (val-1 > val-2) $\vee$

        is-LE (rel) $\wedge$ (val-1 $\leq$ val-2) $\vee$

        is-LT (rel) $\wedge$ (val-1 < val-2) $\vee$

        is-GE (rel) $\wedge$ (val-1 $\geq$ val-2) $\vee$

        is-NE (rel) $\wedge$ (val-1 $\neq$ val-2) $\longrightarrow$ PASS: T

    T $\longrightarrow$ PASS: F

eval-expr (expr) =

    is-intg (expr) $\longrightarrow$ PASS: expr

    is-var (expr) $\longrightarrow$ **eval-var** (expr)

    is-infix-expr (expr) $\longrightarrow$

        calculate (a, b, s-opr (expr));

            a: **eval-expr** (s-left-opd (expr)),

            b: **eval-expr** (s-right-opd (expr))

eval-var (var) =

    is-UNDEFINED (elem (s-addr (var)) (s-stg (ξ))) $\longrightarrow$ **error**

    T $\longrightarrow$ PASS: elem (s-addr (var)) (s-stg (ξ))

calculate (val-1, val-2, opr) =

    is-PLUS (opr) $\longrightarrow$ PASS: val-1 + val-2

    is-MINUS (opr) $\longrightarrow$ PASS: val-1 $-$ val-2

    is-TIMES (opr) $\longrightarrow$ PASS: val-1 $\times$ val-2

    is-OVER (opr) $\longrightarrow$ PASS: val-1 $\div$ val-2

store (loc, val) =

    s-stg: μ(s-stg(ξ); $\langle$elem (loc) : val$\rangle$)

read (vars) =

    is-$\langle\rangle$ (vars) $\longrightarrow$ **null**

    T $\longrightarrow$ **read** (tail (vars));

            store (s-addr $\circ$ head (vars), val);

                val: **input-val**

input-val =

    is-$\langle\rangle$ $\circ$ s-input (ξ) $\longrightarrow$ **error**

    T $\longrightarrow$ PASS: head $\circ$ s-input (ξ)

        s-input: tail $\circ$ s-input (ξ)

TABLE 4.1   (Continued)

---

write (vars) =

    is-$\langle\rangle$ (vars) $\longrightarrow$ **null**

    T $\longrightarrow$ **write** (tail (vars));

                output-val (val);

                      val: **eval-expr** (head (vars))

output-val (val) =

    s-output: s-output(ζ)$\frown$val

EXERCISES

1. Describe the general conditions under which a VDL control tree will truly be a tree, with multiple branching, as opposed to a mere chain. Of the programming languages you know, which would result in this multiple branching to the greatest extent and which to the least extent?

2. Referring to Table 4.1, trace the interpretation of the program

$$n := 2 ;$$
$$\textbf{to } n \textbf{ do write } n \ ; \ n := n + 1 \textbf{ end}$$

4.1.3   A Semantic Specification for Eva

The definition of the semantics of Eva shown in Table 4.2, pp. 162–66, provides a second example of the use of the Vienna Definition Language. It may be seen immediately that these specifications are considerably longer than those for Pam and that, in particular, the structure of the abstract machine is much more elaborate. Also, a few notational devices not yet introduced have been employed. As is generally the case with VDL specifications, the key to understanding the interpreter is to familiarize oneself thoroughly with the predicate definitions for the abstract machine and the abstract syntax of the subject language.

Since Eva deals with character and string data only, the contents of the 'input', 'output', and 'store' components of the abstract machine are defined in terms of the predicate 'is-char', which is satisfied by the 27 elementary objects SPACE, A, B, . . . , Z. The 'store' component consists of a list of values conforming to the predicate defined by

$$\text{is-value} = \text{is-UNDEFINED} \lor \text{is-char} \lor \text{is-char-list} \lor \text{is-proc-rec}$$

The first two alternatives correspond to variables of type **char** and the third to variables of type **string**, the empty list representing the null string. Procedure names will be associated with "procedure records" satisfying the predicate

$$\text{is-proc-rec} = (\langle\text{s-attr} : \text{is-proc-attr}\rangle, \langle\text{s-env} : \text{is-env}\rangle)$$

where 'is-proc-attr' is defined by the following rules of abstract syntax:

$$\text{is-proc-attr} = (\langle\text{s-params} : \text{is-param-list}\rangle, \langle\text{s-body} : \text{is-st}\rangle)$$
$$\text{is-param} = (\langle\text{s-type} : \text{is-valtype}\rangle, \langle\text{s-name} : \text{is-name}\rangle)$$
$$\text{is-valtype} = \text{is-CHAR} \ \lor \ \text{is-STRING}$$
$$\text{is-name} = \text{is-letter-list}$$

(Note that, whereas Pam variables in their abstract form were represented by integer "addresses", Eva names are being represented by lists of letters corresponding closely to their textual form.) Basically, we are saying that the value of a procedure name comprises the parameter list and procedure body contained in the declaration of the name. (If the procedure has no parameters, the 'params' component will be the empty list.) Additionally, however, a procedure record has an "environment" ('env') component, which brings into the discussion a critically important concept.

An *environment* is a mapping that associates a unique storage location with each distinct name of interest. It may thus be represented by a VDL object of the form

$$\{\langle n_1 : a_1\rangle, \langle n_2 : a_2\rangle, \ldots, \langle n_m : a_m\rangle\}$$

where each n_i is a name and each a_i is the "address" of the storage location associated with n_i. The predicate characterizing these objects is defined with the aid of some new notation:

$$\text{is-env} = (\{\langle\text{name} : \text{is-intg}\rangle \ || \ \text{is-name (name)}\})$$

This equation states that an object satisfying 'is-env' consists of an arbitrary number of integer components selected by *objects* satisfying 'is-name'. The use of VDL objects as selectors in other objects is something new.

One of the immediate components of the Eva abstract machine is an environment. In any given state, the names contained (as selectors) in it will be those that are accessible ("in scope") at that time during the interpretation of the program. Whenever a block (**begin** . . . **end**) of the program is entered, the environment is generally enlarged (adding new addresses) to accommodate the names declared in the block. However, if the block contains a declaration of a name that was already present, the corresponding address given in the environment must be *replaced* by a new one, reflecting the fact that the name represents two different variables in different parts of the program and that the outer one is inaccessible in the inner block. As an example, suppose that the program has the following form:

> **begin**
>> **char** *a*, *b*
>>
>> . . .   (Point A)
>>
>> **begin**
>>> **string** *b*, *c*
>>>
>>> . . .   (Point B)
>>
>> **end**
>>
>> . . .   (Point C)
>
> **end**

At Point A, the environment will be

$$\{\langle\langle A\rangle : 1\rangle, \langle\langle B\rangle : 2\rangle\}$$

meaning that the variable *a* is associated with the first element of the store and the variable *b* with the second. At Point B, the environment will be

$$\{\langle\langle A\rangle : 1\rangle, \langle\langle B\rangle : 3\rangle, \langle\langle C\rangle : 4\rangle\}$$

When interpretation of an inner block is completed, the local variables disappear and the environment reverts to the form it had just before the block was entered. Thus the environment at Point C will again be

$$\{\langle\langle A\rangle : 1\rangle, \langle\langle B\rangle : 2\rangle\}$$

In order to make this restoration of an earlier environment possible, upon entry to a block the current environment will be copied and "saved" before updating it according to the new declarations. Since blocks may be nested to any depth, any number of earlier environments may have to be stored away at any given time. Therefore, the abstract machine contains a 'stack' component satisfying the predicate

$$\text{is-stack} = \text{is-}\Omega \ \lor \ (\langle\text{s-top} : \text{is-env}\rangle, \langle\text{s-rest} : \text{is-stack}\rangle)$$

Whenever a block is entered, a copy of the 'env' component before updating is pushed on the stack, and whenever a block is completed, the top environment is popped from the stack and substituted for the 'env' component.

Whereas in the definition of Pam there was a direct and static mapping from variables to storage locations, the mapping here is indirect and dynamic, with an environment providing an intermediate stage. As may or may not be obvious to the reader at this point, the existence of recursive procedures in Eva implies that there is no upper limit to the number of storage locations containing values that, at any given time, must be kept intact for possible later use. To keep track of the total number of locations that are or have been associated with names, the machine contains an integer 'counter' component. In general, some of the used storage locations will be "dead" (not associated with any name in either the current environment or the stack) and could be reused. It is simpler, however, to leave them as they are and to allocate completely new locations by incrementing the counter whenever the environment is updated. (This is an example of a situation that would have to be handled in a more complicated way in an actual implementation of the subject language. Similarly, the 'store' and 'stack' components of our abstract machine for Eva are impractical simplifications of the analogous aspects of a real implementation.)

When a procedure is called, the current environment generally must be stacked and replaced by the environment determined by the static position of the procedure's declaration, because, as the following example illustrates, these two environments may be different:

begin

    proc p (**char** x) $=$

      . . .

    string a (Point A)

    begin

      char a, b

      . . .   (Point B)

      call p (b)

      . . .   (Point C)

    end

    . . .   (Point D)

end

The body of the procedure p can access the outer a (of type **string**) but not the inner one (of type **char**), whereas the inner block from which p is called can access the inner a but not the outer one. The purpose of the 'env' component of a procedure record is to store the procedure's environment, including the procedure's own name and any names declared *after* the procedure at the same level, for retrieval whenever the procedure is called. If the procedure has parameters, this environment will be updated to include the parameter names when the procedure is called. In the example above, just before the inner block is entered (Point A) the current environment will be

$$\{\langle\langle P\rangle : 1\rangle, \langle\langle A\rangle : 2\rangle\}$$

and a copy of this will form the 'env' component of p's procedure record (the first element of the 'store' component). At Point B, the current environment will be

$$\{\langle\langle P\rangle : 1\rangle, \langle\langle A\rangle : 3\rangle, \langle\langle B\rangle : 4\rangle\}$$

When the call is interpreted, (1) the argument b is evaluated in this environment, (2) this environment is stacked and $\{\langle\langle P\rangle : 1\rangle, \langle\langle A\rangle : 2\rangle\}$ installed, (3) the latter environment is updated to

$$\{\langle\langle P\rangle : 1\rangle, \langle\langle A\rangle : 2\rangle, \langle\langle X\rangle : 5\rangle\}$$

(4) x is assigned the result of the earlier argument evaluation (i.e., the fifth element of the 'store' component is altered), and (5) the body of the procedure is interpreted. When the procedure returns (Point C), the current environment reverts to

$$\{\langle\langle P\rangle : 1\rangle, \langle\langle A\rangle : 3\rangle, \langle\langle B\rangle : 4\rangle\}$$

which was saved on the stack. At Point D, the environment will again be $\{\langle\langle P\rangle : 1\rangle, \langle\langle A\rangle : 2\rangle\}$.

The reader should be able to convince herself that this mechanism is general enough to handle all possibilities, including a procedure containing blocks, one procedure calling another, a procedure calling itself (simple recursion), and two or more procedures calling each other (mutual recursion).

Having obtained an informal overview of the critical aspects of the definition, we may now examine the remainder of the abstract syntax specifications in order to extract the full details from the instruction definitions.

An abstract program will satisfy the predicate 'is-block' defined by

$$\text{is-block} = (\langle\text{s-decl-part} : \text{is-decl-part}\rangle, \langle\text{s-stmt-part} : \text{is-st-list}\rangle)$$

The declaration part of a block is regarded as a mapping from the names declared to the attributes specified in their declarations; i.e., it is represented by an object consisting of attributes selected by names:

$$\text{is-decl-part} = (\{\langle\text{name} : \text{is-attr}\rangle \mid\mid \text{is-name (name)}\})$$
$$\text{is-attr} = \text{is-valtype} \lor \text{is-proc-attr}$$

The rules defining the abstract form of statements and expressions are quite straightforward:

is-st $=$ is-input-st $\lor$ is-output-st $\lor$ is-call $\lor$ is-block $\lor$ is-st-list $\lor$

      is-cond-st $\lor$ is-cons-st

is-input-st $= (\langle$s-var : is-name$\rangle)$

is-output-st $= (\langle$s-expr : is-expr$\rangle)$

is-call $= (\langle$s-procname : is-name$\rangle, \langle$s-args : is-expr-list$\rangle)$

is-cond-st $= (\langle$s-test : is-EQ $\lor$ is-NEQ$\rangle, \langle$s-left-opd : is-expr$\rangle,$

      $\langle$s-right-opd : is-expr$\rangle, \langle$s-inner-part : is-st$\rangle)$

is-cons-st $= (\langle$s-char : is-expr$\rangle, \langle$s-var : is-name$\rangle)$

is-expr $=$ is-name $\lor$ is-char $\lor$ is-char-list $\lor$ is-head-expr $\lor$ is-tail-expr

is-head-expr $= (\langle$s-h : is-expr$\rangle)$

is-tail-expr $= (\langle$s-t : is-expr$\rangle)$

Clearly, these abstract syntax specifications do not in themselves rule out programs that are illegal with respect to the context-sensitive aspects of the Eva language. In other words, not all objects satisfying 'is-block' are valid programs. A complete syntactic and semantic definition of Eva would have to include a component that had the effect of imposing the required restrictions. Since we are concentrating our attention on semantics in this chapter, we shall merely assume that these additional specifications exist and that violations of static structure will never appear in abstract programs.

In an initial state of the machine, the 'input' component contains the complete sequence of input characters, the 'output', 'store', 'env', and 'stack' components are empty, the 'counter' component is 0, and the only instruction in the control component is **exec-block**(t), where t is the abstract program.

The instructions **exec-block, push-stack, pop-stack, prepare-env, update-env, prepare-store**, and **update-store**, defined in Table 4.2, are mainly concerned with environment management. The notation

$$\mu_0(\langle s : a \rangle)$$

is merely an abbreviation for

$$\mu(\Omega; \langle s : a \rangle)$$

i.e., a completely new object $\{\langle s : a \rangle\}$ is created. In general, an expression of the form

$$\mu_0(\langle s_1 : a_1 \rangle, \ldots, \langle s_n : a_n \rangle)$$

creates a new object of the form $\{\langle s_1 : a_1 \rangle, \ldots, \langle s_n : a_n \rangle\}$. Thus the instruction defined by

> **push-stack** =
>
> s-stack: $\mu_0(\langle$s-top : s-env$(\xi)\rangle$, $\langle$s-rest : s-stack$(\xi)\rangle)$

has the effect of pushing a copy of the current environment on the stack.
The body of the instruction definition

> **prepare-env** (decs) =
>
> {**update-env** (name) | name (decs) $\neq \Omega$}

where 'decs' is assumed to satisfy 'is-decl-part', stands for a self-replacing
group of the form

> **update-env** (n_1),
>
> **update-env** (n_2),
>
> . . .
>
> **update-env** (n_m)

where $n_1, n_2, \ldots, n_m$ are all the different names occurring as selectors in the
value of 'decs'. Each **update-env** instruction increments the 'counter' component by 1 and makes it the address associated with the argument name in the
current environment.

When updating of the environment is complete, the instructions **prepare-
store** and **update-store** are used to initialize the storage locations allocated to
each new name. For **char** names, the initial value is UNDEFINED, for
string names it is the empty list of characters, and for procedure names it is
a procedure record consisting of the procedure's attribute (parameters and
body) and the recently updated environment.

After all this housekeeping has been done, the statement part of the block
is interpreted. The final action is to restore the original environment by means
of the instruction

> **pop-stack** =
>
> s-env: s-top ∘ s-stack (ξ)
>
> s-stack: s-rest ∘ s-stack (ξ)

The definitions of the instructions **exec-st-list**, **exec-stmt**, **exec-cond-st**,
read, **write**, **assign**, **pass-head**, and **pass-tail** are all quite straightforward. The
instructions **concatenate** and **eval-expr** make use of an auxiliary *function*
(not an instruction) defined as

> value (val) =
>
> is-UNDEFINED (val) $\rightarrow$ error
>
> T $\rightarrow$ val

where 'error' is a primitive, undefined function analogous to the instruction **error**. Such function definitions occur quite frequently in VDL definitions of realistic programming languages.

The arguments of an **exec-call** instruction are the call statement itself and the procedure record for the procedure being called. First, the instructions **eval-args** and **send-vals** are used to evaluate the arguments, if any, of the call in the existing environment and to form a list 'arg-vals' of the resulting values. After the environment is pushed on the stack, the instruction **establish-env** is used to install the environment stored in the procedure record. Then a **pass-args** instruction carries out the environment updating and store initialization involving the procedure's parameters, if any. The procedure body is then interpreted, and interpretation of the call is completed by restoring the original environment.

This completes the discussion of the VDL definition of the semantics of Eva shown in Table 4.2. The zealous or incredulous reader may wish to simulate the detailed operation of the interpreter on a small example.

TABLE 4.2 VDL Definition of the Semantics of Eva

Abstract Machine

is-ξ = ($\langle$s-c : is-c$\rangle$, $\langle$s-input : is-char-list$\rangle$,

   $\langle$s-output : is-char-list$\rangle$, $\langle$s-store : is-value-list$\rangle$,

   $\langle$s-counter : is-intg$\rangle$, $\langle$s-env : is-env$\rangle$, $\langle$s-stack : is-stack$\rangle$)

is-env = ($\{\langle$name : is-intg$\rangle$ || is-name (name)$\}$)

is-stack = ($\langle$s-top : is-env$\rangle$, $\langle$s-rest : is-stack$\rangle$) $\lor$ is-Ω

is-value = is-UNDEFINED $\lor$ is-char $\lor$ is-char-list $\lor$ is-proc-rec

is-proc-rec = ($\langle$s-attr : is-proc-attr$\rangle$, $\langle$s-env : is-env$\rangle$)

is-char = is-letter $\lor$ is-SPACE

is-letter = is-A $\lor$ is-B $\lor$ is-C $\lor$ is-D $\lor$ is-E $\lor$ is-F $\lor$ is-G $\lor$

   is-H $\lor$ is-I $\lor$ is-J $\lor$ is-K $\lor$ is-L $\lor$ is-M $\lor$ is-N $\lor$ is-O $\lor$

   is-P $\lor$ is-Q $\lor$ is-R $\lor$ is-S $\lor$ is-T $\lor$ is-U $\lor$ is-V $\lor$ is-W $\lor$

   is-X $\lor$ is-Y $\lor$ is-Z

Abstract Syntax

is-block = ($\langle$s-decl-part : is-decl-part$\rangle$, $\langle$s-stmt-part : is-st-list$\rangle$)

is-decl-part = ($\{\langle$name : is-attr$\rangle$ || is-name (name)$\}$)

is-attr = is-valtype $\lor$ is-proc-attr

is-valtype = is-CHAR $\lor$ is-STRING

is-proc-attr = ($\langle$s-params : is-param-list$\rangle$, $\langle$s-body : is-st$\rangle$)

TABLE 4.2 (Continued)

is-param = ($\langle$s-type : is-valtype$\rangle$, $\langle$s-name : is-name$\rangle$)

is-name = is-letter-list

is-st = is-input-st $\lor$ is-output-st $\lor$ is-call $\lor$ is-block $\lor$ is-st-list $\lor$
    is-cond-st $\lor$ is-cons-st

is-input-st = ($\langle$s-var : is-name$\rangle$)

is-output-st = ($\langle$s-expr : is-expr$\rangle$)

is-call = ($\langle$s-procname : is-name$\rangle$, $\langle$s-args : is-expr-list$\rangle$)

is-cond-st = ($\langle$s-test : is-EQ $\lor$ is-NEQ$\rangle$, $\langle$s-left-opd : is-expr$\rangle$,
    $\langle$s-right-opd : is-expr$\rangle$, $\langle$s-inner-part : is-st$\rangle$)

is-cons-st = ($\langle$s-char : is-expr$\rangle$, $\langle$s-var : is-name$\rangle$)

is-expr = is-name $\lor$ is-char $\lor$ is-char-list $\lor$ is-head-expr $\lor$ is-tail-expr

is-head-expr = ($\langle$s-h : is-expr$\rangle$)

is-tail-expr = ($\langle$s-t : is-expr$\rangle$)

Instruction Definitions

exec-block (block) =
    pop-stack;
        exec-st-list (s-stmt-part (block));
            prepare-store (s-decl-part (block));
                prepare-env (s-decl-part (block));
                    push-stack

push-stack =
    s-stack: μ_0($\langle$s-top : s-env(ξ)$\rangle$, $\langle$s-rest : s-stack(ξ)$\rangle$)

pop-stack =
    s-env: s-top $\circ$ s-stack (ξ)
    s-stack: s-rest $\circ$ s-stack (ξ)

prepare-env (decs) =
    {**update-env** (name) | name (decs) $\neq \Omega$}

update-env (name) =
    s-counter: s-counter(ξ) $+$ 1
    s-env: μ(s-env(ξ); $\langle$name : s-counter(ξ)$\rangle$)

prepare-store (decs) =
    {**update-store** (name, name (decs)) | name (decs) $\neq \Omega$}

TABLE 4.2   (Continued)

update-store (name, attr) $=$

    is-CHAR (attr) $\longrightarrow$

        s-store: μ(s-store(ξ); $\langle$elem (name $\circ$ s-env (ξ)) : UNDEFINED$\rangle$)

    is-STRING (attr) $\longrightarrow$

        s-store: μ(s-store(ξ); $\langle$elem (name $\circ$ s-env(ξ)) : $\langle\rangle\rangle$)

    is-proc-attr (attr) $\longrightarrow$

        s-store: μ(s-store(ξ); $\langle$elem (name $\circ$ s-env (ξ)) : μ_0($\langle$s-attr : attr$\rangle$,

            $\langle$s-env : s-env(ξ)$\rangle$)$\rangle$)

exec-st-list (stmts) $=$

    is-$\langle\rangle$ (stmts) $\longrightarrow$ **null**

    T $\longrightarrow$ **exec-st-list** (tail (stmts));

                exec-stmt (head (stmts))

exec-stmt (stmt) $=$

    is-input-st (stmt) $\longrightarrow$

        assign (s-var (stmt), char);

            char: **read**

    is-output-st (stmt) $\longrightarrow$

        write (char);

            char: **eval-expr** (s-expr (stmt))

    is-call (stmt) $\longrightarrow$

        exec-call (stmt, elem (s-procname (stmt) $\circ$ s-env (ξ))(s-store(ξ)))

    is-block (stmt) $\longrightarrow$ **exec-block** (stmt)

    is-st-list (stmt) $\longrightarrow$ **exec-st-list** (stmt)

    is-cond-st (stmt) $\longrightarrow$

        exec-cond-st (a, b, stmt);

            a: **eval-expr** (s-left-opd (stmt)),

            b: **eval-expr** (s-right-opd (stmt))

    is-cons-st (stmt)

        concatenate (char, s-var (stmt));

            char: **eval-expr** (s-char (stmt))

TABLE 4.2   (Continued)

exec-call (call, proc-rec) =
  pop-stack;
    exec-stmt (s-body ∘ s-attr (proc-rec));
      pass-args (s-params ∘ s-attr (proc-rec), arg-vals);
        establish-env (s-env (proc-rec));
          push-stack;
            arg-vals: **eval-args** (s-args (call))

eval-args (arglist) =
  is-⟨⟩ (arglist) ⟶ PASS: ⟨⟩
  T ⟶ **send-vals** (v, vlist);
        vlist: **eval-args** (tail (arglist));
          v: **eval-expr** (head (arglist))

send-vals (v, vlist) =
  PASS: ⟨v⟩⌢vlist

establish-env (env) =
  s-env: env

pass-args (params, arg-vals) =
  is-⟨⟩ (params) ⟶ **null**
  T ⟶ **pass-args** (tail (params), tail (arg-vals));
        assign (s-name ∘ head (params), head (arg-vals));
          update-env (s-name ∘ head (params))

exec-cond-st (a, b, cond-st) =
  is-EQ ∘ s-test (cond-st) ∧ a = b ⟶ **exec-stmt** (s-inner-part (cond-st))
  is-NEQ ∘ s-test (cond-st) ∧ a ≠ b ⟶ **exec-stmt** (s-inner-part (cond-st))
  T ⟶ **null**

read =
  is-⟨⟩ ∘ s-input (ξ) ⟶ **error**
  T ⟶ PASS: head ∘ s-input (ξ)
        s-input: tail ∘ s-input (ξ)

write (char) =
  s-output: s-output(ξ)⌢⟨char⟩

TABLE 4.2   (Continued)

---

concatenate (char, name) =

    assign (name, ⟨char⟩⌢value (elem (name ∘ s-env (ξ))(s-store(ξ))))

assign (name, val) =

    s-store: μ(s-store(ξ); ⟨elem (name ∘ s-env (ξ)) : val⟩)

eval-expr (expr) =

    is-name (expr) ⟶ PASS: value (elem (expr ∘ s-env (ξ))(s-store(ξ)))

    is-char (expr) ⟶ PASS: expr

    is-char-list (expr) ⟶ PASS: expr

    is-head-expr (expr) ⟶

        pass-head (v);

            v: **eval-expr** (s-h (expr))

    is-tail-expr (expr) ⟶

        pass-tail (v)

            v: **eval-expr** (s-t (expr))

value (val) =

    is-UNDEFINED (val) ⟶ error

    T ⟶ val

pass-head (val) =

    PASS: head (val)

pass-tail (val) =

    PASS: tail (val)

EXERCISES

1. Draw a tree diagram for the VDL object satisfying 'is-block' and corresponding to the Eva program

```
begin
    proc p (char x) =
        cons x, a
    string a
    begin
        char a, b
        input a, b
        call p (b)
    end
    output head a
end
```

2. Trace the interpretation of the program in Exercise 1 as specified by Table 4.2, given that the 'input' component of the initial state consists of the characters *m* and *n*.

For Further Information

The Vienna Definition Language is treated at length in the article by Wegner (1972a) and in the books by Lee (1972) and Ollongren (1974). VDL includes more facilities than have been described here. In particular, the complete metalanguage incorporates a means of completely specifying syntax (including context conditions) as well as semantics; a small example of a complete language definition using these tools is given by Marcotty et al. (1976). The complete, formal definition of PL/I referred to by Lucas and Walk (1969) is the prime example of a large-scale VDL specification of a real language. Specifications for several other languages, such as Basic (Lee, 1972) and a subset of SNOBOL4 (Pagan, 1978), have also been constructed. The operational definition of standard PL/I, as supported by the American National Standards Institute and the European Computer Manufacturers' Association, employs a semiformal notation similar in many respects to VDL (Marcotty and Sayward, 1977).

Some alternative forms of the operational approach to formal semantics, analyses of their theoretical aspects, and further references, may be found in the papers by Landin (1964), Reynolds (1972), and Anderson et al. (1976). Wegner (1972b) offers an extended treatment of operational semantics in general.

4.2

THE DENOTATIONAL APPROACH

4.2.1 Concepts and Characteristics

The denotational approach, also known as the "mathematical" approach, to formal semantics is fundamentally more abstract than the operational methods. In this approach, the meanings of language constructs are explicated in terms of various mathematical objects, especially *functions*, which provide appropriate models for them. Unlike the operational approaches, there is no explicit modeling of computational processes such as the compilation or interpretation of programs. The meanings of abstract programs or program segments are expressed in terms of *semantic functions* which map them into various *semantic domains*, the members of which are usually themselves functions. The main part of a denotational specification of the semantics of a subject language consists of a set of *semantic equations* which define the semantic functions.

The denotational approach is based on some rather deep mathematical concepts, and much of the literature on the subject has been more concerned with exploring and explaining these concepts than with standardizing the metalinguistic notation, of which there are several variations. In keeping with the style and character of this book, we shall take a greatly simplified view of the underlying theory and concentrate on the application of one of the most commonly used notations.

For our purposes, a *domain* is basically a set (finite or infinite) of objects, including two special objects $\bot$ ("bottom") and $\top$ ("top").[1] Roughly speaking, $\bot$ represents an undefined value and $\top$ an inconsistent or erroneous value. In specifying simple domains by enumeration of their elements, an expression of the form $\{...\}^\circ$ is short for $\{..., \bot, \top\}$; for example, the domain of truth values is

$$\{true, false\}^\circ = \{true, false, \bot, \top\}$$

There are several ways of constructing new domains from simpler domains. First, given n (≥ 2) domains $D_1, D_2, \ldots, D_n$, the elements of the *product domain*

$$P = D_1 \times D_2 \times \ldots \times D_n$$

are ordered *n*-tuples which may be written in the form

$$\langle d_1, d_2, \ldots, d_n \rangle$$

where d_1 is an element of D_1, d_2 is an element of D_2, and so forth. Given an element p of P, an expression of the form

$$p \downarrow i$$

($1 \leq i \leq n$) represents the *i*th component (an element of D_i) of p. In the special case where $D_1, D_2, \ldots, D_n$ are all the same domain D, the product domain may be written as D^n and thought of as a set of fixed-length lists of elements of D.

Domains may be "added," so that each element of a *sum domain* such as

$$S = D_1 + D_2 + \ldots + D_n$$

corresponds to an element of one of the n given domains. If d_i is an element of the summand D_i, the expression

$$d_i \text{ in } S$$

---

[1]Technically, domains are defined not as sets but as *complete lattices* with certain mathematical properties. In some more recent versions of denotational semantics, $\top$ elements are not used.

yields the corresponding element s of the larger domain S; conversely, the expression $s \mid D_i$ yields the corresponding element d_i of the smaller domain D_i. The boolean expression $s \in D_i$ ("s is squarely in D_i") is true if and only if s corresponds to an element of D_i as opposed to one of the other summands. The technical terms for the three operations 'in', '$\mid$', and '$\in$' are *injection*, *projection*, and *inspection*, respectively.

If D_1 and D_2 are two domains, then each element of the *function domain*

$$F = D_1 \longrightarrow D_2$$

is a function which maps elements of D_1 to elements of D_2. If f is an element of F and d_1 is an element of D_1, then the *application* $f(d_1)$ yields an element of D_2.[2] Function values (i.e., values that are functions—elements of function domains such as F) are sometimes written as *abstractions* or *lambda-expressions* of the form $\lambda p . e$, where p is a parameter name and e is an expression. For example, $\lambda x . x \times x$ is a direct (anonymous) representation of the squaring function and could represent a member of the domain $N \longrightarrow N$, where N is the domain of integers.

It is important to realize that a domain may have an arbitrarily complex structure. Expressions for domains may contain several operators, with '$\times$' taking precedence over '$+$' and '$+$' taking precedence over '$\longrightarrow$'. Thus

$$D_1 \times D_2 \longrightarrow D_3 + D_4 \times D_5$$

means

$$(D_1 \times D_2) \longrightarrow (D_3 + (D_4 \times D_5))$$

rather than, say,

$$D_1 \times (D_2 \longrightarrow (D_3 + D_4)) \times D_5$$

which would also be a possible domain. Frequent use is made of domains such as

$$D_1 \longrightarrow (D_2 \longrightarrow D_3)$$

whose elements are functions that map elements of D_1 into functions which are elements of $D_2 \longrightarrow D_3$. The domain operator '$\longrightarrow$' associates to the right, so that $D_1 \longrightarrow (D_2 \longrightarrow D_3)$ may be rewritten as

$$D_1 \longrightarrow D_2 \longrightarrow D_3$$

Similarly,

$$D_1 \longrightarrow D_2 \longrightarrow D_3 \longrightarrow D_4$$

---

[2]Technically, a function domain includes only those functions which are *monotonic* and *continuous*, in accordance with certain definitions of these terms. For a function f, it is usually the case that $f(\perp) = \perp$ and $f(\top) = \top$.

means

$$D_1 \longrightarrow (D_2 \longrightarrow (D_3 \longrightarrow D_4))$$

Given a domain **D**, **D*** represents the domain of all finite *lists* of elements of **D**, including the empty list 'nil'. Thus **D*** is equivalent to

$$\{nil\} + D + D^2 + D^3 + \cdots$$

As in other formalisms, it is useful to have primitive functions available for extracting the "head" and "tail" of a list and adding an element to a list. Given any domain **D**, we may assume that *hd* denotes an element of the domain $D^* \longrightarrow D$ such that $hd(l)$ produces the element of **D** which is the first item in the list *l*, and that *tl* denotes an element of $D^* \longrightarrow D^*$ such that $tl(l)$ produces the sublist of *l* following the first item; if $l =$ nil, both $hd(l)$ and $tl(l)$ yield $\top$. The function *append* is an element of $D^* \times D \longrightarrow D^*$ such that $append(l, d)$ is the list obtained by joining *d* to the end of *l*, and the function *prefix* is an element of $D \times D^* \longrightarrow D^*$ such that $prefix\,(d, l)$ is the list obtained by joining *d* to the beginning of *l*.

The abstract syntax of a subject language may be expressed in terms of a set of related *syntactic domains*, conventionally represented by boldface words of three or more letters the first of which is capitalized. Thus **Var** could denote the domain of all variables in a language. When defining a domain, we normally also specify a symbol which will represent a typical member of that domain, i.e., act as a metavariable over the domain. In the case of syntactic domains, the convention is to use uppercase Greek letters as metavariables; for example,

$$\Xi: \textbf{Var}$$

specifies that Ξ will be used to represent an arbitrary element of **Var**. If more than one metavariable is needed for the same domain, primes or subscripts may be used, so that Ξ' and Ξ'' or Ξ_1 and Ξ_2 would represent any two elements of **Var**.

Compound syntactic entities may be modeled by product or list domains. For example, if **Var** is the domain of variables and **Exp** is the domain of expressions, assignment statements might be regarded as elements of **Var** $\times$ **Exp**. Further, if a loop statement consists of a **to**-part which is an expression and a **do**-part which is a statement, and if assignments and loops are the only types of statement, then the domain of statements might be recursively formulated as

$$\Sigma: \textbf{Stmt} = \textbf{Var} \times \textbf{Exp} + \textbf{Exp} \times \textbf{Stmt}$$

For purposes of defining semantic functions, however, this notation for abstract syntax is not particularly convenient. Given a simple list of domains such as

$$\Sigma: \textbf{Stmt}$$
$$\Xi: \textbf{Var}$$
$$E: \textbf{Exp}$$

it will be preferable to express the relationships in terms of BNF-like production rules such as

$$\Sigma ::= \Xi := E \mid \textbf{to } E \textbf{ do } \Sigma$$

The meanings of constructs are given in terms of *semantic domains*, the names of which consist of one or two letters only. As far as metavariables over semantic domains are concerned, the convention is to use lowercase Greek letters. Thus the domain of integer values could be specified as

$$v: \textbf{N} = \{\ldots, -2, -1, 0, 1, 2, \ldots\}^\circ$$

As another example of a semantic domain, memory states could in simple cases be modeled by

$$\sigma: \textbf{S} = \textbf{Var} \longrightarrow \textbf{N}$$

so that a particular state σ would be some function mapping variables into integers.

A *semantic function*, represented by an uppercase script letter, is typically a member of a domain of the form **Syn** $\longrightarrow$ **Se**, where **Syn** is a syntactic domain and **Se** is a semantic domain. For example, by writing

$$\mathcal{S}: \textbf{Stmt} \longrightarrow \textbf{S} \longrightarrow \textbf{S}$$

we specify that the semantic function $\mathcal{S}$ is a member of the domain **Stmt** $\longrightarrow$ **S** $\longrightarrow$ **S** [which is the same as **Stmt** $\longrightarrow$ (**Var** $\longrightarrow$ **N**) $\longrightarrow$ (**Var** $\longrightarrow$ **N**)]. The significance of this is that the meaning of a statement is to be regarded as some function mapping states into states.

Having specified the "type" of a semantic function, we must give its detailed definition by writing a set of *semantic equations*, one for each summand of the syntactic domain involved. The left side of a semantic equation begins with an application of the semantic function to an argument consisting of a representative element of the syntactic domain. The argument is expressed in the notation used for the abstract syntax rules and is enclosed by the special brackets $\llbracket$ and $\rrbracket$ instead of by parentheses. For example, the application $\mathcal{S}\llbracket \Xi := E \rrbracket$ is formally equivalent to $\mathcal{S}(\langle \Xi, E \rangle)$ and yields some function in the domain **S** $\longrightarrow$ **S**. If we can give an expression that represents this function directly, the equation can take the form

$$S[\![\Xi := E]\!] = \ldots$$

Alternatively, the equation can take the form

$$S[\![\Xi := E]\!](\sigma) = \ldots$$

where the right side is an expression for the state yielded when the $S \longrightarrow S$ function is applied to a typical argument σ. A further notational convention permits us to omit parentheses enclosing single-symbol arguments such as σ, so that the left side of the equation may be abbreviated to $S[\![\Xi := E]\!]\sigma$. The definition of S would be completed by a second equation with $S[\![$to E do $\Sigma]\!]\sigma$ on the left side.

Several additional notational devices may be used in an expression on the right side of a semantic equation. Among these are "update" expressions of the form $f[a/b]$, which denotes a function f' which is the same as the function f except that it maps the argument b into the value of a. An expression of the form f^n, where f is a function belonging to a domain of the form $D \longrightarrow D$ and n is a nonnegative integer, denotes the function in $D \longrightarrow D$ obtained by composing f with itself n times. Conditional expressions are written in the form

$$t \longrightarrow e_1, e_2$$

where the value of the expression e_1 is yielded if the boolean expression t is true and the value of e_2 is yielded otherwise. Such devices are employed in the denotational specifications of Pam and Eva which follow.

EXERCISES

1. If you have read Sec. 4.1, identify the Vienna Definition Language features that are roughly analogous to each of the following concepts and metalinguistic devices in the denotational approach, given that VDL predicates roughly correspond to domains:
   (a) product domains
   (b) sum domains
   (c) $p \downarrow i$
   (d) $s \in D_i$
   (e) list domains and associated functions
   (f) $t \longrightarrow e_1, e_2$

2. Before continuing with the next subsection, review the conventions we are adopting for the use of each of the following:

(a) boldface "words" of three or more letters
(b) boldface "words" of one or two letters
(c) uppercase Greek letters
(d) lowercase Greek letters
(e) script letters
(f) special double brackets
(g) expressions of the form $f[a/b]$

4.2.2 The Denotational Semantics of Pam

A denotational definition of the semantics of Pam is shown in Table 4.3, pp. 178–80. There the following syntactic domains and corresponding metavariables are listed:

Ψ:	**Prog**	programs
Σ:	**Stmt**	statements
Ξ:	**Var**	variables
Λ:	**Vars**	lists of one or more variables
E:	**Exp**	expressions
K:	**Comp**	comparisons
P:	**Rel**	relations
Θ:	**Opr**	operators
N:	**Num**	integer constants
Δ:	**Dig**	decimal digits

The necessity for a domain of series of statements has been eliminated by permitting a statement to consist of a sequence of two other statements, as implied by the following abstract syntax rules:

$$\Psi ::= \Sigma$$
$$\Sigma ::= \Sigma_1 ; \Sigma_2 \mid \textbf{read} \wedge \mid \textbf{write} \wedge \mid \Xi := E \mid$$
$$\textbf{if } K \textbf{ then } \Sigma \textbf{ fi} \mid \textbf{if } K \textbf{ then } \Sigma_1 \textbf{ else } \Sigma_2 \textbf{ fi} \mid$$
$$\textbf{to } E \textbf{ do } \Sigma \textbf{ end} \mid \textbf{while } K \textbf{ do } \Sigma \textbf{ end}$$

The ambiguity inherent in this formulation is of no consequence, and the set of legal programs is the same as it was before. A similar device is used in the rule for lists of variables:

$$\Lambda ::= \Xi \mid \Lambda_1, \Lambda_2$$

The remaining rules are straightforward:

$$K ::= E_1 \ P \ E_2$$
$$E ::= E_1 \ \Theta \ E_2 \mid \Xi \mid N$$
$$N ::= \Delta \mid N \Delta$$
$$P ::= \ = \mid > \mid < \mid = < \mid > = \mid \neq$$
$$\Theta ::= \ + \mid - \mid * \mid /$$
$$\Delta ::= 0 \mid 1 \mid 2 \mid 3 \mid 4 \mid 5 \mid 6 \mid 7 \mid 8 \mid 9$$

No rule is given for Ξ, because the internal structure of variables is not semantically relevant.

The primitive semantic domains are those of truth values and integers:

$$\tau: \mathbf{T} = \{true, false\}^\circ$$
$$v: \mathbf{N} = \{\ldots, -2, -1, 0, 1, 2, \ldots\}^\circ$$

As for the other semantic domains, a *state* is a function from variables to integers, a *file* is a list of integers, and a *configuration* is a combination of a state, an input file, and an output file:

$$\sigma: \mathbf{S} = \mathbf{Var} \longrightarrow \mathbf{N}$$
$$\phi: \mathbf{Fi} = \mathbf{N}^*$$
$$\gamma: \mathbf{Cf} = \mathbf{S} \times \mathbf{Fi} \times \mathbf{Fi}$$

Given a configuration γ, $\gamma \downarrow 1$ gives the memory state, $\gamma \downarrow 2$ the input file, and $\gamma \downarrow 3$ the output file.

The "topmost" semantic function $\mathfrak{M}$ is stated to be a member of the domain $\mathbf{Prog} \longrightarrow \mathbf{Fi} \longrightarrow \mathbf{Fi}$; i.e., the meaning $\mathfrak{M}[\![\Psi]\!]$ of an entire program Ψ is some function mapping (input) files into (output) files. The nature of this function is spelled out by the semantic equation

$$\mathfrak{M}[\![\Psi]\!]\phi_i = (\mathbb{S}[\![\Psi]\!](\langle \lambda\Xi.\bot, \phi_i, \text{nil}\rangle)) \downarrow 3$$

where $\mathbb{S}: \mathbf{Stmt} \longrightarrow \mathbf{Cf} \longrightarrow \mathbf{Cf}$ is the semantic function for statements. The equation states that the output file produced by a program with initial input file ϕ_i is given by the third component of the configuration produced by Ψ considered as a statement from the initial configuration $\langle \lambda\Xi.\bot, \phi_i, \text{nil}\rangle$, where the input file component is ϕ_i, the output file component is empty, and the state component $\lambda\Xi.\bot$ is such that all variables have undefined values.

Thus the meaning of the program

read x, y ; **write** y

is the **Fi** $\longrightarrow$ **Fi** function $\mathfrak{M}[\![\text{read } x, y; \text{ write } y]\!]$ such that

$$\mathfrak{M}[\![\text{read } x, y \text{ ; write } y]\!]\phi_i = (\mathcal{S}[\![\text{read } x, y \text{ ; write } y]\!](\langle\lambda\Xi.\bot, \phi_i, \text{nil}\rangle)) \downarrow 3$$

Either side of this equation is an expression for the output produced by the program when given the input file ϕ_i; if $\phi_i = \langle-2, 7, 1\rangle$, for example, $\langle 7\rangle$ should be yielded. Our next task is to define $\mathcal{S}$ in such a way as to produce this result and to produce appropriate results for all cases.

$\mathcal{S}$ is defined by a number of semantic equations, each dealing with a different kind of statement. For statements that are sequences, we have

$$\mathcal{S}[\![\Sigma_1; \Sigma_2]\!] = \mathcal{S}[\![\Sigma_2]\!] \circ \mathcal{S}[\![\Sigma_1]\!]$$

which states that the **Cf** $\longrightarrow$ **Cf** function denoted by '$\Sigma_1; \Sigma_2$' is the **Cf** $\longrightarrow$ **Cf** function denoted by Σ_2 composed with the **Cf** $\longrightarrow$ **Cf** function denoted by Σ_1. (In operational terms, the transformation specified by Σ_1 precedes the transformation specified by Σ_2.) For our example,

$$\mathcal{S}[\![\text{read } x, y \text{ ; write } y]\!] = \mathcal{S}[\![\text{write } y]\!] \circ \mathcal{S}[\![\text{read } x, y]\!]$$

and hence

$$\mathfrak{M}[\![\text{read } x, y \text{ ; write } y]\!]\phi_i$$
$$= ((\mathcal{S}[\![\text{write } y]\!] \circ \mathcal{S}[\![\text{read } x, y]\!])(\langle\lambda\Xi.\bot, \phi_i, \text{nil}\rangle)) \downarrow 3$$
$$= (\mathcal{S}[\![\text{write } y]\!](\mathcal{S}[\![\text{read } x, y]\!](\langle\lambda\Xi.\bot, \phi_i, \text{nil}\rangle))) \downarrow 3$$

Input and output statements containing lists of more than one variable may be trivially expanded, so that we have the semantic equations

$$\mathcal{S}[\![\text{read } \Lambda_1, \Lambda_2]\!] = \mathcal{S}[\![\text{read } \Lambda_1 \text{ ; read } \Lambda_2]\!]$$
$$\mathcal{S}[\![\text{write } \Lambda_1, \Lambda_2]\!] = \mathcal{S}[\![\text{write } \Lambda_1 \text{ ; write } \Lambda_2]\!]$$

Thus, in our example,

$$\mathcal{S}[\![\text{read } x, y]\!]$$
$$= \mathcal{S}[\![\text{read } x \text{ ; read } y]\!]$$
$$= \mathcal{S}[\![\text{read } y]\!] \circ \mathcal{S}[\![\text{read } x]\!]$$

and hence

$$\mathfrak{M}[\![\text{read } x, y \text{ ; write } y]\!]\phi_i$$
$$= \mathcal{S}([\![\text{write } y]\!](\mathcal{S}[\![\text{read } y]\!](\mathcal{S}[\![\text{read } x]\!](\langle\lambda\Xi.\bot, \phi_i, \text{nil}\rangle)))) \downarrow 3$$

The semantic equation for a simple input statement is

$$\mathcal{S}[\![\text{read } \Xi]\!]\gamma = (\phi_1 = \text{nil} \longrightarrow \top, \langle\sigma[hd(\phi_1)/\Xi], tl(\phi_1), \phi_2\rangle)$$
$$\text{where } \sigma = \gamma \downarrow 1, \phi_1 = \gamma \downarrow 2, \phi_2 = \gamma \downarrow 3$$

This states that the configuration produced when the $\mathbf{Cf} \rightarrow \mathbf{Cf}$ function denoted by a statement **read** Ξ is applied to a configuration $\gamma = \langle \sigma, \phi_1, \phi_2 \rangle$ consists of (1) a state which is the same as σ except that it maps Ξ into the head of ϕ_1, (2) an input file component which is the tail of ϕ_1, and (3) an output file component which is the same as ϕ_2. Note that $\top$ corresponds to an erroneous situation. For our example, let σ' be the state that maps x into the first element of ϕ_i and all other variables into $\bot$, and let σ'' be the state that maps x into the first element of ϕ_i, y into the second element of ϕ_i, and all other variables into $\bot$. Then we have

$$\mathfrak{M}[\![\textbf{read } x, y \; ; \; \textbf{write } y]\!]\phi_i$$
$$= (\mathcal{S}[\![\textbf{write } y]\!](\mathcal{S}[\![\textbf{read } y]\!](\langle\sigma', tl(\phi_i), \text{nil}\rangle))) \downarrow 3$$
$$= (\mathcal{S}[\![\textbf{write } y]\!](\langle\sigma'', tl(tl\phi_i)), \text{nil}\rangle)) \downarrow 3$$

The semantic function for a simple output statement is

$$\mathcal{S}[\![\textbf{write } \Xi]\!]\gamma = (\sigma[\![\Xi]\!] = \bot \rightarrow \top, \langle\sigma, \phi_1, append(\phi_2, \sigma[\![\Xi]\!])\rangle)$$
$$\text{where } \sigma = \gamma \downarrow 1, \; \phi_1 = \gamma \downarrow 2, \; \phi_2 = \gamma \downarrow 3$$

In other words, the $\mathbf{Cf} \rightarrow \mathbf{Cf}$ function denoted by **write** Ξ appends the current value $\sigma[\![\Xi]\!]$ of the variable Ξ to the output file component, and the configuration is otherwise unchanged. The analysis of our example can now be completed:

$$\mathfrak{M}[\![\textbf{read } x, y \; ; \; \textbf{write } y]\!]\phi_i$$
$$= \langle\sigma'', tl(tl(\phi_i)), \langle\sigma''[\![y]\!]\rangle\rangle \downarrow 3$$
$$= \langle\sigma'', tl(tl(\phi_i)), \langle hd(tl(\phi_i))\rangle\rangle \downarrow 3$$
$$= \langle hd(tl(\phi_i))\rangle$$

Thus we are able to say that the program

$$\textbf{read } x, y \; ; \; \textbf{write } y$$

denotes the function $hd \circ tl$ of the domain $\mathbf{Fi} \rightarrow \mathbf{Fi}$ provided that the input file has at least two values.

The semantic equation for assignment statements is

$$\mathcal{S}[\![\Xi := E]\!]\gamma = \langle\sigma[\mathcal{E}[\![E]\!]\sigma/\Xi], \phi_1, \phi_2\rangle$$
$$\text{where } \sigma = \gamma \downarrow 1, \phi_1 = \gamma \downarrow 2, \phi_2 = \gamma \downarrow 3$$

This makes use of a semantic function $\mathcal{E}: \mathbf{Exp} \rightarrow \mathbf{S} \rightarrow \mathbf{N}$, the definition of which will imply that the expression $\mathcal{E}[\![E]\!]\sigma$ yields the value of the expression E in the context of the state σ. Thus the $\mathbf{Cf} \rightarrow \mathbf{Cf}$ function denoted by

$\Xi := E$ updates the state so that Ξ is mapped into a new value and leaves the two file components unchanged.

For conditional statements, we need to make use of another semantic function $\mathcal{C}: \mathbf{Comp} \longrightarrow \mathbf{S} \longrightarrow \mathbf{T}$ which will be defined in such a way as to ensure that $\mathcal{C}[\![K]\!]\sigma$ yields *true* if and only if the comparison K holds in the context of the state σ. The semantic equation for **if-then-fi** statements is

$$\mathcal{S}[\![\text{if K then } \Sigma \text{ fi}]\!]\gamma = (\mathcal{C}[\![K]\!](\gamma \downarrow 1) \longrightarrow \mathcal{S}[\![\Sigma]\!]\gamma, \gamma)$$

where the right side is a conditional expression which yields either the configuration yielded by $\mathcal{S}[\![\Sigma]\!]\gamma$ if K holds in the current state $(\gamma \downarrow 1)$ or the original configuration γ otherwise. (In operational terms, the transformation specified by **if K then Σ fi** is the transformation specified by Σ if K holds in the current state and the identity transformation otherwise.) The extension to **if-then-else-fi** statements is straightforward:

$$\mathcal{S}[\![\text{if K then } \Sigma_1 \text{ else } \Sigma_2 \text{ fi}]\!]\gamma = (\mathcal{C}[\![K]\!](\gamma \downarrow 1) \longrightarrow \mathcal{S}[\![\Sigma_1]\!]\gamma, \mathcal{S}[\![\Sigma_2]\!]\gamma)$$

The transformation specified by a definite loop is the identity transformation if the value v of its limit expression is zero or negative (0 repetitions) and the transformation specified by its body repeated v times otherwise:

$$\mathcal{S}[\![\text{to E do } \Sigma \text{ end}]\!]\gamma = (v < 1 \longrightarrow \gamma, (\mathcal{S}[\![\Sigma]\!])^v\gamma)$$
$$\text{where } v = \mathcal{E}[\![E]\!](\gamma \downarrow 1)$$

The semantic equation defining indefinite loops should by this time be almost obvious:

$$\mathcal{S}[\![\text{while K do } \Sigma \text{ end}]\!]\gamma = (\mathcal{C}[\![K]\!](\gamma \downarrow 1) \longrightarrow (\mathcal{S}[\![\text{while K do } \Sigma \text{ end}]\!] \circ \mathcal{S}[\![\Sigma]\!])\gamma, \gamma)$$

Having completed the definition of $\mathcal{S}$, we turn now to the function $\mathcal{C}$, which maps comparisons $(K :: = E_1 \ P \ E_2)$ into functions in the domain $\mathbf{S} \longrightarrow \mathbf{T}$; i.e., the meaning of a comparison is a function mapping states into truth values. $\mathcal{C}$ is easily defined in terms of $\mathcal{E}$ by the following six equations:

$$\mathcal{C}[\![E_1 = E_2]\!]\sigma = (\mathcal{E}[\![E_1]\!]\sigma = \mathcal{E}[\![E_2]\!]\sigma \longrightarrow \textit{true, false})$$
$$\mathcal{C}[\![E_1 > E_2]\!]\sigma = (\mathcal{E}[\![E_1]\!]\sigma > \mathcal{E}[\![E_2]\!]\sigma \longrightarrow \textit{true, false})$$
$$\mathcal{C}[\![E_1 < E_2]\!]\sigma = (\mathcal{E}[\![E_1]\!]\sigma < \mathcal{E}[\![E_2]\!]\sigma \longrightarrow \textit{true, false})$$
$$\mathcal{C}[\![E_1 =< E_2]\!]\sigma = (\mathcal{E}[\![E_1]\!]\sigma \leq \mathcal{E}[\![E_2]\!]\sigma \longrightarrow \textit{true, false})$$
$$\mathcal{C}[\![E_1 >= E_2]\!]\sigma = (\mathcal{E}[\![E_1]\!]\sigma \geq \mathcal{E}[\![E_2]\!]\sigma \longrightarrow \textit{true, false})$$
$$\mathcal{C}[\![E_1 <> E_2]\!]\sigma = (\mathcal{E}[\![E_1]\!]\sigma \neq \mathcal{E}[\![E_2]\!]\sigma \longrightarrow \textit{true, false})$$

The function $\mathcal{E}$, as we have seen, maps expressions into functions in the domain $\mathbf{S} \rightarrow \mathbf{N}$; i.e., the meaning of an expression is a function mapping states into integers. The semantic equations for compound expressions are as follows:

$$\mathcal{E}[\![E_1 + E_2]\!]\sigma = \mathcal{E}[\![E_1]\!]\sigma + \mathcal{E}[\![E_2]\!]\sigma$$
$$\mathcal{E}[\![E_1 - E_2]\!]\sigma = \mathcal{E}[\![E_1]\!]\sigma - \mathcal{E}[\![E_2]\!]\sigma$$
$$\mathcal{E}[\![E_1 * E_2]\!]\sigma = \mathcal{E}[\![E_1]\!]\sigma \times \mathcal{E}[\![E_2]\!]\sigma$$
$$\mathcal{E}[\![E_1 / E_2]\!]\sigma = (\mathcal{E}[\![E_2]\!]\sigma = 0 \rightarrow \top, \mathcal{E}[\![E_1]\!]\sigma \div \mathcal{E}[\![E_2]\!]\sigma)$$

If an expression is a variable, we must check that it has a defined value:

$$\mathcal{E}[\![\Xi]\!]\sigma = (\sigma[\![\Xi]\!] = \bot \rightarrow \top, \sigma[\![\Xi]\!])$$

The value of a constant is independent of the state and is obtained in the obvious way from the decimal representation:

$$\mathcal{E}[\![N\Delta]\!]\sigma = 10 \times \mathcal{E}[\![N]\!]\sigma + \mathcal{E}[\![\Delta]\!]\sigma$$
$$\mathcal{E}[\![0]\!]\sigma = 0$$
$$\mathcal{E}[\![1]\!]\sigma = 1$$
$$\cdots$$
$$\mathcal{E}[\![9]\!]\sigma = 9$$

TABLE 4.3 Denotational Definition of the Semantics of Pam

Syntactic Domains

Ψ:	**Prog**	programs
Σ:	**Stmt**	statements
Ξ:	**Var**	variables
Λ:	**Vars**	lists of one or more variables
E:	**Exp**	expressions
K:	**Comp**	comparisons
P:	**Rel**	relations
Θ:	**Opr**	operators
N:	**Num**	integer constants
Δ:	**Dig**	decimal digits

Abstract Production Rules

$\Psi ::= \Sigma$

$\Sigma ::= \Sigma_1 \; ; \; \Sigma_2 \mid \textbf{read } \Lambda \mid \textbf{write } \Lambda \mid \Xi := E \mid$
$\quad \textbf{if } K \textbf{ then } \Sigma \textbf{ fi} \mid \textbf{if } K \textbf{ then } \Sigma_1 \textbf{ else } \Sigma_2 \textbf{ fi} \mid$
$\quad \textbf{to } E \textbf{ do } \Sigma \textbf{ end} \mid \textbf{while } K \textbf{ do } \Sigma \textbf{ end}$

$\Lambda ::= \Xi \mid \Lambda_1 \, , \, \Lambda_2$

TABLE 4.3 (Continued)

$$K ::= E_1 \ P \ E_2$$
$$E ::= E_1 \ \Theta \ E_2 \mid \Xi \mid N$$
$$N ::= \Delta \mid N \ \Delta$$
$$P ::= \ = \mid > \mid < \mid =< \mid >= \mid <>$$
$$\Theta ::= \ + \mid - \mid * \mid /$$
$$\Delta ::= \ 0 \mid 1 \mid 2 \mid 3 \mid 4 \mid 5 \mid 6 \mid 7 \mid 8 \mid 9$$

Semantic Domains

τ: $\mathbf{T} = \{true, false\}^\circ$	truth values
ν: $\mathbf{N} = \{\dots, -2, -1, 0, 1, 2, \dots\}^\circ$	integers
σ: $\mathbf{S} = \mathbf{Var} \longrightarrow \mathbf{N}$	states
ϕ: $\mathbf{Fi} = \mathbf{N}^*$	files
γ: $\mathbf{Cf} = \mathbf{S} \times \mathbf{Fi} \times \mathbf{Fi}$	configurations

Semantic Functions

$$\mathfrak{M}: \mathbf{Prog} \longrightarrow \mathbf{Fi} \longrightarrow \mathbf{Fi}$$
$$\mathfrak{S}: \mathbf{Stmt} \longrightarrow \mathbf{Cf} \longrightarrow \mathbf{Cf}$$
$$\mathfrak{C}: \mathbf{Comp} \longrightarrow \mathbf{S} \longrightarrow \mathbf{T}$$
$$\mathfrak{E}: \mathbf{Exp} \longrightarrow \mathbf{S} \longrightarrow \mathbf{N}$$

Semantic Equations

$\mathfrak{M}[\![\Psi]\!]\phi_i = (\mathfrak{S}[\![\Psi]\!](\langle\lambda\Xi.\bot, \phi_i, \text{nil}\rangle)) \downarrow 3$

$\mathfrak{S}[\![\Sigma_1 ; \Sigma_2]\!] = \mathfrak{S}[\![\Sigma_2]\!] \circ \mathfrak{S}[\![\Sigma_1]\!]$

$\mathfrak{S}[\![\text{read } \Lambda_1, \Lambda_2]\!] = \mathfrak{S}[\![\text{read } \Lambda_1 \ ; \ \text{read } \Lambda_2]\!]$

$\mathfrak{S}[\![\text{write } \Lambda_1, \Lambda_2]\!] = \mathfrak{S}[\![\text{write } \Lambda_1 \ ; \ \text{write } \Lambda_2]\!]$

$\mathfrak{S}[\![\text{read } \Xi]\!]\gamma = (\phi_1 = \text{nil} \longrightarrow \top, \langle\sigma[hd(\phi_1)/\Xi], tl(\phi_1), \phi_2\rangle)$
  where $\sigma = \gamma \downarrow 1, \phi_1 = \gamma \downarrow 2, \phi_2 = \gamma \downarrow 3$

$\mathfrak{S}[\![\text{write } \Xi]\!]\gamma = (\sigma[\![\Xi]\!] = \bot \longrightarrow \top, \langle\sigma, \phi_1, append(\phi_2, \sigma[\![\Xi]\!])\rangle)$
  where $\sigma = \gamma \downarrow 1, \phi_1 = \gamma \downarrow 2, \phi_2 = \gamma \downarrow 3$

$\mathfrak{S}[\![\Xi := E]\!]\gamma = \langle\sigma[\mathfrak{E}[\![E]\!]\sigma/\Xi], \phi_1, \phi_2\rangle$
  where $\sigma = \gamma \downarrow 1, \phi_1 = \gamma \downarrow 2, \phi_2 = \gamma \downarrow 3$

$\mathfrak{S}[\![\text{if K then } \Sigma \text{ fi}]\!]\gamma = (\mathfrak{C}[\![K]\!](\gamma \downarrow 1) \longrightarrow \mathfrak{S}[\![\Sigma]\!]\gamma, \gamma)$

$\mathfrak{S}[\![\text{if K then } \Sigma_1 \text{ else } \Sigma_2 \text{ fi}]\!]\gamma = (\mathfrak{C}[\![K]\!](\gamma \downarrow 1) \longrightarrow \mathfrak{S}[\![\Sigma_1]\!]\gamma, \mathfrak{S}[\![\Sigma_2]\!]\gamma)$

$\mathfrak{S}[\![\text{to E do } \Sigma \text{ end}]\!]\gamma = (\nu < 1 \longrightarrow \gamma, (\mathfrak{S}[\![\Sigma]\!])^\nu\gamma)$
  where $\nu = \mathfrak{E}[\![E]\!](\gamma \downarrow 1)$

$\mathfrak{S}[\![\text{while K do } \Sigma \text{ end}]\!]\gamma = (\mathfrak{C}[\![K]\!](\gamma \downarrow 1) \longrightarrow (\mathfrak{S}[\![\text{while K do } \Sigma \text{ end}]\!] \circ \mathfrak{S}[\![\Sigma]\!])\gamma, \gamma)$

$\mathfrak{C}[\![E_1 = E_2]\!]\sigma = (\mathfrak{E}[\![E_1]\!]\sigma = \mathfrak{E}[\![E_2]\!]\sigma \longrightarrow true, false)$

$\mathfrak{C}[\![E_1 > E_2]\!]\sigma = (\mathfrak{E}[\![E_1]\!]\sigma > \mathfrak{E}[\![E_2]\!]\sigma \longrightarrow true, false)$

TABLE 4.3   (Continued)

$\mathcal{C}[\![E_1 < E_2]\!]\sigma = (\mathcal{E}[\![E_1]\!]\sigma < \mathcal{E}[\![E_2]\!]\sigma \longrightarrow true, false)$

$\mathcal{C}[\![E_1 =< E_2]\!]\sigma = (\mathcal{E}[\![E_1]\!]\sigma \le \mathcal{E}[\![E_2]\!]\sigma \longrightarrow true, false)$

$\mathcal{C}[\![E_1 >= E_2]\!]\sigma = (\mathcal{E}[\![E_1]\!]\sigma \ge \mathcal{E}[\![E_2]\!]\sigma \longrightarrow true, false)$

$\mathcal{C}[\![E_1 <> E_2]\!]\sigma = (\mathcal{E}[\![E_1]\!]\sigma \neq \mathcal{E}[\![E_2]\!]\sigma \longrightarrow true, false)$

$\mathcal{E}[\![E_1 + E_2]\!]\sigma = \mathcal{E}[\![E_1]\!]\sigma + \mathcal{E}[\![E_2]\!]\sigma$

$\mathcal{E}[\![E_1 - E_2]\!]\sigma = \mathcal{E}[\![E_1]\!]\sigma - \mathcal{E}[\![E_2]\!]\sigma$

$\mathcal{E}[\![E_1 * E_2]\!]\sigma = \mathcal{E}[\![E_1]\!]\sigma \times \mathcal{E}[\![E_2]\!]\sigma$

$\mathcal{E}[\![E_1 / E_2]\!]\sigma = (\mathcal{E}[\![E_2]\!]\sigma = 0 \longrightarrow \top, \mathcal{E}[\![E_1]\!]\sigma \div \mathcal{E}[\![E_2]\!]\sigma)$

$\mathcal{E}[\![E]\!]\sigma = (\sigma[\![\Xi]\!] = \perp \longrightarrow \top, \sigma[\![\Xi]\!])$

$\mathcal{E}[\![N\Delta]\!]\sigma = 10 \times \mathcal{E}[\![N]\!]\sigma + \mathcal{E}[\![\Delta]\!]\sigma$

$\mathcal{E}[\![0]\!]\sigma = 0$

$\mathcal{E}[\![1]\!]\sigma = 1$

$\dots$

$\mathcal{E}[\![9]\!]\sigma = 9$

EXERCISES

1. If it were possible for Pam expressions to have state-altering side effects, as is the case in several common languages, then it might be appropriate to redefine the functionality of $\mathcal{E}$ as $\mathbf{Exp} \longrightarrow \mathbf{S} \longrightarrow \mathbf{N} \times \mathbf{S}$. Under this assumption, rewrite the semantic equations for $\mathcal{E}[\![0]\!]$ and $\mathcal{S}[\![\Xi := E]\!]$.

2. Referring to Table 4.3, give detailed elaborations of the meanings of the following programs:
   (a) **read** a ;
       if $a = 0$ **then read** b ; **write** b **else write** a **fi**
   (b) $n := 2$;
       to n **do write** n ; $n := n + 1$ **end**
   (c) **read** k ;
       while $k > 0$ **do** $k := k - 1$ **end** ;
       write k

4.2.3 The Denotational Semantics of Eva

Moving on to the more difficult of our miniature languages, the following syntactic domains and corresponding metavariables are suitable for purposes of a denotational definition of Eva:

Ψ:	**Prog**	programs
B:	**Blo**	blocks
Δ:	**Dec**	declarations
I:	**Ide**	identifiers (names)
T:	**Type**	data types
Σ:	**Stmt**	statements
E:	**Exp**	expressions
Ξ:	**Str**	literal strings
Λ:	**Let**	letters

In the following abstract syntax rules, declaration sequences and statement sequences are specified in a simple and harmlessly ambiguous manner, while parameter and argument lists are specified by a simple elliptic notational device where it is assumed that $n \geq 1$:

$$\Psi ::= B$$
$$B ::= \textbf{begin } \Delta \ \Sigma \ \textbf{end}$$
$$\Delta ::= \Delta_1 \ \Delta_2 \mid T \ I \mid \textbf{proc } I = \Sigma \mid$$
$$\textbf{proc } I \ (T_1 \ I_1, \ \ldots, \ T_n \ I_n) = \Sigma$$
$$T ::= \textbf{char} \mid \textbf{string}$$
$$\Sigma ::= \Sigma_1 \ \Sigma_2 \mid \textbf{input } I \mid \textbf{output } E \mid \textbf{call } I \mid$$
$$\textbf{call } I \ (E_1, \ \ldots, \ E_n) \mid B \mid \textbf{eq } E_1, E_2: \Sigma \mid$$
$$\textbf{neq } E_1, E_2: \Sigma \mid \textbf{cons } E, I$$
$$E ::= I \mid \text{""} \mid \text{"}\Lambda\text{"} \mid \text{"}\Xi\text{"} \mid \textbf{space} \mid \textbf{head } E \mid \textbf{tail } E$$
$$\Xi ::= \Lambda \mid \Xi\Lambda$$
$$\Lambda ::= a \mid b \mid \ldots \mid z$$

These abstract production rules do not enforce the various context conditions of Eva's syntax. A truly complete definition of the language would have to include a component dealing with this aspect, but, since we are concentrating our attention on semantics in this chapter, we shall merely assume that the additional specifications exist and that abstract programs will always be syntactically valid.

Values of Eva variables are either character values or string values. The former may be modeled by the primitive semantic domain **H** and the latter by the list domain **Z**:

$$\eta: \textbf{H} = \{a, \ b, \ \ldots, \ z, \ space\}^\circ$$
$$\zeta: \textbf{Z} = \textbf{H}^*$$

Because the same identifiers may represent different variables (or procedures) in different parts of an Eva program, we cannot simply define a "state" domain as a domain of functions mapping identifiers into values, as we did in the case of Pam. Instead, it is necessary to introduce a primitive domain **L** of *locations*, such as

$$\alpha: \mathbf{L} \,=\, \{1,\ 2,\ 3,\ \ldots\}^{\circ}$$

into which identifiers are mapped by an *environment* function ρ and which is itself mapped into a domain of values by a *store* function σ. Thus $\rho[\![I]\!]$ could be a location α "allocated" to the name I (double brackets are used because I belongs to a syntactic domain) and $\sigma(\rho[\![I]\!])\ (=\ \sigma\alpha)$ the character or string value of I, given a particular environment ρ and a particular store σ. Formally, the domain of stores is defined by

$$\sigma: \mathbf{S} \,=\, \mathbf{L} \longrightarrow \mathbf{V}$$

where **V**, the domain of storable values, is defined by

$$\beta: \mathbf{V} \,=\, \mathbf{H} \,+\, \mathbf{Z} \,+\, \{unallocated\}^{\circ}$$

We shall arrange that, if $\alpha \neq \rho[\![I]\!]$ for any identifier I and a given environment ρ, then the value of $\sigma\alpha$ will be *unallocated*. In operational terms, the current store may be irreversibly altered by each execution of a statement, whereas the current environment changes (reversibly) only when there is a shift from one scope level to another, as determined by the static structure of the program. Thus it is appropriate to regard procedures not as storable values but as entities which, like locations, are directly represented by identifiers and hence retrievable from an environment alone. The domain **U** of environments, then, is not simply **Ide** $\longrightarrow$ **L** but **Ide** $\longrightarrow$ **P** + **L**, where **P** is a domain of procedure values still to be defined. It is convenient to introduce **D** as the domain of denotable values—values directly representable by identifiers—and specify

$$\rho: \mathbf{U} \,=\, \mathbf{Ide} \longrightarrow \mathbf{D}$$
$$\delta: \mathbf{D} \,=\, \mathbf{P} \,+\, \mathbf{L}$$

Now, if a certain identifier I is known to be a variable as opposed to a procedure name, it will be necessary to write $\sigma(\rho[\![I]\!] \mid \mathbf{L})$ instead of simply $\sigma(\rho[\![I]\!])$.

As in the denotational definition of Pam, we define a domain **Cf** of configurations; here each configuration γ will consist of a store, an input file, and an output file, where each file is a string of characters:

$$\gamma: \mathbf{Cf} \,=\, \mathbf{S} \,\times\, \mathbf{Z} \,\times\, \mathbf{Z}$$

Now the domain **P** of procedure values is defined as

$$\pi: \mathbf{P} = \mathbf{L}^* \rightarrow \mathbf{Cf} \rightarrow \mathbf{Cf}$$

That is to say, a procedure value is basically a $\mathbf{Cf} \rightarrow \mathbf{Cf}$ function given by the procedure's body, but this function also depends on the arguments supplied when the procedure is called. A common model for the call-by-value discipline for argument-parameter correspondence is that, whenever a procedure is called, its parameters are allocated new locations which are initialized with the values of the arguments. A procedure value π will have to be supplied with a list of these locations before it will yield a particular $\mathbf{Cf} \rightarrow \mathbf{Cf}$ function.

Moving on from semantic domains to semantic functions now, the meaning $\mathfrak{M}[\![\Psi]\!]$ of a program Ψ is considered to be a function mapping input files into output files:

$$\mathfrak{M}: \mathbf{Prog} \rightarrow \mathbf{Z} \rightarrow \mathbf{Z}$$

The meanings of individual statements and expressions are also analogous to those of the Pam constructs, except that they depend on an environment value:

$$\mathfrak{S}: \mathbf{Stmt} \rightarrow \mathbf{U} \rightarrow \mathbf{Cf} \rightarrow \mathbf{Cf}$$

$$\mathfrak{E}: \mathbf{Exp} \rightarrow \mathbf{U} \rightarrow \mathbf{S} \rightarrow \mathbf{V}$$

Thus, the meaning $\mathfrak{S}[\![\Sigma]\!]$ of a statement Σ is a function mapping environments into $\mathbf{Cf} \rightarrow \mathbf{Cf}$ functions and, given a particular environment ρ, $\mathfrak{S}[\![\Sigma]\!]\rho$ is the $\mathbf{Cf} \rightarrow \mathbf{Cf}$ function denoted by Σ in the context of ρ. Similarly, the meaning $\mathfrak{E}[\![E]\!]$ of an expression E is a function mapping environments into $\mathbf{S} \rightarrow \mathbf{V}$ functions and, given a particular environment ρ, $\mathfrak{E}[\![E]\!]\rho$ is the $\mathbf{S} \rightarrow \mathbf{V}$ function denoted by E relative to ρ. To deal with declarations and the construction of environments, we also need a fourth semantic function $\mathfrak{D}$ to be described below.

For any program Ψ, the initial store is that in which all locations are unallocated, and the initial configuration is

$$\langle \lambda\alpha.unallocated, \zeta_i, nil \rangle$$

where ζ_i is the initial input file. The final configuration is obtained by supplying this as an argument to the $\mathbf{Cf} \rightarrow \mathbf{Cf}$ function denoted by Ψ considered as a statement relative to an initial environment $(\lambda I. \bot)$ in which all identifiers have undefined denotations. The third component of the final configuration is the output of the program, so that the semantic equation for $\mathfrak{M}$ may be written as

$$\mathfrak{M}[\![\Psi]\!]\zeta_i = (\mathfrak{S}[\![\Psi]\!](\lambda I.\bot)(\langle \lambda\alpha.unallocated, \zeta_i, nil \rangle)) \downarrow 3$$

In this equation, Ψ considered as a statement is a block of the form **begin** Δ Σ **end**. Intuitively, the $\mathbf{Cf} \longrightarrow \mathbf{Cf}$ transformation denoted by the block is just the $\mathbf{Cf} \longrightarrow \mathbf{Cf}$ transformation denoted by Σ; however, while the former has to be defined in the context of some outer environment ρ, the latter must be defined in the context of a modified environment ρ' in which the declarations Δ are taken into account. Moreover, the store component σ' of the initial configuration for Σ differs from that (σ) of the initial configuration for the entire block in that it maps the new locations associated with identifiers in ρ' into values other than *unallocated*, viz., $\perp$ for character variables and 'nil' for string variables. Thus we need a semantic equation along the lines of

$$\mathcal{S}[\![\text{begin } \Delta \Sigma \text{ end}]\!]\rho(\langle\sigma, \zeta_1, \zeta_2\rangle) = \mathcal{S}[\![\Sigma]\!]\rho'(\langle\sigma', \zeta_1, \zeta_2\rangle)$$

where ρ' and σ' are obtained by modifying ρ and σ in accordance with Δ. The equation will define the $\mathbf{U} \longrightarrow \mathbf{Cf} \longrightarrow \mathbf{Cf}$ function denoted by the block in terms of the $\mathbf{Cf} \longrightarrow \mathbf{Cf}$ function produced from a typical argument ρ, and the $\mathbf{Cf} \longrightarrow \mathbf{Cf}$ function will itself be defined in terms of the configuration produced from a typical argument $\langle\sigma, \zeta_1, \zeta_2\rangle$.

It is the task of the semantic function $\mathcal{D}$ to modify environments and stores as indicated above. Let us first try specifying the meanings of declarations as functions mapping pairs of the form $\langle\rho, \sigma\rangle$ into pairs of the form $\langle\rho', \sigma'\rangle$, so that we would have

$$\mathcal{D}: \mathbf{Dec} \longrightarrow (\mathbf{U} \times \mathbf{S}) \longrightarrow (\mathbf{U} \times \mathbf{S})$$

For a declaration of the form **char** I, ρ' should be the same as ρ except that it maps I into some location α which was mapped into *unallocated* by the old state σ, and σ' should be the same as σ except that it maps α into the $\perp$ element of the domain $\mathbf{H}$; i.e., we would have the equation

$$\mathcal{D}[\![\text{char } I]\!](\langle\rho, \sigma\rangle) = \langle\rho[\alpha \text{ in } D/I], \sigma[\perp/\alpha]\rangle$$
$$\text{where } \sigma\alpha = \textit{unallocated}$$

The equation for **string** I would be similar, except that σ' would map α into 'nil' of the domain $\mathbf{Z}$. The meaning of a sequence of declarations would be obtained simply by composing the meanings of its constituents:

$$\mathcal{D}[\![\Delta_1\Delta_2]\!] = \mathcal{D}[\![\Delta_2]\!] \circ \mathcal{D}[\![\Delta_1]\!]$$

When we consider procedure declarations, however, we run into trouble. The declaration of a procedure with no parameters, for example, should involve no change in the store, and the equation should be along the lines of

$$\mathcal{D}[\![\text{proc } I = \Sigma]\!](\langle\rho, \sigma\rangle) = \langle\rho[\pi \text{ in } D/I], \sigma\rangle$$

where the procedure value π is a $\mathbf{L^*} \rightarrow \mathbf{Cf} \rightarrow \mathbf{Cf}$ function which, given the argument 'nil', produces the $\mathbf{Cf} \rightarrow \mathbf{Cf}$ function denoted by Σ. But, since a procedure may be recursive and may reference names whose declarations occur after the procedure in the program, the latter function must be defined relative to the environment which incorporates *all* the declarations at the current level; the only environment, ρ, that we have available incorporates only those declarations preceding the procedure declaration.

To get around this difficulty, we respecify the functionality of $\mathfrak{D}$ as

$$\mathfrak{D}: \mathbf{Dec} \longrightarrow \mathbf{U} \longrightarrow (\mathbf{U} \times \mathbf{S}) \longrightarrow (\mathbf{U} \times \mathbf{S})$$

and arrange that the argument given to $\mathfrak{D}[\![\Delta]\!]$ will always be the environment incorporating the entire sequence of declarations of which Δ is a part. In the semantic equation for blocks, then, we specify that

$$\rho' = \mathfrak{D}[\![\Delta]\!]\rho'(\langle\rho, \sigma\rangle) \downarrow 1$$

and that

$$\sigma' = \mathfrak{D}[\![\Delta]\!]\rho'(\langle\rho, \sigma\rangle) \downarrow 2$$

Now a procedure value can always be defined relative to the correct environment, and we have the equations

$$\mathfrak{D}[\![\Delta_1 \, \Delta_2]\!]\rho' = \mathfrak{D}[\![\Delta_2]\!]\rho' \circ \mathfrak{D}[\![\Delta_1]\!]\rho'$$

$$\mathfrak{D}[\![\mathbf{char} \; I]\!]\rho'(\langle\rho, \sigma\rangle) = \langle\rho[\alpha \text{ in } \mathbf{D}/I], \sigma[\perp/\alpha]\rangle$$
$$\text{where } \sigma\alpha = \textit{unallocated}$$

$$\mathfrak{D}[\![\mathbf{string} \; I]\!]\rho'(\langle\rho, \sigma\rangle) = \langle\rho[\sigma \text{ in } \mathbf{D}/I], \sigma[\text{nil}/\alpha]\rangle$$
$$\text{where } \sigma\alpha = \textit{unallocated}$$

$$\mathfrak{D}[\![\mathbf{proc} \; I = \Sigma]\!]\rho'(\langle\rho, \sigma\rangle) = \langle\rho[\pi \text{ in } \mathbf{D}/I], \sigma\rangle$$
$$\text{where } \pi(\text{nil}) = \mathbf{S}[\![\Sigma]\!]\rho'$$

For a procedure with n parameters, the procedure value is a $\mathbf{L^*} \rightarrow \mathbf{Cf} \rightarrow \mathbf{Cf}$ function which, given as argument a list of n (new) locations, produces the $\mathbf{Cf} \rightarrow \mathbf{Cf}$ function denoted by the body relative to the environment obtained by updating ρ' so that the parameter names are mapped into these locations:

$$\mathfrak{D}[\![\mathbf{proc} \; I \; (T_1 \; I_1, \ldots, T_n \; I_n) = \Sigma]\!]\rho'(\langle\rho, \sigma\rangle) = \langle\rho[\pi \text{ in } \mathbf{D}/I], \sigma\rangle$$
$$\text{where } \pi(\langle\alpha_1, \ldots, \alpha_n\rangle) = \mathbf{S}[\![\Sigma]\!](\rho'[\alpha_1 \text{ in } \mathbf{D}/I_1, \ldots, \alpha_n \text{ in } \mathbf{D}/I_n])$$

The allocation and initialization of the parameter locations will be handled by the semantic specification for call statements.

In order to gain a better feeling for these equations, let us consider a program Ψ of the following form:

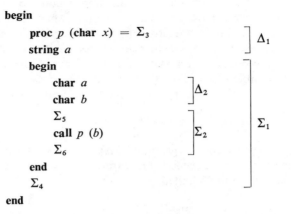

```
begin
    proc p (char x) = Σ₃
    string a
    begin
        char a
        char b
        Σ₅
        call p (b)
        Σ₆
    end
    Σ₄
end
```

Let ρ_0 be $\lambda I.\bot$ and σ_0 be $\lambda\alpha.unallocated$. Then the semantic equation for blocks tells us that

$$\mathcal{S}[\![\Psi]\!]\rho_0(\langle\sigma_0, \zeta_1, \zeta_2\rangle) = \mathcal{S}[\![\Sigma_1]\!]\rho_1(\langle\sigma_1, \zeta_1, \zeta_2\rangle)$$
$$\text{where } \langle\rho_1, \sigma_1\rangle = \mathcal{D}[\![\Delta_1]\!]\rho_1(\langle\rho_0, \sigma_0\rangle)$$

Now, using the equations for $\mathcal{D}$,

$$\mathcal{D}[\![\Delta_1]\!]\rho_1(\langle\rho_0, \sigma_0\rangle)$$
$$= (\mathcal{D}[\![\textbf{string } a]\!]\rho_1 \circ \mathcal{D}[\![\textbf{proc } p \text{ (char } x) = \Sigma_3]\!]\rho_1)(\langle\rho_0, \sigma_0\rangle)$$
$$= \mathcal{D}[\![\textbf{string } a]\!]\rho_1(\mathcal{D}[\![\textbf{proc } p \text{ (char } x) = \Sigma_3]\!]\rho_1(\langle\rho_0, \sigma_0\rangle))$$
$$= \mathcal{D}[\![\textbf{string } a]\!]\rho_1(\langle\rho_0[\pi/p], \sigma_0\rangle)$$
$$\text{(where } \pi(\langle\alpha\rangle) = \mathcal{S}[\![\Sigma_3]\!](\rho_1[\alpha/x]))$$
$$= \langle\rho_0[\pi/p, \alpha_1/a], \sigma_0[nil/\alpha_1]\rangle$$

Thus $\sigma_1 = \sigma_0[nil/\alpha_1]$ and

$$\rho_1 = \rho_0[\pi/p, \alpha_1/a]$$
$$\text{where } \pi(\langle\alpha\rangle) = \mathcal{S}[\![\Sigma_3]\!](\rho_1[\alpha/x])$$

The semantic equation for statement sequences is

$$\mathcal{S}[\![\Sigma_1 \ \Sigma_2]\!]\rho = \mathcal{S}[\![\Sigma_2]\!]\rho \circ \mathcal{S}[\![\Sigma_1]\!]\rho$$

Thus, for our example,

$$\mathcal{S}[\![\Sigma_1]\!]\rho_1(\langle\sigma_1, \zeta_1, \zeta_2\rangle)$$
$$= \mathcal{S}[\![\textbf{begin } \Delta_2 \ \Sigma_2 \textbf{ end } \Sigma_4]\!]\rho_1(\langle\sigma_1, \zeta_1, \zeta_2\rangle)$$

$$= (S[\![\Sigma_4]\!]\rho_1 \circ S[\![\text{begin } \Delta_2\ \Sigma_2\ \text{end}]\!]\rho_1)(\langle\sigma_1, \zeta_1, \zeta_2\rangle)$$
$$= S[\![\Sigma_4]\!]\rho_1(S[\![\text{begin } \Delta_2\ \Sigma_2\ \text{end}]\!]\rho_1(\langle\sigma_1, \zeta_1, \zeta_2\rangle))$$
$$= S[\![\Sigma_4]\!]\rho_1(S[\![\Sigma_2]\!]\rho_2(\langle\sigma_2, \zeta_1, \zeta_2\rangle))$$
$$\text{where } \langle\rho_2, \sigma_2\rangle = \mathfrak{D}[\![\Delta_2]\!]\rho_2(\langle\rho_1, \sigma_1\rangle)$$

Note that the meaning of Σ_4 is defined relative to a different environment (ρ_1) from that (ρ_2) used for Σ_2; this corresponds to the concept of local declarations losing their effect upon exit from a block. Now let us compute ρ_2 and σ_2:

$$\mathfrak{D}[\![\Delta_2]\!]\rho_2(\langle\rho_1, \sigma_1\rangle)$$
$$= (\mathfrak{D}[\![\text{char } b]\!]\rho_2 \circ \mathfrak{D}[\![\text{char } a]\!]\rho_2)(\langle\rho_1, \sigma_1\rangle)$$
$$= \mathfrak{D}[\![\text{char } b]\!]\rho_2(\mathfrak{D}[\![\text{char } a]\!]\rho_2(\langle\rho_1, \sigma_1\rangle))$$
$$= \mathfrak{D}[\![\text{char } b]\!]\rho_2(\langle\rho_1[\alpha_2/a], \sigma_1[\bot/\alpha_2]\rangle)$$
$$= \langle\rho_1[\alpha_2/a, \alpha_3/b], \sigma_1[\bot/\alpha_2, \bot/\alpha_3]\rangle$$
$$= \langle\rho_0[\pi/p, \alpha_2/a, \alpha_3/b], \sigma_0[\text{nil}/\alpha_1, \bot/\alpha_2, \bot/\alpha_3]\rangle$$
$$(\text{where } \alpha_1 \neq \alpha_2 \neq \alpha_3)$$

As we would expect, the location (α_1) corresponding to the outer a is not accessible in the inner block, where all references to a will access α_2.

According to the equation for statement sequences, and assuming that $S[\![\Sigma_5]\!]\rho_2(\langle\sigma_2, \zeta_1, \zeta_2\rangle)$ results in $\langle\sigma_3, \zeta_3, \zeta_4\rangle$, the expression

$$S[\![\Sigma_4]\!]\rho_1(S[\![\Sigma_2]\!]\rho_2(\langle\sigma_2, \zeta_1, \zeta_2\rangle))$$

becomes

$$S[\![\Sigma_4]\!]\rho_1(S[\![\Sigma_6]\!]\rho_2(S[\![\text{call } p(b)]\!]\rho_2(\langle\sigma_3, \zeta_3, \zeta_4\rangle)))$$

The semantic equation for calls of procedures with parameters expresses the fact that the procedure value $(\rho[\![I]\!] \mid \mathbf{P},$ where ρ is the environment of the call) must be supplied with a list of new, distinct locations followed by a configuration which differs from the given one in that these locations are mapped into the values obtained by evaluating the argument expressions in the environment ρ:

$$S[\![\text{call } I\ (E_1, \ldots, E_n)]\!]\rho\gamma = (\rho[\![I]\!] \mid \mathbf{P})(\langle\alpha_1, \ldots, \alpha_n\rangle)(\sigma', \zeta_1, \zeta_2)$$
$$\text{where } \zeta_1 = \gamma\downarrow 2, \zeta_2 = \gamma\downarrow 3, \sigma' = \sigma[\mathcal{E}[\![E_1]\!]\rho\sigma/\alpha_1, \ldots, \mathcal{E}[\![E_n]\!]\rho\sigma/\alpha_n]$$
$$\text{where } \sigma = \gamma\downarrow 1, \sigma\alpha_i = \textit{unallocated}\ (1 \leq i \leq n), \alpha_i \neq \alpha_j \text{ if}$$
$$i \neq j (1 \leq i \leq n, 1 \leq j \leq n)$$

Thus we have, for our example,

$$S[\![\Sigma_4]\!]\rho_1(S[\![\Sigma_6]\!]\rho_2(S[\![\text{call } p\ (b)]\!]\rho_2(\langle\sigma_3, \zeta_3, \zeta_4\rangle)))$$
$$= S[\![\Sigma_4]\!]\rho_1(S[\![\Sigma_6]\!]\rho_2(\pi(\langle\alpha_4\rangle)(\langle\sigma_3[\mathcal{E}[\![b]\!]\rho_2\sigma_3/\alpha_4], \zeta_3, \zeta_4\rangle)))$$
$$= S[\![\Sigma_4]\!]\rho_1(S[\![\Sigma_6]\!]\rho_2(S[\![\Sigma_3]\!](\rho_1[\alpha_4/x])(\langle\sigma_3[\mathcal{E}[\![b]\!]\rho_2\sigma_3/\alpha_4], \zeta_3, \zeta_4\rangle)))$$

Since we have not specified what the statements Σ_3 through Σ_6 are, there is little more that we can get out of this example, but the important thing to note is how the meaning of each statement is defined relative to the environment appropriate to it and how the store is expanded and altered in an irreversible manner.

The semantic equation for calls of parameterless procedures is simply

$$\mathcal{S}[\![\mathbf{call}\ I]\!]\rho = (\rho[\![I]\!] \mid \mathbf{P})(\text{nil})$$

and the equations for the remaining types of statement are relatively straight-forward:

$\mathcal{S}[\![\mathbf{input}\ I]\!]\rho\gamma = (\zeta_1 = \text{nil} \longrightarrow \top, \langle\sigma[(hd(\zeta_1)\ \text{in}\ \mathbf{V})/(\rho[\![I]\!]\mid\mathbf{L})],\ tl(\zeta_1),\ \zeta_2\rangle$

    where $\sigma = \gamma\downarrow 1,\ \zeta_1 = \gamma\downarrow 2,\ \zeta_2 = \gamma\downarrow 3$

$\mathcal{S}[\![\mathbf{output}\ E]\!]\rho\gamma = \langle\sigma,\ \zeta_1,\ append\ (\zeta_2,\ \mathcal{E}[\![E]\!]\rho\sigma \mid \mathbf{H})\rangle$

    where $\sigma = \gamma\downarrow 1,\ \zeta_1 = \gamma\downarrow 2,\ \zeta_2 = \gamma\downarrow 3$

$\mathcal{S}[\![\mathbf{eq}\ E_1, E_2: \Sigma]\!]\rho\gamma = (\mathcal{E}[\![E_1]\!]\rho\sigma = \mathcal{E}[\![E_2]\!]\rho\sigma \longrightarrow \mathcal{S}[\![\Sigma]\!]\rho\gamma,\ \gamma)$

    where $\sigma = \gamma\downarrow 1$

$\mathcal{S}[\![\mathbf{neq}\ E_1, E_2: \Sigma]\!]\rho\gamma = (\mathcal{E}[\![E_1]\!]\rho\sigma \neq \mathcal{E}[\![E_2]\!]\rho\sigma \longrightarrow \mathcal{S}[\![\Sigma]\!]\rho\gamma,\ \gamma)$

    where $\sigma = \gamma\downarrow 1$

$\mathcal{S}[\![\mathbf{cons}\ E, I]\!]\rho\gamma = \langle\sigma[(prefix(\mathcal{E}[\![E]\!]\rho\sigma\mid\mathbf{H},\ \sigma(\rho[\![I]\!]\mid\mathbf{L})\mid\mathbf{Z})\ \text{in}\ \mathbf{V})/\rho[\![I]\!]\mid\mathbf{L})],\ \zeta_1, \zeta_2\rangle$

    where $\sigma = \gamma\downarrow 1,\ \zeta_1 = \gamma\downarrow 2,\ \zeta_2 = \gamma\downarrow 3$

Finally, the following equations specify the semantics of expressions:

$$\mathcal{E}[\![I]\!]\rho\sigma = (\sigma(\rho[\![I]\!]\mid\mathbf{L}) = \bot \longrightarrow \top, \sigma(\rho[\![I]\!]\mid\mathbf{L}))$$

$$\mathcal{E}[\![``"]\!]\rho\sigma = \text{nil in}\ \mathbf{V}$$

$$\mathcal{E}[\![``a"]\!]\rho\sigma = a\ \text{in}\ \mathbf{V}$$

$$\ldots$$

$$\mathcal{E}[\![``z"]\!]\rho\sigma = z\ \text{in}\ \mathbf{V}$$

$$\mathcal{E}[\![``\Xi a"]\!]\rho\sigma = append(\mathcal{E}[\![``\Xi"]\!]\rho\sigma\mid\mathbf{Z}, a)\ \text{in}\ \mathbf{V}$$

$$\ldots$$

$$\mathcal{E}[\![``\Xi z"]\!]\rho\sigma = append(\mathcal{E}[\![``\Xi"]\!]\rho\sigma\mid\mathbf{Z}, z)\ \text{in}\ \mathbf{V}$$

$$\mathcal{E}[\![\mathbf{space}]\!]\rho\sigma = space\ \text{in}\ \mathbf{V}$$

$\mathcal{E}[\![\mathbf{head}\ E]\!]\rho\sigma = (\zeta \neq \text{nil} \longrightarrow hd(\zeta), \top)\ \text{in}\ \mathbf{V}$

    where $\zeta = \mathcal{E}[\![E]\!]\rho\sigma\mid\mathbf{Z}$

$\mathcal{E}[\![\mathbf{tail}\ E]\!]\rho\sigma = (\zeta \neq \text{nil} \longrightarrow tl(\zeta), \top)\ \text{in}\ \mathbf{V}$

    where $\zeta = \mathcal{E}[\![E]\!]\rho\sigma\mid\mathbf{Z}$

The complete denotational definition of Eva is summarized in Table 4.4, pp. 190–92.

As a simple illustration of the fact that our equations correctly define the meanings of constructs involving recursive procedures, consider the following program Ψ:

> **begin**
>
> > **proc** p = (
> >
> > > **input** c
> > >
> > > **eq** c, "z": **call** p)
> >
> > **char** c
> >
> > **call** p
>
> **end**

Letting $\rho_0 = \lambda I.\bot$ and $\sigma_0 = \lambda\alpha.unallocated$ as before, we would expect $\mathcal{S}[\![\Psi]\!]\rho_0(\langle\sigma_0, \langle z, y, x\rangle, \text{nil}\rangle)$ to evaluate to a configuration of the form $\langle\sigma_1, \langle x\rangle, \text{nil}\rangle$. Taking $\sigma' = \sigma_0[\bot/\alpha_1]$, $\sigma'' = \sigma_0[z/\alpha_1]$, $\sigma''' = \sigma_0[y/\alpha_1]$, and

$$\rho' = \rho_0[\pi/p, \alpha/c]$$
$$\text{where } \pi(\text{nil}) = \mathcal{S}[\![\text{input } c \text{ eq } c, \text{"}z\text{": call } p]\!]\rho'$$

the following evaluation sequence may be verified:

$$\mathcal{S}[\![\Psi]\!]\rho_0(\langle\sigma_0, \langle z, y, x\rangle, \text{nil}\rangle)$$
$$= \mathcal{S}[\![\text{call } p]\!]\rho'(\langle\sigma', \langle z, y, x\rangle, \text{nil}\rangle)$$
$$= \pi(\text{nil})(\langle\sigma', \langle z, y, x\rangle, \text{nil}\rangle)$$
$$= \mathcal{S}[\![\text{input } c \text{ eq } c, \text{"}z\text{": call } p]\!]\rho'(\langle\sigma', \langle z, y, x\rangle, \text{nil}\rangle)$$
$$= \mathcal{S}[\![\text{eq } c, \text{"}z\text{": call } p]\!]\rho'(\mathcal{S}[\![\text{input } c]\!]\rho'(\langle\sigma', \langle z, y, x\rangle, \text{nil}\rangle))$$
$$= \mathcal{S}[\![\text{eq } c, \text{"}z\text{": call } p]\!]\rho'(\langle\sigma'', \langle y, x\rangle, \text{nil}\rangle)$$
$$= \mathcal{S}[\![\text{call } p]\!]\rho'(\langle\sigma'', \langle y, x\rangle, \text{nil}\rangle)$$
$$= \pi(\text{nil})(\langle\sigma'', \langle y, x\rangle, \text{nil}\rangle)$$
$$= \mathcal{S}[\![\text{input } c \text{ eq } c, \text{"}z\text{": call } p]\!]\rho'(\langle\sigma'', \langle y, x\rangle, \text{nil}\rangle)$$
$$= \mathcal{S}[\![\text{eq } c, \text{"}z\text{": call } p]\!]\rho'(\mathcal{S}[\![\text{input } c]\!]\rho'(\langle\sigma'', \langle y, x\rangle, \text{nil}\rangle))$$
$$= \mathcal{S}[\![\text{eq } c, \text{"}z\text{": call } p]\!]\rho'(\langle\sigma''', \langle x\rangle, \text{nil}\rangle)$$
$$= \langle\sigma''', \langle x\rangle, \text{nil}\rangle$$

The reader should be aware that our treatment of the denotational approach has been quite incomplete and very much simplified compared with the descriptions of other approaches in this book. The devices we have used to write the sample specifications are merely the tip of a mathematical iceberg; in many cases, especially those involving the use of metalinguistic recursion, the devices can be mathematically justified on the basis of the underlying theory to guarantee that the specifications do indeed adequately map the various constructs into well-defined, abstract mathematical objects. It should also be noted that our sample evaluations of functions are not typical of the general mathematical analyses of program properties carried out by language theorists; these evaluations merely provided a simple means of gaining an intuitive feeling for the semantic equations. For the semantic specification of more realistic languages, additional theoretical and notational devices and methods of using these devices must be brought into play. In order to deal with **goto** statements and related control structures, for example, it is necessary to introduce domains of special functions known as *continuations*. All these topics, although very important, are beyond the scope of this primer; those readers with sufficient motivation and aptitude should consult the literature sources devoted to the denotational approach.

TABLE 4.4   Denotational Definition of the Semantics of Eva

Syntactic Domains

Ψ:	**Prog**	programs
B:	**Blo**	blocks
Δ:	**Dec**	declarations
I:	**Ide**	identifiers (names)
T:	**Type**	data types
Σ:	**Stmt**	statements
E:	**Exp**	expressions
Ξ:	**Str**	literal strings
Λ:	**Let**	letters

Abstract Production Rules

$\Psi ::= B$

$B ::= $ **begin** Δ Σ **end**

$\Delta ::= \Delta_1 \Delta_2 \mid T I \mid$ **proc** $I = \Sigma \mid$
$\qquad$ **proc** $I (T_1 I_1, \ldots, T_n I_n) = \Sigma$

$T ::= $ **char** $\mid$ **string**

$\Sigma ::= \Sigma_1 \Sigma_2 \mid$ **input** $I \mid$ **output** $E \mid$ **call** $I \mid$
$\qquad$ **call** $I (E_1, \ldots, E_n) \mid B \mid$ **eq** $E_1, E_2 : \Sigma \mid$
$\qquad$ **neq** $E_1, E_2 : \Sigma \mid$ **cons** E, I

$E ::= I \mid$ "" $\mid$ "Λ" $\mid$ "Ξ" $\mid$ **space** $\mid$ **head** $E \mid$ **tail** E

$\Xi ::= \Lambda \mid \Xi\Lambda$

$\Lambda ::= a \mid b \mid \ldots \mid z$

TABLE 4.4 (Continued)

Semantic Domains

$$\eta: \mathbf{H} = \{a, b, \ldots, z, \textit{space}\}^\circ \qquad \text{characters}$$
$$\zeta: \mathbf{Z} = \mathbf{H}^* \qquad\qquad\qquad\qquad \text{strings}$$
$$\pi: \mathbf{P} = \mathbf{L}^* \longrightarrow \mathbf{Cf} \longrightarrow \mathbf{Cf} \qquad \text{procedures}$$
$$\alpha: \mathbf{L} = \{1, 2, 3, \ldots\}^\circ \qquad\qquad \text{locations}$$
$$\sigma: \mathbf{S} = \mathbf{L} \longrightarrow \mathbf{V} \qquad\qquad \text{stores}$$
$$\rho: \mathbf{U} = \mathbf{Ide} \longrightarrow \mathbf{D} \qquad\qquad \text{environments}$$
$$\delta: \mathbf{D} = \mathbf{P} + \mathbf{L} \qquad\qquad\quad \text{denotable values}$$
$$\beta: \mathbf{V} = \mathbf{H} + \mathbf{Z} + \{\textit{unallocated}\}^\circ \quad \text{storable values}$$
$$\gamma: \mathbf{Cf} = \mathbf{S} \times \mathbf{Z} \times \mathbf{Z} \qquad\qquad \text{configurations}$$

Semantic Functions

$$\mathfrak{M}: \mathbf{Prog} \longrightarrow \mathbf{Z} \longrightarrow \mathbf{Z}$$
$$\mathfrak{S}: \mathbf{Stmt} \longrightarrow \mathbf{U} \longrightarrow \mathbf{Cf} \longrightarrow \mathbf{Cf}$$
$$\mathfrak{D}: \mathbf{Dec} \longrightarrow \mathbf{U} \longrightarrow (\mathbf{U} \times \mathbf{S}) \longrightarrow (\mathbf{U} \times \mathbf{S})$$
$$\mathcal{E}: \mathbf{Exp} \longrightarrow \mathbf{U} \longrightarrow \mathbf{S} \longrightarrow \mathbf{V}$$

Semantic Equations

$\mathfrak{M}[\![\Psi]\!]\zeta_i = (\mathfrak{S}[\![\Psi]\!](\lambda \mathrm{I}.\bot)(\langle \lambda \alpha.\textit{unallocated}, \zeta_i, \mathrm{nil}\rangle)) \downarrow 3$

$\mathfrak{S}[\![\Sigma_1 \Sigma_2]\!]\rho = \mathfrak{S}[\![\Sigma_2]\!]\rho \circ \mathfrak{S}[\![\Sigma_1]\!]\rho$

$\mathfrak{S}[\![\textbf{input } \mathrm{I}]\!]\rho\gamma = (\zeta_1 = \mathrm{nil} \longrightarrow \top, \langle \sigma[(hd(\zeta_1) \text{ in } \mathbf{V})/(\rho[\![\mathrm{I}]\!] \,|\, \mathbf{L})], \, tl(\zeta_1), \zeta_2\rangle)$

    where $\sigma = \gamma \downarrow 1, \zeta_1 = \gamma \downarrow 2, \zeta_2 = \gamma \downarrow 3$

$\mathfrak{S}[\![\textbf{output } \mathrm{E}]\!]\rho\gamma = \langle \sigma, \zeta_1, \textit{append}\,(\zeta_2, \mathcal{E}[\![\mathrm{E}]\!]\rho\sigma \,|\, \mathbf{H})\rangle$

    where $\sigma = \gamma \downarrow 1, \zeta_1 = \gamma \downarrow 2, \zeta_2 = \gamma \downarrow 3$

$\mathfrak{S}[\![\textbf{call } \mathrm{I}]\!]\rho = (\rho[\![\mathrm{I}]\!] \,|\, \mathbf{P})(\mathrm{nil})$

$\mathfrak{S}[\![\textbf{call } \mathrm{I}\, (\mathrm{E}_1, \ldots, \mathrm{E}_n)]\!]\rho\gamma = (\rho[\![\mathrm{I}]\!] \,|\, \mathbf{P})(\langle \alpha_1, \ldots, \alpha_n\rangle)(\langle \sigma', \zeta_1, \zeta_2\rangle)$

    where $\zeta_1 = \gamma \downarrow 2, \zeta_2 = \gamma \downarrow 3, \sigma' = \sigma[\mathcal{E}[\![\mathrm{E}_1]\!]\rho\sigma/\alpha_1, \ldots, \mathcal{E}[\![\mathrm{E}_n]\!]\rho\sigma/\alpha_n]$

        where $\sigma = \gamma \downarrow 1, \sigma\alpha_i = \textit{unallocated } (1 \leq i \leq n), \; \alpha_i \neq \alpha_j$

                                  if $i \neq j\,(1 \leq i \leq n, 1 \leq j \leq n)$

$\mathfrak{S}[\![\textbf{begin } \Delta \Sigma \textbf{ end}]\!]\rho\gamma = \mathfrak{S}[\![\Sigma]\!]\rho'(\langle \sigma', \zeta_1, \zeta_2\rangle)$

    where $\zeta_1 = \gamma \downarrow 2, \zeta_2 = \gamma \downarrow 3, \langle \rho', \sigma'\rangle = \mathfrak{D}[\![\Delta]\!]\rho'(\langle \rho, \sigma\rangle)$

        where $\sigma = \gamma \downarrow 1$

$\mathfrak{S}[\![\textbf{eq } \mathrm{E}_1, \mathrm{E}_2 \colon \Sigma]\!]\rho\gamma = (\mathcal{E}[\![\mathrm{E}_1]\!]\rho\sigma = \mathcal{E}[\![\mathrm{E}_2]\!]\rho\sigma \longrightarrow \mathfrak{S}[\![\Sigma]\!]\rho\gamma, \gamma)$

    where $\sigma = \gamma \downarrow 1$

$\mathfrak{S}[\![\textbf{neq } \mathrm{E}_1, \mathrm{E}_2 \colon \Sigma]\!]\rho\gamma = (\mathcal{E}[\![\mathrm{E}_1]\!]\rho\sigma \neq \mathcal{E}[\![\mathrm{E}_2]\!]\rho\sigma \longrightarrow \mathfrak{S}[\![\Sigma]\!]\rho\gamma, \gamma)$

    where $\sigma = \gamma \downarrow 1$

$\mathfrak{S}[\![\textbf{cons } \mathrm{E}, \mathrm{I}]\!]\rho\gamma = \langle \sigma[(\textit{prefix }(\mathcal{E}[\![\mathrm{E}]\!]\rho\sigma \,|\, \mathbf{H}, \sigma(\rho[\![\mathrm{I}]\!] \,|\, \mathbf{L}) \,|\, \mathbf{Z}) \text{ in } \mathbf{V})/(\rho[\![\mathrm{I}]\!] \,|\, \mathbf{L})], \zeta_1, \zeta_2\rangle$

    where $\sigma = \gamma \downarrow 1, \zeta_1 = \gamma \downarrow 2, \zeta_2 = \gamma \downarrow 3$

TABLE 4.4   (Continued)

$\mathfrak{D}[\![\Delta_1 \Delta_2]\!]\rho' = \mathfrak{D}[\![\Delta_2]\!]\rho' \circ \mathfrak{D}[\![\Delta_1]\!]\rho'$

$\mathfrak{D}[\![\text{char I}]\!]\rho'(\langle\rho, \sigma\rangle) = \langle\rho[\alpha \text{ in } \mathbf{D}/\mathrm{I}], \sigma[\bot/\alpha]\rangle$

    where $\sigma\alpha = $ *unallocated*

$\mathfrak{D}[\![\text{string I}]\!]\rho'(\langle\rho, \sigma\rangle) = \langle\rho[\alpha \text{ in } \mathbf{D}/\mathrm{I}], \sigma[\text{nil}/\alpha]\rangle$

    where $\sigma\alpha = $ *unallocated*

$\mathfrak{D}[\![\text{proc I} = \Sigma]\!]\rho'(\langle\rho, \sigma\rangle) = \langle\rho[\pi \text{ in } \mathbf{D}/\mathrm{I}], \sigma\rangle$

    where $\pi(\text{nil}) = \mathcal{S}[\![\Sigma]\!]\rho'$

$\mathfrak{D}[\![\text{proc I} (\mathrm{T}_1\,\mathrm{I}_1, \ldots, \mathrm{T}_n\,\mathrm{I}_n) = \Sigma]\!]\rho'(\langle\rho, \sigma\rangle) = \langle\rho[\pi \text{ in } \mathbf{D}/\mathrm{I}], \sigma\rangle$

    where $\pi(\langle\alpha_1, \ldots, \alpha_n\rangle) = \mathcal{S}[\![\Sigma]\!](\rho'[\alpha_1 \text{ in } \mathbf{D}/\mathrm{I}_1, \ldots, \alpha_n \text{ in } \mathbf{D}/\mathrm{I}_n])$

$\mathcal{E}[\![\mathrm{I}]\!]\rho\sigma = (\sigma(\rho[\![\mathrm{I}]\!] \mid \mathbf{L}) = \bot \longrightarrow \top, \sigma(\rho[\![\mathrm{I}]\!] \mid \mathbf{L}))$

$\mathcal{E}[\![\text{""}]\!]\rho\sigma = \text{nil in } \mathbf{V}$

$\mathcal{E}[\![\text{"}a\text{"}]\!]\rho\sigma = a \text{ in } \mathbf{V}$

$\cdots$

$\mathcal{E}[\![\text{"}z\text{"}]\!]\rho\sigma = z \text{ in } \mathbf{V}$

$\mathcal{E}[\![\text{"}\Xi a\text{"}]\!]\rho\sigma = append\,(\mathcal{E}[\![\text{"}\Xi\text{"}]\!]\rho\sigma \mid \mathbf{Z}, a) \text{ in } \mathbf{V}$

$\cdots$

$\mathcal{E}[\![\text{"}\Xi z\text{"}]\!]\rho\sigma = append\,(\mathcal{E}[\![\text{"}\Xi\text{"}]\!]\rho\sigma \mid \mathbf{Z}, z) \text{ in } \mathbf{V}$

$\mathcal{E}[\![\text{space}]\!]\rho\sigma = space \text{ in } \mathbf{V}$

$\mathcal{E}[\![\text{head E}]\!]\rho\sigma = (\zeta \neq \text{nil} \longrightarrow hd\,(\zeta), \top) \text{ in } \mathbf{V}$

    where $\zeta = \mathcal{E}[\![\mathrm{E}]\!]\rho\sigma \mid \mathbf{Z}$

$\mathcal{E}[\![\text{tail E}]\!]\rho\sigma = (\zeta \neq \text{nil} \longrightarrow tl\,(\zeta), \top) \text{ in } \mathbf{V}$

    where $\zeta = \mathcal{E}[\![\mathrm{E}]\!]\rho\sigma \mid \mathbf{Z}$

EXERCISES

1. Determine what modifications to the semantic equations of Table 4.4 would be necessary if Eva followed the "call-by-reference" parameter discipline, as found in PL/I and other common languages, instead of the "call-by-value" discipline.

2. By giving a detailed elaboration of each according to the semantic equations, show that the following programs are semantically equivalent:

  (a) **begin**
        char c
        input c
        output c
   end

  (b) **begin**
        string s
        proc $p = ($
           char c
           input c
           cons c, s)
        call p
        output head s
   end

The denotational approach is introduced very briefly in the book by Brady (1977) and more thoroughly in the tutorial paper by Tennent (1976). As for book-length treatments, there is the text by Stoy (1977) and the rather formidable, two-volume monograph by Milne and Strachey (1976). References to the basic literature on the mathematical theory, developed by D. Scott and others, may be found in these sources. Mosses (1976) discusses one way in which the approach might be applied to the problem of compiler generation, while Tennent (1977) and Donahue (1977) are concerned with its implications for language design. An alternative metalinguistic notation and examples of its use, including a denotational definition of Algol 60, are described by Bjørner and Jones (1978).

4.3

THE AXIOMATIC APPROACH

4.3.1 Concepts and Characteristics

The *axiomatic* approach described in this part is by far the most abstract and "high-level" of all the semantic definition methods considered in this book. One of its basic tenets is that the semantics of a programming language may be considered to be sufficiently defined if the specifications enable one to prove any true statement (and no false statements) about the effect of executing any program or program segment. Accordingly, the specifications are somewhat analogous to the axioms and rules of inference of a logical calculus and constitute a formal system in which there is no explicit notion of the "state of a machine". They prescribe, in an abstract way, a minimal set of constraints that any implementation of the subject language must satisfy in its treatment of the various types of construct but say nothing about the details of how this might be achieved. The application for which axiomatic semantics is most useful is construction (by programmers) of proofs that programs possess various formal properties. Indeed, a set of axiomatic specifications for a particular subject language is sometimes said to constitute a *proof theory* for that language.

There is no single, comprehensive metalanguage for axiomatic semantics that is generally regarded as "standard", but the notational conventions adopted by different authors have many properties in common. In the first place, all the standard notation for logical expressions is available, including logical operators ($\wedge$, $\vee$, $\neg$, $\supset$, $=$ or $\equiv$), quantifiers ($\exists$, $\forall$), and logical constants (*true, false*). The purpose of forming a logical expression in this context is usually to make an *assertion* about the values of one or more program variables or the relationship between such values. Thus it is convenient to permit variables and constants of the subject language to appear within metalinguistic expressions; for example,

$$x + y < 10$$

could be an assertion about a program segment involving the integer variables x and y. Assuming that the subject language includes operators such as '$+$' and '$<$' conforming to the standard precedence conventions, etc., it may be possible to say that the metalanguage includes the logical expressions (and hence expressions of other types) of the subject language as a subset, thus removing the need to explicitly define the meaning of subject-language expressions.

In a sense, this may appear to be a form of "cheating" that will result in language specifications which are less complete or less detailed than those generated by other approaches. All we are doing, however, is to assume the existence of some trivial conversion functions which map the subject-language expressions into the corresponding metalanguage expressions. If the former are mathematically nonstandard, we may define the conversion functions explicitly in such a way that, for example, the Fortran expression X .LE. SQRT(Y) could appear as $x \leq \sqrt{y}$ in an assertion. We may also provide sets of axioms to characterize the properties of data types and operations that do not ordinarily appear in mathematical notation. It is true nonetheless that the version of the axiomatic approach to be described and illustrated here is strongly oriented toward the semantic description of statements as opposed to expressions and that it is less adaptable and less generally applicable than the other types of approach. With regard to the latter point, one restriction that is often imposed on the subject language is that expressions cannot have side effects (e.g., a function subprogram cannot change the value of a nonlocal variable). If the language does not satisfy all the restrictions of this sort, the method can still be used to give a partial (incomplete) specification of its semantics, i.e., a specification for that subset of the language consisting of programs in which the restrictions *are* satisfied. In such a case, it may be possible to augment the partial specification with some scheme for transforming an arbitrary program into an equivalent program belonging to the subset.

However these issues are resolved, we extend the class of assertions to include formulas of the form

$$\{P\} \, S \, \{Q\}$$

where P and Q are logical expressions as described above and S is a construct (usually a statement) of the subject language. (In some publications, the notation $P\{S\}Q$ is used instead of $\{P\}S\{Q\}$.) The interpretation of such an assertion is as follows:

> 'if P is true before the execution of S and if the execution of S terminates, then Q is true after the execution of S'.

P is said to be the *precondition* of the assertion and Q the *postcondition*. A particular assertion of this form may be either true or false. For example, we would certainly expect

$$\{x = 5\}\, x := x + 1\, \{x = 6\}$$

to be true and

$$\{y = 5\}\, x := x + 1\, \{y = 6\}$$

to be false. The basic aim of an axiomatic definition is to specify which assertions are true; these will be the ones that are the provable "theorems" of the formal system.

If the execution of S fails to terminate, then $\{P\}S\{Q\}$ is trivially true for any conditions P and Q. A proof of "correctness" of a program using these tools alone is actually only a proof of *partial correctness*, i.e., correctness subject to the *assumption* of termination. To verify the *total correctness* of a program, it is necessary to supplement the proof of partial correctness with a separate proof of termination constructed by other means.

The semantics of simple, unstructured statement forms can often be defined by *axiom schemata* consisting of generalized assertions. To start with a trivial example, the CONTINUE statement of Fortran, which is a dummy or "do-nothing" statement, can be defined by

$$\{P\}\ \text{CONTINUE}\ \{P\} \qquad\qquad \text{(Dummy)}$$

This tells us that any specific assertion about a CONTINUE statement is true if its precondition and postcondition are the same, so that the following assertions are among the (infinitely many) axioms we have specified:

$\{x = 1\}\,\text{CONTINUE}\,\{x = 1\}$

$\{(\forall k)(1 \leq k \leq n \supset a_k > b)\}\,\text{CONTINUE}\,\{(\forall k)(1 \leq k \leq n \supset a_k > b)$

$\{true\}\,\text{CONTINUE}\,\{true\}$

Since we obviously do not want any other assertions, such as

$$\{x = 1\}\,\text{CONTINUE}\,\{y = 1\}$$

to be true, the Dummy rule precisely captures our intuitive concept of what a CONTINUE statement means.

In writing specifications for other statement types, we shall assume a rudimentary form of abstract syntax in which single, uppercase letters (possibly primed or subscripted) correspond to BNF nonterminal symbols (except for P, Q, and R, which we reserve for use as symbols standing for arbitrary logical expressions). Thus $V := E$ is a typical form for assignment statements. Before giving an axiom schema for this construct, we introduce the notation P_E^V to stand for the logical expression obtained from P by substituting the expression E for all occurrences, if any, of the variable V.[3] More generally, $P_{E_1 \ldots E_n}^{V_1 \ldots V_n}$, where $V_1, \ldots, V_n$ are all distinct variables, stands for the expression obtained from P by simultaneous substitution of E_i for $V_i, i = 1, \ldots, n$.

The meaning of the assignment construct may now be specified as

$$\{P_E^V\}\ V := E\{P\} \qquad \text{(Assignment)}$$

For example, each of the following assertions holds:

$$\{a > b\}\, c := 5\, \{a > b\}$$
$$\{a > b + 5\}\, b := b + 5\, \{a > b\}$$
$$\{a > b\}\, b := b + 5\, \{a > b - 5\}$$

(where the precondition is obtained by simplifying $a > (b + 5) - 5$)

$$\{true\}\, c := 5\, \{c = 5\}$$

(where $true$ is obtained by simplifying $5 = 5$)

It may seem strange at first that the precondition should be derived from the postcondition rather than vice versa, but it turns out that this Assignment rule, as well as being simple, is very convenient to apply in constructing proofs about programs.

In addition to axiom schemata, an axiomatic specification of a programming language includes a number of *rules of inference* (also called *proof rules* or *deduction rules*), which enable the truth of certain assertions to be deduced from the truth of certain other assertions. Specifically, a rule of inference of the form

$$\frac{H_1, H_2, \ldots, H_n}{H}$$

where $H_1, H_2, \ldots, H_n, H$ are all generalized assertions, has the following interpretation:

'given that $H_1, H_2, \ldots, H_n$ are true, that H is true may be deduced'.

Further, a rule of inference of the form

$$\frac{H_1, H_2, \ldots, H_n \vdash H_{n+1}}{H}$$

[3] Strictly speaking, only the *free* (unquantified) occurrences of V are replaced by E. If P is $x = k \land (\exists k)(a_k > x)$, for example, then P_y^k is $x = y \land (\exists k)(a_k > x)$. Also, it may be necessary to rename some of P's quantified variables so as to avoid conflicts; in this example, P_k^x could be written as $k = k \land (\exists j)(a_j > k)$ but not as $k = k \land (\exists k)(a_k > k)$.

states that

> 'if the truth of H_{n+1} can be deduced by assuming the truth of $H_1, H_2, \ldots, H_n$, then the truth of H may be deduced'.

There are some useful rules of inference which are independent of the language being defined. First, it is intuitively obvious that the postcondition of an assertion may be "weakened" and that its precondition may be "strengthened" without jeopardizing its truth:

$$\frac{\{P\}\ S\ \{Q\},\ Q \supset R}{\{P\}S\{R\}} \qquad \text{(Consequence}_1)$$

$$\frac{P \supset Q,\ \{Q\}\ S\ \{R\}}{\{P\}S\{R\}} \qquad \text{(Consequence}_2)$$

To illustrate the use of these rules, we know from the Assignment rule that the following assertion holds:

$$\{x + y = a \wedge y > b\}\, x := x + y\, \{x = a \wedge y > b\}$$

Taking P to be $x + y = a \wedge y > b \wedge z < c$, Q to be $x + y = a \wedge y > b$, and R to be $x = a \wedge y > b$, we have $P \supset Q$ and hence, by the second Consequence rule,

$$\{x + y = a \wedge y > b \wedge z < c\}\, x := x + y\, \{x = a \wedge y > b\}$$

Now taking P to be $x + y = a \wedge y > b \wedge z < c$, Q to be $x = a \wedge y > b$, and R to be $x = a$, we have $Q \supset R$ and hence, by the first Consequence rule,

$$\{x + y = a \wedge y > b \wedge z < c\}\, x := x + y\, \{x = a\}$$

Another pair of general inference rules are the following:

$$\frac{\{P\}\ S\ \{Q\},\ \{P'\}\ S\ \{Q'\}}{\{P \wedge P'\}S\{Q \wedge Q'\}} \qquad \text{(And)}$$

$$\frac{\{P\}\ S\ \{Q\},\ \{P'\}\ S\ \{Q'\}}{\{P \vee P'\}\ S\ \{Q \vee Q'\}} \qquad \text{(Or)}$$

As an example, since we have both

$$\{x + y = a\}\, x := x + y\, \{x = a\}$$

and

$$\{x + y < b\}\, x := x + y\, \{x < b\}$$

by the Assignment rule, the Or rule permits us to conclude that

$$\{x + y = a \lor x + y < b\} \, x := x + y \, \{x = a \lor x < b\}$$

(This does not illustrate the real utility of the Or rule, however, since the final result also follows directly from the Assignment rule.)

Almost every programming language allows statements to be strung together in a sequence. We may regard the abstract syntax as permitting a statement S to consist of an ordered pair of statements $S_1 S_2$, where each of these could be another pair, etc. Thus any statement sequence can be analyzed in terms of pairs in various ways (Fig. 4.13), but the ambiguity is irrelevant as

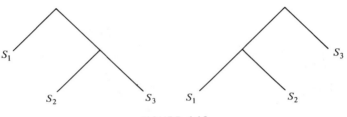

FIGURE 4.13

far as the semantics is concerned. With this in mind, the following rule of inference specifies the semantics of statement sequences:

$$\frac{\{P\} \, S_1 \, \{Q\}, \, \{Q\} \, S_2 \, \{R\}}{\{P\} \, S_1 \, S_2 \, \{R\}} \qquad \text{(Composition)}$$

As a simple example, if S_1 is $x := a$ and S_2 is $x := x + b$, then by the Assignment rule we have $\{true\} \, S_1 \, \{x = a\}$ and $\{x = a\} \, x := x + b \, \{x = a + b\}$ (after simplifying the second precondition $x + b = a + b$), so that the Composition rule permits us to deduce $\{true\} \, S_1 \, S_2 \, \{x = a + b\}$. This rule of inference is typical in that it defines the properties of a composite construct in terms of the properties of its constituents. Structured statement types such as loops and conditionals are generally specified in this way.

We have now been exposed to the basic ideas and notational conventions of the axiomatic approach and have seen some very elementary applications of them. An axiomatic specification of a subject language basically consists of a collection of axiom schemata and inference rules similar to the Dummy, Assignment, Consequence, And, Or, and Composition rules given above. In order to be certain that the specifications "make sense" and adequately characterize the semantics of the subject language, we really should give formal proofs of some sort that the individual rules are logically sound and that collectively they are both complete and consistent. Important as these concerns are, however, they are beyond the scope of this book. We shall confine ourselves to working through some examples of the use of the rules in correctness proofs, and even then the examples will be very short and simple.

EXERCISES

1. Give an example of an assertion about the statement

$$a := b - c + a$$

which is true by the Assignment rule. Give another assertion which follows from the first by virtue of
(a) the Consequence$_1$ rule,
(b) the Consequence$_2$ rule,
(c) the And rule, and
(d) the Or rule.

2. Using the Composition rule as well as the Assignment rule, give examples of true assertions of the form

$$\{P\}\, a := b - c + a \; ; \; a := b - c + a \; \{Q\}$$

4.3.2 The Axiomatic Semantics of Pam

The axiomatic specifications for Pam as summarized in Table 4.5, p. 204, are based upon the following rules of abstract syntax:

$$S ::= S_1; S_2 \mid \textbf{read } W \mid \textbf{write } W \mid V := E \mid$$
$$\textbf{if } B \textbf{ then } S \textbf{ fi} \mid \textbf{if } B \textbf{ then } S_1 \textbf{ else } S_2 \textbf{ fi} \mid$$
$$\textbf{to } E \textbf{ do } S \textbf{ end} \mid \textbf{while } B \textbf{ do } S \textbf{ end}$$
$$W ::= V \mid W_1, W_2$$

where S corresponds to ⟨series⟩ and ⟨statement⟩,
  W corresponds to ⟨variable list⟩,
  V corresponds to ⟨variable⟩,
  E corresponds to ⟨expression⟩,
  B corresponds to ⟨comparison⟩

We do not bother to spell out the alternatives for E and B or the mapping rules which ensure that such expressions will be written in standard mathematical notation when used metalinguistically within assertions (e.g., $a = < c * d$ would appear as $a \leq c \times d$). This rather cavalier treatment of the "lower" constructs of a language is customary in the axiomatic approach.

The Consequence, And, Or, Composition, and Assignment rules are the same as in Sec. 4.3.1. In order to define the meaning of **read** and **write** statements, we introduce the following notational conventions: (1) K stands for any integer value; (2) L stands for any sequence of zero or more integer values; (3) $\langle K_1, \ldots, K_n \rangle$ stands for the sequence composed of the values $K_1, \ldots, K_n$, and $\langle \rangle$ stands for the empty sequence; (4) concatenation of sequences is denoted by simple juxtaposition, so that, if $L = \langle K_1, K_2 \rangle$, then $L \langle K_3 \rangle L = \langle K_1, K_2, K_3, K_1, K_2 \rangle$; (5) the special variables IN and OUT correspond to the input and output files (sequences of integers), respectively. A **read** statement has the effect of removing the first value from the input file and assigning it to a certain variable; this is captured by the axiom schema

$$\{\text{IN} = \langle K \rangle L \wedge P_K^V\} \text{ read } V \{\text{IN} = L \wedge P\} \qquad \text{(Input)}$$

An output statement appends the current value of a certain variable to the output file and leaves everything else unchanged; one way of expressing this is as follows:

$$\{\text{OUT} = L \wedge P \wedge V = K\} \text{ write } V \{\text{OUT} = L \langle K \rangle \wedge P \wedge V = K\} \qquad \text{(Output)}$$

The following simple rules of inference imply that a **read** or **write** statement containing more than one variable is equivalent to a sequence of separate statements:

$$\frac{\{P\} \text{ read } W_1 \text{ ; read } W_2 \{Q\}}{\{P\} \text{ read } W_1, W_2 \{Q\}} \qquad \text{(Input Combination)}$$

$$\frac{\{P\} \text{ write } W_1 \text{ ; write } W_2 \{Q\}}{\{P\} \text{ write } W_1, W_2 \{Q\}} \qquad \text{(Output Combination)}$$

Before examining the remaining rules of Table 4.5, p. 204, let us check that the specifications we have introduced so far can indeed be used to verify the partial correctness of a simple example. We shall consider a program S consisting of

$$\text{read } x, y \text{ ; write } y$$

and prove the assertion

$$\{\text{IN} = \langle -2, 7, 1 \rangle \wedge \text{OUT} = \langle \rangle\} S \{\text{OUT} = \langle 7 \rangle\} \qquad (1)$$

The Composition rule tells us that, to deduce this result, it is sufficient to establish the validity of

$$\{\text{IN} = \langle -2, 7, 1 \rangle \wedge \text{OUT} = \langle \rangle\} \text{ read } x, y \{Q\} \qquad (2a)$$

for some logical expression Q, and of

$$\{Q\} \text{ write } y \{\text{OUT} = \langle 7 \rangle\} \qquad (2b)$$

for the same Q. If we take Q to be $y = 7 \wedge \text{OUT} = \langle \rangle$ (the obvious choice!), then (2b) becomes

$$\{y = 7 \wedge \text{OUT} = \langle \rangle\} \text{ write } y \{\text{OUT} = \langle 7 \rangle\} \qquad (2b')$$

By the first Consequence rule, this is deducible from

$$\{OUT = \diamondsuit \wedge \textit{true} \wedge y = 7\} \textbf{ write } y \{OUT = \langle 7 \rangle \wedge \textit{true} \wedge y = 7\} \quad (3)$$

which holds by virtue of the Output rule (since the precondition simplifies to $OUT = \diamondsuit \wedge y = 7$). It remains only to prove

$$\{IN = \langle -2, 7, 1 \rangle \wedge OUT = \diamondsuit\} \textbf{ read } x, y \{y = 7 \wedge OUT = \diamondsuit\} \quad (2a')$$

or rather, by the Input Combination rule,

$$\{IN = \langle -2, 7, 1 \rangle \wedge OUT = \diamondsuit\} \textbf{ read } x \textbf{ ; read } y \{y = 7 \wedge OUT = \diamondsuit\} \quad (4)$$

By the Composition rule again, it is sufficient to prove, for some Q,

$$\{IN = \langle -2, 7, 1 \rangle \wedge OUT = \diamondsuit\} \textbf{ read } x \{Q\} \quad (5a)$$

$$\{Q\} \textbf{ read } y \{y = 7 \wedge OUT = \diamondsuit\} \quad (5b)$$

Taking Q to be $IN = \langle 7, 1 \rangle \wedge OUT = \diamondsuit$, (5a) holds by virtue of the Input rule (using $OUT = \diamondsuit$ for both P and P_K^v), and the only thing that must now be proved is

$$\{IN = \langle 7, 1 \rangle \wedge OUT = \diamondsuit\} \textbf{ read } y \{y = 7 \wedge OUT = \diamondsuit\} \quad (5b')$$

According to the first Consequence rule, this is deducible from

$$\{IN = \langle 7, 1 \rangle \wedge OUT = \diamondsuit\} \textbf{ read } y \{IN = \langle 1 \rangle \wedge y = 7 \wedge OUT = \diamondsuit\} \quad (6)$$

which holds by virtue of the Input rule.

It may be noted that the foregoing argument proceeded in a "backwards", "outside-in", or "top-down" fashion; this approach is quite natural and correlates well with the precepts of structured programming. If we wish, we can go back and piece together a normal, "forward" version of the proof in which (1) appears as the theorem at the end:

Assertion	Justification
(6)	Input
(5b')	(6), Consequence$_1$
(5a')	Input
(4)	(5a'), (5b'), Composition
(2a')	(4), Input Combination
(3)	Output
(2b')	(3), Consequence$_1$
(1)	(2a'), (2b'), Composition

We will not bother to do this in subsequent examples.

Moving on to the remaining statement types, the rule of inference for constructs of the form **if** B **then** S_1 **else** S_2 **fi** is

$$\frac{\{P \wedge B\}\ S_1\ \{Q\},\ \{P \wedge \neg B\}\ S_2\ \{Q\}}{\{P\}\ \textbf{if}\ B\ \textbf{then}\ S_1\ \textbf{else}\ S_2\ \textbf{fi}\ \{Q\}} \qquad \text{(Selection}_2)$$

Essentially, this reflects the fact that the effect (precondition P, postcondition Q) of executing an entire conditional statement is the same as the effect of executing one of its constituents S_1 and S_2, with the added twist that S_1 is executed only if B (as well as P) is true initially and S_2 is executed only if B is false initially. As an elementary example, we certainly want to be able to deduce the truth of

$$\{true\}\ \textbf{if}\ a > b\ \textbf{then}\ x := 1\ \textbf{else}\ x := 2\ \textbf{fi}$$
$$\{(a > b \wedge x = 1) \vee (\neg(a > b) \wedge x = 2)\}$$

The Selection$_2$ rule does permit this, since the assertions

$$\{true \wedge a > b\}\ x := 1\ \{(a > b \wedge x = 1) \vee (\neg(a > b) \wedge x = 2)\}$$
$$\{true \wedge \neg(a > b)\}\ x := 2\ \{(a > b \wedge x = 1) \vee (\neg(a > b) \wedge x = 2)\}$$

both hold by virtue of the Assignment and Consequence$_1$ rules. The inference rule for statements of the form **if** B **then** S **fi** is a straightforward special case of Selection$_2$:

$$\frac{\{P \wedge B\}\ S\ \{Q\},\ P \wedge \neg B \supset Q}{\{P\}\ \textbf{if}\ B\ \textbf{then}\ S\ \textbf{fi}\ \{Q\}} \qquad \text{(Selection}_1)$$

A statement of the form **to** E **do** S **end** is equivalent to a statement sequence consisting of K copies of S, where K is the initial value of the expression E. Thus we should be able to infer the truth of an assertion $\{P\}$ **to** E **do** S **end** $\{Q\}$ from the truth of the K assertions $\{P\}S\{P_1\}$, $\{P_1\}\ S\{P_2\}$, ..., $\{P_{K-1}\}\ S\ \{Q\}$. The value of K is crucial here and we will stipulate that it must be determinable from the first precondition P. Renaming P as P_0 and Q as P_K, we have the rule of inference

$$\frac{P_0 \supset (E > 0 \wedge E = K),\ \{P_{i-1}\}\ S\ \{P_i\}\ \text{for}\ i = 1, \ldots, K}{\{P_0\}\ \textbf{to}\ E\ \textbf{do}\ S\ \textbf{end}\ \{P_K\}} \qquad \text{(Repetition}_2)$$

If K is zero or negative, the loop acts as a dummy statement:

$$\frac{P \supset E \leq 0}{\{P\}\ \textbf{to}\ E\ \textbf{do}\ S\ \textbf{end}\ \{P\}} \qquad \text{(Repetition}_1)$$

The final construct to be defined is **while** B **do** S **end**. Its rule of inference may be neatly formulated as follows:

$$\frac{\{P \wedge B\}\, S\, \{P\}}{\{P\}\, \textbf{while}\ B\ \textbf{do}\ S\ \textbf{end}\ \{P \wedge \neg B\}} \qquad \text{(Iteration)}$$

Here P is some *invariant* condition whose truth is unaffected by an execution of the loop body S and hence by any number of executions of S. Since S is only executed as long as B is true, B appears as well as P in its precondition. When execution of the entire construct is complete, P still holds but B is necessarily false. Of all the rules given in Table 4.5, the Iteration rule is the most powerful as far as program proving is concerned. It can also be the most difficult to apply, because it is not always easy to see what the invariant condition is in any particular case. The construction of significant proofs about substantial program segments is beyond the scope of this discussion, but, in order to gain a better feeling for the soundness of the Iteration rule, it is a worthwhile exercise to work through an example which, though small, is not entirely trivial.

The following statements S are intended to assign the quotient of $x \div 5$ to q and the corresponding remainder to r:

$$r := x\ ;\ q := 0\ ;$$
$$\textbf{while}\ 5\ =< \ r\ \textbf{do}\ r := r - 5\ ;\ q := q + 1\ \textbf{end}$$

Thus it should be possible to prove the assertion

$$\{true\}\, S\, \{(x = r + 5 \times q) \wedge \neg(5 \le r)\} \qquad (1)$$

By the Composition rule, it is sufficient to prove, for some Q,

$$\{true\}\, r := x\ ;\ q := 0\, \{Q\} \qquad (2a)$$

$$\{Q\}\, \textbf{while}\ 5\ =< \ r\ \textbf{do}\ r := r - 5\ ;\ q := q + 1\ \textbf{end}$$
$$\{(x = r + 5 \times q) \wedge \neg(5 \le r)\} \qquad (2b)$$

It is now quite obvious from (2b) and the Iteration rule that Q should be taken to be $x = r + 5 \times q$ and that this condition is the loop invariant. First, (2a) may be deduced by applying the Composition rule to the assertions

$$\{true\}\, r := x\, \{x = r + 0\} \qquad (3a)$$
$$\{x = r + 0\}\, q := 0\, \{x = r + 5 \times q\} \qquad (3b)$$

which, by carrying out some trivial algebraic manipulation, can be seen to follow from the Assignment rule. Turning to (2b), the Iteration rule tells us that we need only prove

$$\{(x = r + 5 \times q) \wedge (5 \le r)\}\, r := r - 5\ ;\ q := q + 1\, \{x = r + 5 \times q\} \qquad (4)$$

Now, by the Composition rule, it is sufficient to establish (5a) and (5b) for some Q:

$$\{(x = r + 5 \times q) \wedge (5 \leq r)\} \, r := r - 5 \, \{Q\} \tag{5a}$$

$$\{Q\} \, q := q + 1 \, \{x = r + 5 \times q\} \tag{5b}$$

Taking Q to be $x = r + 5 \times (q + 1)$, (5b) holds by the Assignment rule and (5a) becomes

$$\{(x = r + 5 \times q) \wedge (5 \leq r)\} \, r := r - 5 \, \{x = r + 5 \times (q + 1)\} \tag{5a'}$$

By the Assignment rule, we have

$$\{x = (r - 5) + 5 \times (q + 1)\} \, r := r - 5 \, \{x = r + 5 \times (q + 1)\} \tag{6}$$

From this, finally, the second Consequence rule permits us to deduce (5a'), since it can easily be shown that

$$((x = r + 5 \times q) \wedge (5 \leq r)) \supset (x = (r - 5) + 5 \times (q + 1))$$

TABLE 4.5   Axiomatic Definition of the Semantics of Pam

$\dfrac{\{P\} \, S \, \{Q\}, \ Q \supset R}{\{P\} \, S \, \{R\}}$	(Consequence₁)
$\dfrac{P \supset Q, \ \{Q\} \, S \, \{R\}}{\{P\} \, S \, \{R\}}$	(Consequence₂)
$\dfrac{\{P\} \, S \, \{Q\}, \ \{P'\} \, S \, \{Q'\}}{\{P \wedge P'\} \, S \, \{Q \wedge Q'\}}$	(And)
$\dfrac{\{P\} \, S \, \{Q\}, \ \{P'\} \, S \, \{Q'\}}{\{P \vee P'\} \, S \, \{Q \vee Q'\}}$	(Or)
$\dfrac{\{P\} \, S_1 \, \{Q\}, \ \{Q\} \, S_2 \, \{R\}}{\{P\} \, S_1 \, ; \, S_2 \, \{R\}}$	(Composition)
$\dfrac{\{P\} \, \textbf{read} \, W_1 \, ; \, \textbf{read} \, W_2 \, \{Q\}}{\{P\} \, \textbf{read} \, W_1, W_2 \, \{Q\}}$	(Input Combination)
$\dfrac{\{P\} \, \textbf{write} \, W_1 \, ; \, \textbf{write} \, W_2 \, \{Q\}}{\{P\} \, \textbf{write} \, W_1, W_2 \, \{Q\}}$	(Output Combination)
$\{\text{IN} = \langle K \rangle L \wedge P_K^V\} \, \textbf{read} \, V \, \{\text{IN} = L \wedge P\}$	(Input)
$\{\text{OUT} = L \wedge P \wedge V = K\} \, \textbf{write} \, V \, \{\text{OUT} = L\langle K \rangle \wedge P \wedge V = K\}$	(Output)
$\{P_E^V\} \, V := E \, \{P\}$	(Assignment)
$\dfrac{\{P \wedge B\} \, S \, \{Q\}, \ P \wedge \neg B \supset Q}{\{P\} \, \textbf{if} \, B \, \textbf{then} \, S \, \textbf{fi} \, \{Q\}}$	(Selection₁)
$\dfrac{\{P \wedge B\} \, S_1 \, \{Q\}, \ \{P \wedge \neg B\} \, S_2 \, \{Q\}}{\{P\} \, \textbf{if} \, B \, \textbf{then} \, S_1 \, \textbf{else} \, S_2 \, \textbf{fi} \, \{Q\}}$	(Selection₂)
$\dfrac{P \supset E \leq 0}{\{P\} \, \textbf{to} \, E \, \textbf{do} \, S \, \textbf{end} \, \{P\}}$	(Repetition₁)
$\dfrac{P_0 \supset (E > 0 \wedge E = K), \ \{P_{i-1}\} \, S \, \{P_i\} \ \text{for } i = 1, \ldots, K}{\{P_0\} \, \textbf{to} \, E \, \textbf{do} \, S \, \textbf{end} \, \{P_K\}}$	(Repetition₂)
$\dfrac{\{P \wedge B\} \, S \, \{P\}}{\{P\} \, \textbf{while} \, B \, \textbf{do} \, S \, \textbf{end} \, \{P \wedge \neg B\}}$	(Iteration)

1. Referring to Table 4.5, verify the following assertions:
   (a) $\{OUT = \langle\rangle\}\, n := 2$;

           to n **do write** n ; $n := n + 1$ **end**

     $\{OUT = \langle 2,3 \rangle\}$

   (b) $\{n \geq 0\}\, p := 1$; $i := n$;

        while $i > 0$ **do**

           $p := p * x$;

           $i := i - 1$

       end

     $\{p = x^n\}$

2. The rule of inference for the Pascal-type **repeat** statement may be formulated as

$$\frac{\{P\}\, S\, \{Q\},\ Q \wedge \neg B \supset P}{\{P\}\, \textbf{repeat}\ S\ \textbf{until}\ B\ \textbf{end}\ \{Q \wedge B\}}$$

If this construct were added to Pam, verify that the following assertion could be deduced:

$$\{x \geq 5\}\, r := x ; q := 0 ;$$
$$\textbf{repeat}\ r := r - 5 ;$$
$$q := q + 1$$
$$\textbf{until}\ r < 5$$
$$\textbf{end}$$
$$\{x = r + 5 \times q \wedge r < 5\}$$

4.3.3 The Axiomatic Semantics of Eva

For the purpose of giving axiomatic specifications for Eva, we assume the following rules for the abstract syntax of declarations and statements:

$B ::= \textbf{begin}\ D\ S\ \textbf{end}$

$D ::= D_1\ D_2 \mid T\ N \mid \textbf{proc}\ N = S \mid \textbf{proc}\ N\, (T_1\ N_1, \ldots, T_n\ N_n) = S$

$T ::= \textbf{char} \mid \textbf{string}$

$S ::= S_1\ S_2 \mid \textbf{input}\ N \mid \textbf{output}\ E \mid \textbf{call}\ N \mid \textbf{call}\ N\, (E_1, \ldots, E_n) \mid$

     $B \mid \textbf{eq}\ E_1, E_2 \colon S \mid \textbf{neq}\ E_1, E_2 \colon S \mid \textbf{cons}\ E, N$

where B corresponds to $\langle$block$\rangle$,

    D corresponds to $\langle$declaration sequence$\rangle$ and $\langle$declaration$\rangle$,

    T corresponds to $\langle$declarer$\rangle$ ("type"),

    S corresponds to $\langle$statement sequence$\rangle$ and $\langle$statement$\rangle$.

Of course, these rules do not in themselves enforce the context conditions that must be satisfied for a program to be syntactically legal. As usual, we assume that this is done by some independent means and that the semantic rules will never be applied to syntactically invalid programs.

We have seen that formal definitions of Eva are generally more difficult to construct than formal definitions of Pam, and this is especially true for the axiomatic approach. It turns out that one of the major sources of difficulty in this case is the possibility of the same names being used to denote different objects in different parts of a program, as in

```
begin
    string s
    proc p (string s, t) = (
        output head s
        ... )
    ...
    call p ("abc", s)
    ...
end
```

If we were to strengthen the context conditions of the language and insist that no name may be declared (or appear as a formal parameter) more than once in a program, there would be no loss of generality, because any program of the original language could be transformed into an equivalent program of the restricted language by a systematic substitution of names. For example, assuming that u does not appear anywhere in the foregoing program, that program can be transformed into either of the following:

```
begin                             begin
    string s                          string u
    proc p (string u, t) = (           proc p (string s, t) = (
        output head u                      output head s
        ... )                              ... )
    ...                               ...
    call p ("abc", s)                 call p ("abc", u)
    ...                               ...
end                               end
```

In our formulation of the axiomatic specifications (Table 4.6, p. 214) for Eva, it is assumed that all programs satisfy this restriction as well as some further restrictions mentioned later. Viewed by themselves, then, the specifications leave much to be desired with respect to completeness, but we may regard them as being supplemented by a set of rules for mapping arbitrary programs into equivalent restricted programs.

The Consequence, And, Or, Composition, Input, and Output rules are practically the same as before. In the rules

$$\{\text{IN} = \langle C\rangle L \wedge P_C^N\} \text{ input } N\{\text{IN} = L \wedge P\} \qquad \text{(Input)}$$

$$\{\text{OUT} = L \wedge P \wedge E = C\} \text{ output } E \{\text{OUT} = L\langle C\rangle \wedge P \wedge E = C\} \quad \text{(Output)}$$

C stands for any allowed character value and L stands for any sequence of zero or more character values. The construct **cons** E, N is actually a specialized kind of assignment statement and hence may be defined by the axiom schema

$$\{P_{\langle E\rangle N}^N\} \text{ cons } E, N \{P\} \qquad \text{(Concatenation)}$$

The basic rule of inference for blocks is

$$\frac{H \vdash \{P \wedge A\} S \{Q\}}{\{P\} \text{ begin } D S \text{ end } \{Q\}} \qquad \text{(Block)}$$

where A is an assertion and H a set of assertions implied by the set of declarations D. The set of assertions H is defined as follows: (1) each declaration of a parameterless procedure N with body S implies an assertion $body(N) = S$; (2) each declaration of a procedure N with parameters $N_1, \ldots, N_n$ and body S implies an assertion $body(N) = S$ and an assertion $params(N) = \langle N_1, \ldots, N_n\rangle$; (3) H contains only those assertions obtained from D in these ways. The assertion A is a condition of the form $true \wedge N_1 = \text{""} \wedge \ldots \wedge N_n = \text{""}$, where $N_1, \ldots, N_n$ are the string variables declared in D. The Block rule states that if $\{P \wedge A\} S \{Q\}$ can be proved by using the assertions in H as assumptions, then $\{P\}$ **begin** $D S$ **end** $\{Q\}$ may be deduced.

Before going any further, let us see how these specifications apply to the following simple, procedure-free example:

> **begin**
>> **char** c
>>
>> **string** s
>>
>> **input** c
>>
>> **cons** c, s
>>
>> **output head** s
>
> **end**

Suppose that we wish to verify the assertion

$$\{\text{IN} = \langle\text{``}a\text{''}\rangle \wedge \text{OUT} = \langle\rangle\} B \{\text{OUT} = \langle\text{``}a\text{''}\rangle\} \qquad (1)$$

where B is the entire block. According to the Block rule, all we need to prove is

$$\{\text{IN} = \langle \text{``}a\text{''}\rangle \wedge \text{OUT} = \diamondsuit \wedge s = \text{``''}\} \textbf{ input } c \textbf{ cons } c, s$$
$$\textbf{output head } s \{\text{OUT} = \langle \text{``}a\text{''}\rangle\} \qquad (2)$$

The Composition rule permits (2) to be replaced by (3a) and (3b):

$$\{\text{IN} = \langle \text{``}a\text{''}\rangle \wedge \text{OUT} = \diamondsuit \wedge s = \text{``''}\} \textbf{ input } c$$
$$\{c = \text{``}a\text{''} \wedge \text{OUT} = \diamondsuit \wedge s = \text{``''}\} \qquad (3a)$$
$$\{c = \text{``}a\text{''} \wedge \text{OUT} = \diamondsuit \wedge s = \text{``''}\} \textbf{ cons } c, s$$
$$\textbf{output head } s \{\text{OUT} = \langle \text{``}a\text{''}\rangle\} \qquad (3b)$$

Assertion (3a) follows easily from the Input and Consequence rules, and (3b) can be reduced by the Composition rule to

$$\{c = \text{``}a\text{''} \wedge \text{OUT} = \diamondsuit \wedge s = \text{``''}\} \textbf{ cons } c, s \{s = \text{``}a\text{''} \wedge \text{OUT} = \diamondsuit\} \quad (4a)$$
$$\{s = \text{``}a\text{''} < \text{OUT} = \diamondsuit\} \textbf{ output head } s \{\text{OUT} = \langle \text{``}a\text{''}\rangle\} \qquad (4b)$$

The Concatenation rule tells us directly that

$$\{\langle c\rangle s = \text{``}a\text{''} \wedge \text{OUT} = \diamondsuit\} \textbf{ cons } c, s \{s = \text{``}a\text{''} \wedge \text{OUT} = \diamondsuit\} \qquad (5)$$

and since $(\langle c\rangle s = \text{``}a\text{''}) \supset (c = \text{``}a\text{''} \wedge s = \text{``''})$, (4a) is established by the second Consequence rule. The Output rule tells us directly that

$$\{\text{OUT} = \diamondsuit \wedge \textit{true} \wedge \textit{head}(s) = \text{``}a\text{''}\} \textbf{ output head } s$$
$$\{\text{OUT} = \langle \text{``}a\text{''}\rangle \wedge \textit{true} \wedge \textit{head}(s) = \text{``}a\text{''}\} \qquad (6)$$

But $(s = \text{``}a\text{''}) \supset (\textit{head}(s) = \text{``}a\text{''})$ and (4b) follows by the rules of Consequence, thus completing the argument.

The inference rules for conditional statements are similar to the Selection$_1$ rule in the specifications for Pam:

$$\frac{\{P \wedge E_1 = E_2\} S \{Q\}, P \wedge E_1 \neq E_2 \supset Q}{\{P\} \textbf{ eq } E_1, E_2 : S \{Q\}} \qquad (\text{Decision}_1)$$

$$\frac{\{P \wedge E_1 \neq E_2\} S \{Q\}, P \wedge E_1 = E_2 \supset Q}{\{P\} \textbf{ neq } E_1, E_2 : S \{Q\}} \qquad (\text{Decision}_2)$$

The formulation of the rules for procedure invocation is the most significant aspect of the specifications in Table 4.6, p. 214. We consider four separate cases, the simplest of which is invocation of a nonrecursive procedure with no parameters. Intuitively, the effect of executing such a call is identical to the effect of executing the procedure body, and this is just what the following rule specifies:

$$\frac{\{P\}\,S\,\{Q\},\ body(N) = S}{\{P\}\ \textbf{call}\ N\,\{Q\}}\qquad\text{(Invocation}_1\text{)}$$

To take a very simple example, suppose that we have the following situation:

$$\cdots$$

string x

$$\cdots$$

$$
\left.
\begin{array}{l}
\textbf{begin}\\
\quad \textbf{proc}\ p\ =\ \textbf{cons}\ \text{``}a\text{''},\ x\\
\quad \textbf{call}\ p\\
\textbf{end}
\end{array}
\right] B
$$

$$\cdots$$

Clearly, it ought to be possible to verify the assertion

$$\{x = \text{``}b\text{''}\}\ B\ \{x = \text{``}ab\text{''}\}\qquad(1)$$

According to the Block rule, we need only prove

$$\{x = \text{``}b\text{''} \wedge \ true\}\ \textbf{call}\ p\ \{x = \text{``}ab\text{''}\}\qquad(2a)$$

which is the same as

$$\{x = \text{``}b\text{''}\}\ \textbf{call}\ p\ \{x = \text{``}ab\text{''}\}\qquad(2b)$$

under the assumption that

$$body(p) = \textbf{cons}\ \text{``}a\text{''},\ x\qquad(3)$$

Thus the Invocation$_1$ rule implies that it is sufficient to prove

$$\{x = \text{``}b\text{''}\}\ \textbf{cons}\ \text{``}a\text{''},\ x\ \{x = \text{``}ab\text{''}\}\qquad(4)$$

By virtue of the Concatenation rule, we know that

$$\{\langle\text{``}a\text{''}\rangle x = \text{``}ab\text{''}\}\ \textbf{cons}\ \text{``}a\text{''},\ x\ \{x = \text{``}ab\text{''}\}\qquad(5)$$

from which (4) is easily deduced.

The second case to be treated is that of nonrecursive procedures with parameters. The inference rule for this is

$$\frac{\{P\}\,S\,\{Q\},\ body(N) = S,\ params(N) = \langle N_1, \ldots, N_n\rangle}{\{P^{N_1\ldots N_n}_{E_1\ldots E_n}\}\ \textbf{call}\ N\,(E_1, \ldots, E_n)\,\{Q^{N_1\ldots N_n}_{E_1\ldots E_n}\}}\qquad\text{(Invocation}_2\text{)}$$

The reasoning behind this is that the effect of executing a call is the same as the effect of executing a version of the procedure body in which each occurrence of a parameter name has been replaced by the corresponding argument expression. Whereas the conditions P and Q in the assertion about the original procedure body normally involve the procedure's parameter names, the precondition and postcondition in the assertion about the call involve the argument expressions instead. Suppose, for example, that we have

$$\cdots$$

$$\textbf{proc } p \text{ (\textbf{char } } c) = \textbf{cons } c, x$$

$$\textbf{call } p \text{ (“}a\text{”)}$$

and that we wish to verify

$$\{x = \text{“}b\text{”}\} \textbf{ call } p \text{ (“}a\text{”)} \{x = \text{“}ab\text{”}\} \tag{1}$$

The Block rule will have authorized us to make use of the assumption that

$$body(p) = \textbf{cons } c, x \tag{2}$$

and that

$$params(p) = \langle c \rangle \tag{3}$$

and the Concatenation and Consequence rules tell us that

$$\{x = \text{“}b\text{”}\} \textbf{ cons } c, x \{x = \langle c \rangle\text{“}b\text{”}\} \tag{4}$$

Hence, by the Invocation$_2$ rule, we deduce (1) from (2), (3), and (4) (replacing c in the postcondition of (4) by “a” and simplifying $\langle\text{“}a\text{”}\rangle\text{“}b\text{”}$ to “ab”).

With the introduction of the Invocation$_2$ rule, we must bring in two more language restrictions. It will be recalled that the parameter passage discipline for Eva procedures is supposed to be "call by value", meaning that, although a procedure may change the values of its parameters (so that the parameters may be used as if they were local variables after their initial values are no longer required), this has no effect on the values of the arguments in the call. But, given the declaration

$$\textbf{proc } p \text{ (\textbf{char } } c, \textbf{ string } x) = \textbf{cons } c, x$$

for example, the Invocation$_2$ rule permits us to deduce

$$\{y = \text{“}b\text{”}\} \textbf{ call } p \text{ (“}a\text{”, } y) \{y = \text{“}ab\text{”}\}$$

which is false (p has no external effects at all). We can avoid such problems simply by forbidding procedures to change their parameter values. This does not decrease the power of the language, because, by introducing extra local variables, an offending procedure can always be transformed into an equivalent one satisfying the restriction. The other restriction, also a fairly innocuous one, is that arguments may not contain variables that appear globally in the procedure body. Otherwise, given the declaration

$$\textbf{proc } p \textbf{ (char } c) = ($$

$$\textbf{cons } c, x$$

$$\textbf{input } d \,)$$

for example, we would be able to deduce the invalid assertion

$$\{x = \text{“}a\text{”}\} \textbf{ call } p \, (d) \, \{x = \langle d \rangle \text{“}a\text{”}\}$$

Next, consider the case of a recursive procedure with no parameters, such as

$$\textbf{proc } p = ($$

$$\textbf{input } c$$

$$\textbf{eq } c, \text{“}z\text{”}: \textbf{call } p \,)$$

Any attempt to prove an assertion about a call of p using the Invocation$_1$ rule would, because of the inner call, lead to an infinite regress of appeals to that very rule. Thus Invocation$_1$ does not define the semantics of recursive procedures. The solution is to add the following rule of inference:

$$\frac{\{P\} \textbf{ call } N \, \{Q\} \vdash \{P\} \, S \, \{Q\}, \; body(N) = S}{\{P\} \textbf{ call } N \, \{Q\}} \qquad \text{(Recursion}_1)$$

Like Invocation$_1$, this rule basically says that the effect of executing a call is the same as the effect of executing the procedure body; the difference is that here we are permitted to *assume* the desired conclusion about the inner, recursive call(s) for purposes of establishing the assertion about the body. As an example, we shall verify the following general property of the procedure given above:

$$\{\text{IN} = Z\langle Y \rangle L\} \textbf{ call } p \, \{\text{IN} = L \wedge c = Y\} \qquad (1)$$

where Z is any sequence of zero or more "z" characters, Y is any allowed character other than "z", and L is any sequence of zero or more characters. The Recursion$_1$ rule tells us that (1) will be established if, by using it as an assumption, we can prove

$$\{\text{IN} = Z\langle Y \rangle L\} \textbf{ input } c$$

$$\textbf{eq } c, \text{“}z\text{”}: \textbf{call } p \, \{\text{IN} = L \wedge c = Y\} \qquad (2)$$

By the Composition rule, it is sufficient to prove (3a) and (3b) for some Q:

$$\{IN = Z\langle Y\rangle L\} \text{ input } c \{Q\} \tag{3a}$$

$$\{Q\} \text{ eq } c, \text{ "}z\text{": call } p \{IN = L \wedge c = Y\} \tag{3b}$$

We take Q to be

$$IN = Z'\langle Y\rangle L \wedge c = \text{"}z\text{"} \vee IN = L \wedge c = Y$$

where, in the case that Z is nonempty, Z' is the sequence of "z" characters such that $Z = \langle \text{"}z\text{"}\rangle Z'$. Noting that the precondition of (3a) is equivalent to

$$IN = \langle \text{"}z\text{"}\rangle Z'\langle Y\rangle L \vee IN = \langle Y\rangle L$$

we see that (3a) will be established by the Or rule provided that (4a) and (4b) hold:

$$\{IN = \langle \text{"}z\text{"}\rangle Z'\langle Y\rangle L\} \text{ input } c \{IN = Z'\langle Y\rangle L \wedge c = \text{"}z\text{"}\} \tag{4a}$$

$$\{IN = \langle Y\rangle L\} \text{ input } c \{IN = L \wedge c = Y\} \tag{4b}$$

These follow easily from the Input rule and it remains to prove (3b). By the Decision$_1$ rule, the latter reduces to

$$\{Q \wedge c = \text{"}z\text{"}\} \text{ call } p \{IN = L \wedge c = Y\} \tag{5a}$$

$$(Q \wedge c \neq \text{"}z\text{"}) \supset (IN = L \wedge c = Y) \tag{5b}$$

where Q is still

$$IN = Z'\langle Y\rangle L \wedge c = \text{"}z\text{"} \vee IN = L \wedge c = Y$$

Thus it is easily seen that (5b) holds, and (5a) simplifies to

$$\{IN = Z'\langle Y\rangle L \wedge c = \text{"}z\text{"}\} \text{ call } p \{IN = L \wedge c = Y\} \tag{5a$'$}$$

By the second Consequence rule, this will follow from

$$\{IN = Z'\langle Y\rangle L\} \text{ call } p \{IN = L \wedge c = Y\} \tag{6}$$

Now, by comparing it with (1), we see that (6) holds by the assumption that was originally granted for the purpose of proving (2), thus completing the argument.

Invocation of recursive procedures with parameters is the final case we will consider. The rule of inference for this is basically a generalization of Invocation$_2$ and Recursion$_1$:

$$\frac{(\forall N_1, \ldots, N_n)(\{P\} \text{ call } N(N_1, \ldots, N_n) \{Q\}) \vdash \{P\} S \{Q\},}{\{P^{N_1 \ldots N_n}_{E_1 \ldots E_n}\} \text{ call } N(E_1, \ldots, E_n)\{Q^{N_1 \ldots N_n}_{E_1 \ldots E_n}\}} \quad \text{(Recursion}_2\text{)}$$

where $body(N) = S$, $params(N) = \langle N_1, \ldots, N_n\rangle$

Note that the hypothesis

$$(\forall N_1, \ldots, N_n)(\{P\} \text{ call } N\ (N_1, \ldots, N_n)\ \{Q\})$$

permitted for purposes of proving $\{P\}\ S\ \{Q\}$ about the procedure body is a general assertion about calls of the procedure, not the particular one that is to be deduced. Taking as an example the declaration

$$\textbf{proc } p\ (\textbf{string } x) =$$
$$\textbf{neq } x, \text{ ``''}: ($$
$$\textbf{call } p\ (\textbf{tail } x)$$
$$\textbf{cons head } x, y\ )$$

suppose that we wish to verify

$$\{y = \text{``''}\} \text{ call } p\ (\text{``}ab\text{''})\ \{y = \text{``}ab\text{''}\} \tag{1}$$

According to Recursion$_2$, this will be established if, using

$$(\forall x)(\{y = \text{``''}\} \text{ call } p\ (x)\ \{y = x\}) \tag{2}$$

as an assumption, we can prove

$$\{y = \text{``''}\}\ body\ (p)\ \{y = x\} \tag{3}$$

By the Decision$_2$ rule, (3) reduces to

$$\{y = \text{``''} \wedge x \neq \text{``''}\} \text{ call } p\ (\textbf{tail } x)$$
$$\textbf{cons head } x, y\ \{y = x\} \tag{4a}$$
$$y = \text{``''} \wedge x = \text{``''} \supset y = x \tag{4b}$$

Assertion (4b) is obvious, and the Composition rule enables (4a) to be reduced to

$$\{y = \text{``''} \wedge x \neq \text{``''}\} \text{ call } p\ (\textbf{tail } x)\ \{y = tail(x)\} \tag{5a}$$
$$\{y = tail(x)\} \textbf{ cons head } x, y\ \{y = x\} \tag{5b}$$

By the Consequence$_2$ rule, (5a) reduces to

$$\{y = \text{``''}\} \text{ call } p\ (\textbf{tail } x)\ \{y = tail(x)\} \tag{6}$$

which holds by the assumption (2). By the Concatenation rule, we have

$$\{\langle head(x)\rangle y = x\} \textbf{ cons head } x, y\ \{y = x\} \tag{7}$$

But since

$$(y = tail(x)) \supset (\langle head(x)\rangle y = x)$$

(5b) holds, and we are finished.

TABLE 4.6 Partial Axiomatic Definition of the Semantics of Eva

$$\frac{\{P\}\ S\ \{Q\},\ Q \supset R}{\{P\}\ S\ \{R\}} \qquad\qquad\qquad (\text{Consequence}_1)$$

$$\frac{P \supset Q,\ \{Q\}\ S\ \{R\}}{\{P\}\ S\ \{R\}} \qquad\qquad\qquad (\text{Consequence}_2)$$

$$\frac{\{P\}\ S\ \{Q\},\ \{P'\}\ S\ \{Q'\}}{\{P \wedge P'\}\ S\ \{Q \wedge Q'\}} \qquad\qquad\qquad (\text{And})$$

$$\frac{\{P\}\ S\ \{Q\},\ \{P'\}\ S\ \{Q'\}}{\{P \vee P'\}\ S\ \{Q \vee Q'\}} \qquad\qquad\qquad (\text{Or})$$

$$\frac{H \vdash \{P \wedge A\}\ S\ \{Q\}}{\{P\}\ \textbf{begin}\ D\ S\ \textbf{end}\ \{Q\}} \qquad\qquad\qquad (\text{Block})$$

where A is a condition of the form *true* $\wedge\ N_1 = $ "" $\wedge \ldots \wedge\ N_n = $ "", where N_1, $\ldots, N_n$ are the string variables declared in D;

$(\forall N)(\text{'}\textbf{proc}\ N = S\text{'} \in D \supset \text{'}body(N) = S\text{'} \in H)$;
$(\forall N)(\text{'}\textbf{proc}\ N\ (T_1\ N_1, \ldots, T_n\ N_n) = S\text{'} \in D \supset \text{'}body(N) = S\text{'} \in H\ \wedge$
$\quad \text{'}params(N) = \langle N_1, \ldots, N_n\rangle\text{'} \in H)$;

no other assertions are in H.

$$\frac{\{P\}\ S_1\ \{Q\},\ \{Q\}\ S_2\ \{R\}}{\{P\}\ S_1\ S_2\ \{R\}} \qquad\qquad\qquad (\text{Composition})$$

$$\{\text{IN} = \langle C\rangle L \wedge P_C^N\}\ \textbf{input}\ N\ \{\text{IN} = L \wedge P\} \qquad\qquad\qquad (\text{Input})$$

$$\{\text{OUT} = L \wedge P \wedge E = C\}\ \textbf{output}\ E\ \{\text{OUT} = L\langle C\rangle \wedge P \wedge E = C\} \qquad (\text{Output})$$

$$\frac{\{P \wedge E_1 = E_2\}\ S\ \{Q\},\ P \wedge E_1 \neq E_2 \supset Q}{\{P\}\ \textbf{eq}\ E_1, E_2\colon S\ \{Q\}} \qquad\qquad (\text{Decision}_1)$$

$$\frac{\{P \wedge E_1 \neq E_2\}\ S\ \{Q\},\ P \wedge E_1 = E_2 \supset Q}{\{P\}\ \textbf{neq}\ E_1, E_2\colon S\ \{Q\}} \qquad\qquad (\text{Decision}_2)$$

$$\{P_{\langle E\rangle N}^N\}\ \textbf{cons}\ E, N\ \{P\} \qquad\qquad\qquad (\text{Concatenation})$$

$$\frac{\{P\}\ S\ \{Q\},\ body(N) = S}{\{P\}\ \textbf{call}\ N\ \{Q\}} \qquad\qquad\qquad (\text{Invocation}_1)$$

$$\frac{\{P\}\ S\ \{Q\},\ body(N) = S,\ params(N) = \langle N_1, \ldots, N_n\rangle}{\{P_{E_1\ldots E_n}^{N_1\ldots N_n}\}\ \textbf{call}\ N\ (E_1, \ldots, E_n)\ \{Q_{E_1\ldots E_n}^{N_1\ldots N_n}\}} \qquad (\text{Invocation}_2)$$

$$\frac{\{P\}\ \textbf{call}\ N\ \{Q\} \vdash \{P\}\ S\ \{Q\},\ body\ (N) = S}{\{P\}\ \textbf{call}\ N\ \{Q\}} \qquad\qquad (\text{Recursion}_1)$$

$$\frac{(\forall N_1, \ldots, N_n)(\{P\}\ \textbf{call}\ N\ (N_1, \ldots, N_n)\{Q\}) \vdash \{P\}\ S\ \{Q\},}{body\ (N) = S,\ params\ (N) = \langle N_1, \ldots, N_n\rangle} \atop {\{P_{E_1\ldots E_n}^{N_1\ldots N_n}\}\ \textbf{call}\ N\ (E_1, \ldots, E_n)\ \{Q_{E_1\ldots E_n}^{N_1\ldots N_n}\}}} \qquad (\text{Recursion}_2)$$

EXERCISES

1. Give an example of an invalid assertion that could be deduced if names are allowed to be declared more than once in an Eva program.

2. Using the specifications of Table 4.6, show that the following programs are semantically equivalent:

(a) **begin**
    char c
    input c
    output c
end

(b) **begin**
    string s
    proc p = (
        char c
        input c
        cons c, s
    call p
    output head s
end

3. Referring to Table 4.6, verify the assertion

$\{\text{IN} = W\langle\text{"}z\text{"}\rangle \wedge \text{OUT} = \Diamond\}$ **begin**
    char ch
    proc $copy$ = (
        input ch
        neq ch, "z" : (
            output ch
            call $copy$))
    call $copy$
end
$\{\text{OUT} = W\}$

where W is any sequence of zero or more characters other than "z".

For Further Information

The landmark paper by Hoare (1969) is the classic reference for the basic ideas of the axiomatic approach. The best-known application of the technique to an actual programming language is the partial axiomatic definition of the semantics of Pascal (Hoare and Wirth, 1973). This definition, slightly modified, is used in the textbook of Alagić and Arbib (1978) as a tool for program design as well as for program proving. The suitability of the approach for various types of constructs and languages has been built up gradually in a long series of research papers. Clint and Hoare (1972) discuss the axiomatic definition of **goto** statements and functions. The difficult problems posed by procedures and parameter mechanisms are attacked by, among others, Hoare (1971), Igarashi et al. (1975), Gorelick (1975), Ernst (1977), Apt and de Bakker (1977), Cook (1976), Cartwright and Oppen (1978), and Guttag et al. (1978). The handling of expressions with side effects is discussed by Cunningham and Gilford (1976) and by Kowaltowski (1977), while Pritchard (1977) deals with "expression languages" in which imperative constructs can yield values. Owicki and Gries (1976a, 1976b) apply the approach to parallel programs. Fokkinga (1978) discusses the treatment of declarations and an escape construct. Clarke (1979) shows that there are limits on how far the technique can be pushed. Igarashi et al. (1975) describe a system for automating the construction of correctness proofs. Further information on proof methodology may be found in the article by Gerhart (1976) as well as in many of the papers mentioned above.

Dijkstra's (1976) formalism of *weakest preconditions* constitutes a different but related form of axiomatic semantics.

5

programming languages as metalanguages

To a certain extent, we may distinguish between the *basic approach* (translational, denotational, etc.) underlying a set of formal language specifications and the particular *notation* (metalanguage) in which the specifications are expressed. This comparatively brief chapter introduces no new basic approaches and is purely concerned with a notational possibility that may at first seem surprising—the idea of employing programming languages as metalanguages.

This idea does not seem so strange after one has observed the striking similarities between the process of constructing a formal definition and the activity of ordinary computer programming. In both cases, one passes through a series of phases such as overall design, modularization, detailed coding, debugging, and rewriting for greater conciseness and improved style. The analogy holds quite well even for those approaches where the language specifications are almost completely nonalgorithmic in character; anyone who has ever written, debugged, and polished a BNF grammar of substantial size, for example, will appreciate this point. If the task of language specification is essentially one of programming, then, it is reasonable to ask whether it is possible in principle to use some actual programming language as the metalanguage. If it is, and if such a course of action is *reasonable* with respect to qualities of specification such as clarity and conciseness, then two important advantages may accrue.

The first advantage stems from the fact that programming languages in general are familiar entities to all concerned. Formal specifications will be more acceptable and more widely understood by the community of language designers, implementers, and users if they are expressed in a familiar, general-purpose programming language than if they are expressed in an esoteric, specialized, formal metalanguage.

The second advantage is that specifications expressed in a programming language can obviously and easily be subjected to computer-aided testing without the aid of any special tools or preparation—they can be fed to a compiler for the language and perhaps even executed. One facet of the analogy between programming and language definition is that in both cases the "software engineering" problem becomes more and more serious as the size and complexity of the product increase. As is well known, it is extremely difficult to achieve full correctness in a large program without the aid of some debugging runs on a computer. It is just as difficult to achieve total completeness and consistency in a set of language specifications that is not amenable to mechanical checking. Language specifications are "metasoftware", and we can be much more confident of their validity if they have been computer-tested than we ever could be otherwise.

5.1
DEFINITION OF ONE PROGRAMMING LANGUAGE BY ANOTHER

The "definition by processor" idea mentioned at the beginning of Chap. 4 provides the most obvious but least interesting illustration of the possibility of using programming languages as metalanguages. If a high-level language A is considered to be defined by a particular compiler or interpreter P and if P is written in another high-level language B, then B is clearly playing the role of a metalanguage.

A much more interesting possibility is that of using a programming language as a metalanguage for specifying abstract, definitional interpreters of the kind described in Chap. 4 in terms of the Vienna Definition Language. Most of this section will be devoted to a demonstration that this possibility is in fact viable. The particular (meta-) language to be used in the demonstration is Algol 68, chosen because of its powerful, high-level data-structuring facilities and its overall generality and expressiveness compared with other general-purpose languages that are widely available. The object is not to represent Algol 68 as an ideal meta-programming language but only to make it serve to illustrate the principle that *some* sufficiently advanced programming language, perhaps not yet designed, could be at least as suitable as any purely formal metalanguage for writing language specifications. However, we shall see that, as far as the relatively simple problem of writing an operational definition of the semantics of Pam is concerned, Algol 68 is about as good as VDL with respect to ease of writing, conciseness, and understandability. This standard would not be reached in the case of Pascal, for example, and most definitely not in the case of PL/I.

The problem before us is essentially that of expressing predicate definitions and instruction definitions in Algol 68 instead of in VDL. Specifically, the VDL specifications for Pam given in Table 4.1 will be reexpressed in Algol 68. In programming-language terms, a predicate in the VDL sense corresponds to a data type, so that a predicate definition corresponds to a definition of a new data type in terms of existing ones. Data types are termed *modes* in Algol 68, and the programmer is permitted to declare new mode symbols. For example, the declaration

$$\textbf{mode asmtst} = \textbf{struct (var } \textit{lhs}, \textbf{expr } \textit{rhs})$$

where the modes **var** and **expr** must be declared elsewhere, is a close analog of the VDL definition

$$\text{is-asmt-st} = (\langle \text{s-lhs : is-var} \rangle, \langle \text{s-rhs : is-expr} \rangle)$$

As in VDL, *lhs* and *rhs* are termed *selectors*. A value *a* of mode **asmtst** is a data structure corresponding to a VDL object satisfying 'is-asmt-st'. Instead of writing s-lhs(a) to select the 'lhs' component of the object, we write *lhs* **of** *a*; further, s-addr ∘ s-lhs(a) would be rewritten as *addr* **of** *lhs* **of** *a*.

A predicate defined as a disjunction of other predicates corresponds to a *united mode* in Algol 68, meaning that the allowed values may have any of the modes listed. For example,

$$\textbf{mode expr} = \textbf{union (infixexpr, var, int)}$$

is a close analog of

$$\text{is-expr} = \text{is-infix-expr} \lor \text{is-var} \lor \text{is-intg}$$

(**int** is a primitive mode corresponding to integer values). If *e* is a value of mode **expr** and we wish to do different things with it depending on whether it is actually an **int**, a **var**, or an **infixexpr** value, we may write a construct of the form

$$\textbf{case } e \textbf{ in}$$
$$\textbf{(int } e) : \dots ,$$
$$\textbf{(var } e) : \dots ,$$
$$\textbf{(infixexpr } e) : \dots$$
$$\textbf{esac}$$

which corresponds to a VDL conditional expression of the form

$$\text{is-intg (e)} \longrightarrow \ldots$$
$$\text{is-var (e)} \longrightarrow \ldots$$
$$\text{is-infix-expr (e)} \longrightarrow \ldots$$

A predicate defined as a disjunction of elementary predicates is most conveniently realized as the mode **string**, with the understanding, noted in a comment, that only certain string values will ever occur. Thus we would have

$$\textbf{string} \ \# \ \text{one of } \textit{"plus"}, \textit{"minus"}, \ldots \#$$

in place of a predicate of the form

$$\text{is-PLUS } \lor \text{ is-MINUS } \lor \ldots$$

To deal with a particular value *opr* of this type, we could write

> **if** *opr* = *"plus"* **then** . . .
>
> **elif** *opr* = *"minus"* **then** . . .
>
> **elif** . . .
>
> . . .
>
> **fi**

in place of a VDL conditional expression of the form

$$\text{is-PLUS (opr)} \longrightarrow \ldots$$
$$\text{is-MINUS (opr)} \longrightarrow \ldots$$
$$\ldots$$

Pointers to one-dimensional arrays provide a fairly convenient representation for objects that are lists; e.g., the mode **ref[ ]int** corresponds to the predicate 'is-intg-list'. The bounds of an array thus referred to are unrestricted, but in fact the lower bound will always be 1; an upper bound of 0 then means that we have an empty list. Suppose that *file* is a particular list of integers. Then we have the following pairs of equivalent VDL and Algol 68 expressions:

head (file)	*file*[1]
elem(i) (file)	*file*[*i*]
length (file)	**upb** *file*
is-$\diamondsuit$ (file) $\longrightarrow$ . . .	**if upb** *file* = 0 **then** . . .
tail (file)	*file*[2:]

Enlargement of a list by concatenation, unfortunately, is rather awkward in Algol 68. To achieve the equivalent of

$$\text{file} \frown \langle k \rangle$$

for example, it is necessary to create a new, larger array and copy in all the elements appropriately:

$$(\textbf{int } n = \textbf{upb } \textit{file} \; ; \; \textbf{heap}[1:n+1]\textbf{int } f \; ; \; f[1:n] := \textit{file} \; ; \; f[n+1] := k \; ; \; f)$$

The complete abstract syntax of Pam may be specified in Algol 68 as follows:

> **mode series** = **ref[ ] st**,
>
>   **st** = **union** (**readst, writest, asmtst, condst, defloop, indefloop**),
>
>   **readst** = **struct** (**ref [ ] var** *r*),
>
>   **writest** = **struct** (**ref [ ] var** *w*),
>
>   **asmtst** = **struct** (**var** *lhs*, **expr** *rhs*),
>
>   **condst** = **struct** (**comp** *ifpart*, **series** *thenpart*, *elsepart*),
>
>   **defloop** = **struct** (**expr** *limit*, **series** *body*),
>
>   **indefloop** = **struct** (**comp** *test*, **series** *body*),
>
>   **comp** = **struct** (**expr** *left opd, right opd*, **string** *rel* # one
>
>   of *"eq"*, *"gt"*, *"le"*, *"lt"*, *"ge"*, *"ne"* #),
>
>   **expr** = **union** (**infixexpr, var, int**),
>
>   **infixexpr** = **struct** (**ref expr** *left opd, right opd*, **string** *opr*
>
>   # one of *"plus"*, *"minus"*, *"times"*, *"over"* #),
>
>   **var** = **struct** (**int** *addr*)

These definitions are closely analogous to the corresponding VDL predicate definitions in Table 4.1. The **ref** occurring in the definition of **infixexpr** is a rather unfortunate linguistic requirement necessitated by the fact that the definitions of **expr** and **infixexpr** are mutually recursive.

The structure of states of the abstract machine for interpreting Pam programs may be defined as follows:

> **mode state** = **struct** (**ref [ ] value** *stg*, **ref [ ] int** *input, output*),
>
>   **value** = **union** (**int, void**)

Unlike a VDL state object, a value of mode **state** does not contain a "control" component, as this will be implicit in the (real or imagined) execution state of the set of Algol 68 procedures that will replace the VDL instruction definitions. A variable *xi*, assumed to be declared by

state xi

will play the same role in these procedures as the symbol ξ did in the VDL specifications. Thus (**stg of** *xi*)[*i*], for example, is the new way of writing elem(i) ∘ s-stg(ξ). The initial value of *xi* is assumed to be such that the *input* component consists of a complete list of data values for the program to be interpreted, the *output* component is empty, and the length of the *stg* component is given by the number of distinct variables in the program; the actual mode of each element (of mode **value**) in the latter component will be the dummy mode **void** as opposed to the "normal" mode **int**, indicating that the values are initially undefined.

The coding of procedures to define the detailed operation of the abstract interpreter is quite straightforward. The modes of parameters and returned values (**void** indicates there is no returned value) must always be explicitly specified in the procedure headings. Thus the instruction definition

exec-series (ser) =

is-◇ (ser) ⟶ **null**

T ⟶ **exec-series** (tail (ser));

exec-stmt (head (ser))

which contains self-replacing groups only, can now be written as

proc *exec series* = (**series** *ser*) **void** :

    if upb *ser* = 0 **then skip**

    else *exec stmt* (*ser*[1]) ; *exec series* (*ser*[2:])

    fi

or, more simply, as

proc *exec series* = (**series** *ser*) **void** :

    if upb *ser* > 0

    then *exec stmt* (*ser*[1]) ; *exec series* (*ser*[2:])

    fi

It is not usually necessary to make use of extra identifiers to show the disposition of returned values. For example, the instruction definition

eval-comp (comp) =

compare (a, b, s-rel (comp));

a: **eval-expr** (s-left-opd (comp)),

b: **eval-expr** (s-right-opd (comp))

can now be written as

proc *eval comp* = (**comp** *comp*) **bool** :

  compare (*eval expr* (*left opd* **of** *comp*), *eval expr* (*right opd* **of** *comp*), *rel* **of** *comp*)

The simple ways in which the effects of VDL value-returning groups are expressible in Algol 68 can be appreciated by comparing the VDL forms

  eval-expr (expr) =

    is-intg (expr) $\longrightarrow$ PASS: expr

    . . .

  store (loc, val) =

    s-stg: μ(s-stg(ξ)); $\langle$elem (loc) : val$\rangle$

with the corresponding Algol 68 forms

  proc *eval expr* = (**expr** *expr*) **int** :

    case *expr* **in**

      (**int** *e*) : *e*

  proc *store* = (**int** *loc, val*) **void** :

    (*stg* **of** *xi*)[*loc*] := *val*

The complete set of procedures is shown in Table 5.1, pp. 224–27. The only substantial deviation from Table 4.1 is that a procedure corresponding to the **choose** instruction has been eliminated by recoding the parts of *exec stmt* corresponding to conditional statements and indefinite loops. The undefined procedure *error* is assumed to take a parameter of mode **string**.

By comparing Table 5.1 with Table 4.1, we see that Algol 68 can be as good as and perhaps better than VDL as a metalanguage as far as clarity and conciseness are concerned. It would be considerably more difficult to use Algol 68 to define a more realistic subject language than Pam or Eva, and VDL might in some instances prove to be definitely superior, but that provides no evidence against our hypothesis that a general-purpose programming language of sufficiently advanced design would be superior to any purely formal metalanguage for operational semantics. Clarity and conciseness aside, the advantages of machine-aided certification are considerable and should not be underestimated. A large proportion of possible specification errors in Table 5.1, including all type conflicts, would be detected as syntax errors by a compiler for the programming language. Moreover, the effect of interpreting any particular sample program can be verified by constructing the corresponding value *p* of more **series** and executing the call *exec series* (*p*). In other words, with a few minor additions our formal definition becomes an actual processor for abstract Pam programs (albeit a very inefficient one, since there was no consideration of efficiency in its construction).

Although we shall not examine them in detail here, there are other possible ways of using programming languages to define other programming languages. One of the more interesting possibilities is that of expressing functional or denotational (Sec. 4.2) semantic specifications in a programming language; in addition to the types of facility needed for expressing operational semantics, the metalanguage would have to be capable of manipulating functions as first-class values in a highly flexible manner. Programming languages could also be used for the syntactic components of complete language definitions; for example, these components could take the form of high-level, recursive programs defining transformations that map abstract programs (of the subject language) into textual programs. The assertions of axiomatic semantics (Sec. 4.3) and the evaluation rules and auxiliary functions of attribute grammars (Secs. 2.3 and 3.2) provide other possibilities for the metalinguistic use of programming languages. The potential advantages of familiarity and machine processing obtain in each case.

TABLE 5.1   Operational Semantics of Pam Expressed in Algol 68

Abstract Machine

mode state = **struct (ref[ ]value** *stg*, **ref[ ]int** *input, output*),

    value = **union (int, void)**

Abstract Syntax

mode series = **ref [ ] st**,

    st = **union (readst, writest, asmtst, condst, defloop, indefloop)**,

    readst = **struct (ref [ ] var** *r*),

    writest = **struct (ref [ ] var** *w*),

    asmtst = **struct (var** *lhs*, **expr** *rhs*),

    condst = **struct (comp** *ifpart*, **series** *thenpart, elsepart*),

    defloop = **struct (expr** *limit*, **series** *body*),

    indefloop = **struct (comp** *test*, **series** *body*),

    comp = **struct (expr** *left opd, right opd*, **string** *rel* # one of

        "*eq*", "*gt*", "*le*", "*lt*", "*ge*", "*ne*" #),

    expr = **union (infixexpr, var, int)**,

    infixexpr = **struct (ref expr** *left opd, right opd*, **string** *opr*

        # one of "*plus*", "*minus*", "*times*", "*over*" #),

    var = **struct (int** *addr*)

TABLE 5.1　(Continued)

Interpretation Procedures

proc *exec series* = (**series** *ser*) **void** :

    if upb *ser* > 0

    then *exec stmt* (*ser*[1])　; *exec series* (*ser*[2:])

    fi ,

proc *exec stmt* = (**st** *stmt*) **void** :

    case *stmt* **in**

        (**readst** *s*) : *readp* (*r* **of** *s*),

        (**writest** *s*) : *writep* (*w* **of** *s*),

        (**asmtst** *s*) : *store* (*addr* **of** *lhs* **of** *s*, *eval expr* (*rhs* **of** *s*)),

        (**condst** *s*) : **if** *eval comp* (*ifpart* **of** *s*)

            then *exec series* (*thenpart* **of** *s*)

            else *exec series* (*elsepart* **of** *s*)

            fi,

        (**defloop** *s*) : *repeat series* (*body* **of** *s*, *eval expr* (*limit* **of** *s*))

        (**indefloop** *s*) : **if** *eval comp* (*test* **of** *s*)

            then *exec series* (*body* **of** *s*) ; *exec stmt* (*s*)

            fi

    esac ,

proc *repeat series* = (**series** *ser*, **int** *n*) **void** :

    if *n* > 0

    then *exec series* (*ser*) ; *repeat series* (*ser*, *n* − 1)

    fi ,

proc *eval comp* = (**comp** *comp*) **bool** :

    compare (*eval expr* (*left opd* **of** *comp*), *eval expr* (*right opd* **of** *comp*),

        rel **of** *comp*) ,

proc *compare* = (**int** *val1*, *val2*, **string** *rel*) **bool** :

    rel = "*eq*" $\wedge$ *val1* = *val2* $\vee$

    rel = "*gt*" $\wedge$ *val1* > *val2* $\vee$

    rel = "*le*" $\wedge$ *val1* $\leq$ *val2* $\vee$

    rel = "*lt*" $\wedge$ *val1* < *val2* $\vee$

    rel = "*ge*" $\wedge$ *val1* $\geq$ *val2* $\vee$

    rel = "*ne*" $\wedge$ *val1* $\neq$ *val2* ,

TABLE 5.1 (Continued)

proc *eval expr* = (**expr** *expr*) **int** :
    case *expr* **in**
        (**int** *e*) : *e*,
        (**var** *e*) : *eval var* (*e*),
        (**infixexpr** *e*) : *calculate* (*eval expr* (*left opd* **of** *e*),
               eval expr (*right opd* **of** *e*), *opr* **of** *e*)
    esac ,

proc *eval var* = (**var** *var*) *int* :
    case (*stg* **of** *xi*)[*addr* **of** *var*] **in**
        (**void**) : (*error* ("*undefined variable*") ; **skip**),
        (**int** *i*) : *i*
    esac ,

proc *calculate* = (**int** *val1*, *val2*, **string** *opr*) **int** :
    if *opr* = "*plus*" **then** *val1* + *val2*
    elif *opr* = "*minus*" **then** *val1* − *val2*
    elif *opr* = "*times*" **then** *val1* × *val2*
    elif *opr* = "*over*" **then** *val1* ÷ *val2*
    fi ,

proc *store* = (**int** *loc*, *val*) **void** :
    (*stg* **of** *xi*)[*loc*] := *val* ,

proc *readp* = (**ref** [ ] **var** *vars*) **void** :
    if upb *vars* > 0
    then *store* (*addr* **of** *vars*[1], *input val*) ; *readp* (*vars*[2:])
    fi ,

proc *input val* = **int** :
    if upb *input* **of** *xi* = 0
    then *error* ("*end of input file*") ; **skip**
    else int *i* = (*input* **of** *xi*)[1] ;
        input **of** *xi* := (*input* **of** *xi*)[2:] ;
        i
    fi ,
proc *writep* = (**ref** [ ] **var** *vars*) **void** :
    if upb *vars* > 0

TABLE 5.1 (Continued)

---

then *output val (eval expr (vars[1]))* ; *writep (vars[2:])*
fi ,

proc *output val* = (**int** *val*) **void** : (
    int *n* = **upb** *output* **of** *xi* ;
    heap[1:*n*+1]**int** *f* ; *f*[1:*n*] := *output* **of** *xi* ; *f*[*n*+1] := *val* ;
    output **of** *xi* := *f*)

EXERCISES

1. Referring to Table 5.1, draw a suitable tree diagram for the value *t* of mode **series** corresponding to the program

$$n := 2 ;$$
$$\textbf{to } n \textbf{ do write } n ; n := n + 1 \textbf{ end}$$

Trace in detail the interpretation of the call *exec series* (*t*).

2. Investigate the viability of your favorite general-purpose programming language as a metalanguage for specifying VDL-like abstract interpreters. How does it compare with Algol 68 in this respect?

For Further Information

Anderson et al. (1976) discuss the concept of using a programming language as a metalanguage and describe a particular system which implements their ideas. The demonstration that Algol 68 can sometimes be as good a metalanguage as VDL is based on a paper by Pagan (1976). In a further paper (Pagan, 1979), the possible use of an extended version of Algol 68 for writing denotational specifications is discussed.

5.2

SELF-DEFINITION

An interesting special case of the notion of using programming languages as metalanguages is that in which metalanguage and subject language are the same. In the case of the "definition by processor" approach, for instance, a compiler written in the very language it compiles would be an example of such self-definition. (Such compilers are in fact not uncommon, being a product of the implementation technique known as bootstrapping.) For sufficiently advanced languages, self-specification is also possible in the abstract-interpreter approach to operational semantics—the interpreter is specified in the very language it interprets. The most famous example of an actual formal specification using this technique is that of the language Lisp 1.5.

The self-definition of Lisp is remarkably concise and elegant compared with what could be achieved in the case of most other languages. This is made possible by two highly distinctive attributes of Lisp—its reducibility to a very small number of primitives (basic facilities in terms of which all other features of the language may be programmed) and the structural identicality of programs and data. It is only the primitives that have to be defined by the basic interpreter, and the specification of their interpretation is made very straightforward by the fact that all constructs are expressed in a form (S-expressions) which is ideal for manipulation by Lisp programs.

One might wish to object that a self-specification such as that of Lisp is useless as a *definition* because of its circularity—that one cannot use it to gain an understanding of the language unless the language is already understood. The fact is, however, that any approach to formal definition must ultimately rely on some kind of independent knowledge—understanding of a metalanguage, for example. It can be argued that, with self-definition, it is an advantage that no second language is involved and that one is only required to have an independent understanding of one particular program (the definitional interpreter) of the subject language.

To obtain a complete set of specifications for the entire language, the abstract interpreter for the Lisp primitives has to be supplemented by a fairly large set of Lisp routines which define the remainder of the language in terms of the primitives. This is a particular instance of a self-definition technique whereby a language's "higher" facilities are defined in terms of the more basic facilities that form the "core" of the language. This idea is closely related to the concept of language extensibility—a property that gives programmers the ability to define new language facilities by means of certain extension facilities that are part of the language itself. Here, the extension facilities are considered to belong to the core component of the language and hence are to be defined by some independent means. The noncore facilities are, in principle at least, nothing more than extensions which the language definer has "preprogrammed" for the convenience of ordinary programmers, who are free to program further extensions if they so wish.

Algol 68 is a good example of a language whose standard definition makes much use of the technique described above. The language is a fairly extensible one, in that the programmer has the ability to declare procedures, operators, and modes of various kinds (structures, unions, etc.). A very large number of particular facilities provided as part of the language are, strictly speaking, simply objects that have been predeclared using the extension facilities. For example, *read*, *print*, and a host of other routines for input and output are officially defined by a set of Algol 68 declarations, mainly procedure declarations, which together account for a large fraction of the language's defining document. As another example, the data type for complex numbers is implicitly defined as

$$\textbf{mode compl} = \textbf{struct (real } re, im)$$

and a host of associated operators are implicitly defined by declarations such as

$$\textbf{op} = = (\textbf{compl } a, b) \textbf{ bool} :$$
$$(re \textbf{ of } a = re \textbf{ of } b) \textbf{ and } (im \textbf{ of } a = im \textbf{ of } b)$$

(which permits '=' to be used as an operator for testing the equality of complex-valued operands).

Any specification technique in which a programming language is used as a metalanguage has some kind of self-definition as a special case. The extensional approach that we have just been considering may be viewed as an independent technique which can profitably be applied to large, extensible languages, thus greatly reducing the amount of linguistic detail that must be formalized by other means. Whether the core component of a language should also be self-defined is a separate issue.

For Further Information

The self-definition of Lisp 1.5 is presented by McCarthy et al. (1965) and has been reprinted in several other works. Full details of the extensional aspects of the definition of Algol 68 can be found in the defining document (van Wijngaarden et al., 1976) for that language. Some early ideas closely related to the concept of extensional definition are described by van Wijngaarden (1966).

6

epilog

We have encountered in this book a wide variety of techniques and metalanguages for the formal specification of programming languages. While the selection of approaches described is by no means exhaustive, it is representative of much of the work in the field, and each metalanguage is one which (as metalanguages go) has been used to a significant extent and is known to a large and varied group of people. Some concluding observations on the nature and value of all these techniques and metalanguages are now in order.

Leaving aside the very well-known BNF and related metalanguages for writing context-free grammars, two powerful and important syntactic formalisms have been covered in Chap. 2, attribute grammars and two-level grammars. The reader who has studied both of these may well have noticed certain analogies between them; in particular, metanotions such as NEST and TYPE, which serve to embellish various nonterminal symbols in a two-level grammar, correspond to attributes in an attribute grammar, although the inherited/synthesized distinction is not explicit.

In Chap. 3, we have seen how each of these syntactic formalisms can be pushed to the point where the specification of a subject language includes semantics as well as syntax. Translational semantics was illustrated in the context of attribute grammars and interpretive semantics in the context of two-level grammars, but in each case either formalism could have been used. These techniques have the esthetically pleasing property of completely integrating syntax and semantics in a single set of specifications expressed in one metalanguage, but are vulnerable to the criticism that, by forcing semantics into a form suitable for treatment by syntactic tools, they obscure understanding of the most important aspect of a language—its semantics.

The approaches (operational, denotational, and axiomatic) described in Chap. 4 all focus directly on semantics as the primary area of interest, leaving syntax as a secondary concern. The concept of abstract syntax, in one form or another, is common to these approaches. Some discussion of the relationships among the approaches has been given in the introduction to Chap. 4, which may be reread at this point. Some readers will have noticed that various analogies exist between pairs of approaches to formal semantics, including those of Chap. 3, and that some concepts, such as that of a state, seem to occur in almost all the approaches.

It may be recalled that the potential applications of formal language specification were listed as follows in the Prolog:

1. standardization of programming languages
2. reference for users
3. proofs about programs
4. reference for implementers
5. proofs of implementations
6. automatic implementation
7. improved language design

The degree to which application (1) is realizable is largely a function of the completeness and level of detail of the specifications. With the possible exception of axiomatic semantics, all the approaches covered in this book could in principle serve as aids to language standardization.

In considering application (2), it must be borne in mind that, whatever approach is taken, formal definitions of realistic languages are likely to be substantially longer and more complex than those given for Pam and Eva; certain common features and combinations of features, such as the presence of *both* block structure and **goto** statements, are known to give rise to considerable difficulty as far as formal specification is concerned. The only formalisms that have truly found widespread acceptance as notations for user reference are those of BNF and its variants. Many of the other approaches have been specifically criticized as being unsuitable for user consumption, and in most user manuals the use of formal notation is confined to the specification of the context-free aspects of syntax. The extent to which this situation is justified and the question of to what extent the other formalisms *could* be of routine use to programmers are matters of opinion. A possible, but arguable, ranking here would be, in order of decreasing value: attribute grammars, Vienna Definition Language, two-level grammars, axiomatic semantics, denotational semantics. It would seem that the principle of using a programming language as a metalanguage, discussed in Chap. 5, has great potential importance for the widespread user acceptance of formal specifications.

The construction of proofs about programs [application (3)] is facilitated most by the axiomatic approach, with the denotational approach coming in second. All the other approaches are much less suitable for this purpose.

Any kind of formal syntax is of great value to the language implementer [application (4)]. As far as semantics is concerned, the operational variety has often been taken to be the most directly relevant, whether it is specified by grammatical means (attribute grammars, two-level grammars) or otherwise (e.g., VDL). The area of proofs about implementations [application (5)] is rather difficult to evaluate, but it can be said that the operational, denotational, and axiomatic approaches all have some potential relevance here. Automatic implementation [application (6)] has been an area of great success with respect to context-free syntax (BNF, etc.) and of some success with respect to syntax in general (attribute grammars, two-level grammars). The automatic generation of complete compilers from language specifications which include semantics is a much more difficult problem, although progress has been made with some approaches, such as attribute grammars and denotational semantics. The use of a programming language as a metalanguage has special significance in this context, especially in relation to the operational and denotational approaches, because then a formal definition of a language can already *be* an implementation. The task of converting the definition to a practical, efficient processor then reduces to an optimization problem.

All the approaches have some value for the design of better programming languages [application (7)]. Many language theorists are of the opinion that the denotational approach has the greatest potential in this area because of the deep insights it can provide into the fundamental nature of programming languages.

It can be seen that different approaches, at least those concerned with semantics, tend to have different strengths and that different applications tend to be better served by different approaches. This suggests that no single set of specifications for a programming language will be optimal, or even near-optimal, for all purposes. The notion of *complementary definitions* provides a possible means of overcoming this situation: instead of specifying a language by means of one definition technique, the definer constructs two or more sets of specifications using different techniques together with a proof that the different sets of specifications are equivalent or consistent. Essentially, the idea is to achieve flexibility through redundancy; each alternative definition can be used for those purposes to which it is best suited. An example of a scheme for complementary definition can be obtained by considering any combination of the operational, denotational, and axiomatic approaches. Thus a set of operational specifications could be provided for the benefit of implementers and a corresponding set of axiomatic specifications for use by programmers. There is evidence that, because of its high degree of completeness and abstraction, the denotational approach can usefully serve as the means for constructing the "primary" definition from which the other definitions in a complementary set are derived. This may be prove to be one of the major contributions of the denotational approach to the field of formal specification of programming languages.

For Further Information

The notion of complementary definitions is advocated and illustrated briefly by Hoare and Lauer (1974); their ideas and examples are further examined by Greif and Meyer (1979). The complementary use of the denotational and axiomatic approaches is briefly discussed by de Bakker (1977) and investigated in detail in the context of Pascal by Donahue (1976). An example combining the axiomatic and operational approaches is given by Cook (1976). Milne and Strachey (1976) deal with the matter of complementary denotational and operational specifications, using what is essentially the same metalanguage for both, and Stoy (1977) offers some discussion relevant to the potential primary role of denotational semantics in complementary definitions.

bibliography

ALAGIĆ, S., AND M. A. ARBIB, *The Design of Well-Structured and Correct Programs.* New York: Springer-Verlag, 1978.

ANDERSON, E. R., F. C. BELZ, AND E. K. BLUM, "SEMANOL (73) A Metalanguage for Programming the Semantics of Programming Languages," *Acta Informatica,* 6 (1976), 109–31.

ANDERSON, E. R., F. C. BELZ, AND E. K. BLUM, "Issues in the Formal Specification of Programming Languages," in *Formal Description of Programming Concepts,* ed. E. J. Neuhold. Amsterdam: North-Holland Publishing Company, 1978, 1–30.

APT, K. R., AND J. W. DE BAKKER, "Semantics and Proof Theory of PASCAL Procedures," in *Automata, Languages and Programming, 4th Colloquium,* ed. A. Salomaa and M. Steinby. Lecture Notes in Computer Science, no. 52. Berlin: Springer-Verlag, 1977, 30–44.

BJØRNER, D., AND C. B. JONES, eds., *The Vienna Development Method: The Metalanguage.* Lecture Notes in Computer Science, no. 61. Berlin: Springer-Verlag, 1978.

BOCHMANN, G. V., "Semantic Evaluation from Left to Right," *Communications of the ACM,* 19, no. 2 (1976), 55–62.

BRADY, J. M., *The Theory of Computer Science: A Programming Approach.* London: Chapman & Hall Ltd., 1977.

CARTWRIGHT, R., AND D. C. OPPEN, "Unrestricted Procedure Calls in Hoare's Logic," Conference Record of the 5th Annual ACM Symposium on Principles of Programming Languages, 1978, 131–40.

CLARKE, E. M., "Programming Language Constructs for Which It Is Impossible to Obtain Good Hoare-like Axiom Systems," *Journal of the ACM*, 26 (1979), 129–47.

CLEAVELAND, J. C., AND R. C. UZGALIS, *Grammars for Programming Languages.* New York: Elsevier North-Holland, Inc., 1977.

CLINT, M., AND C. A. R. HOARE, "Program Proving: Jumps and Functions," *Acta Informatica*, 1 (1972), 214–24.

COHEN, R., AND E. HARRY, "Automatic Generation of Near-Optimal Translators for Noncircular Attribute Grammars," Conference Record of the 6th Annual ACM Symposium on Principles of Programming Languages, 1979, 121–34.

COOK, S. A., "Soundness and Completeness of an Axiom System for Program Verification," Technical Report no. 95, Dept. of Computer Science, Univ. of Toronto, 1976.

CROWE, D., "Generating Parsers for Affix Grammars," *Communications of the ACM*, 15 (1972), 728–32.

CUNNINGHAM, R. J., AND M. E. J. GILFORD, "A Note on the Semantic Definition of Side Effects," *Information Processing Letters*, 4 (1976), 118–20.

DE BAKKER, J. W., "Semantics and the Foundations of Program Proving," in *Information Processing 77*, ed. B. Gilchrist. Amsterdam: North-Holland Publishing Company, 1977, 279–84.

DIJKSTRA, E. W., *A Discipline of Programming.* Englewood Cliffs, N.J.: Prentice-Hall, Inc., 1976.

DONAHUE, J. E., *Complementary Definitions of Programming Language Semantics.* Lecture Notes in Computer Science, no. 42. Berlin: Springer-Verlag, 1976.

DONAHUE, J. E., "Locations Considered Unnecessary," *Acta Informatica*, 8 (1977), 221–42.

ENGELER, E., ed., *Symposium on Semantics of Algorithmic Languages.* Lecture Notes in Mathematics, no. 188. Berlin: Springer-Verlag, 1971.

ERNST, G. W., "Rules of Inference for Procedure Calls," *Acta Informatica*, 8 (1977), 145–52.

FELDMAN, J. A., "A Formal Semantics for Computer Languages and Its Application in a Compiler–Compiler," *Communications of the ACM*, 9 (1966), 3–9.

FOKKINGA, M., "Axiomatization of Declarations and the Formal Treatment of an Escape Construct," in *Formal Description of Programming Concepts*, ed. E. J. Neuhold. Amsterdam: North-Holland Publishing Company, 1978, 221–35.

GARWICK, J. V., "The Definition of Programming Languages by Their Compilers," in *Formal Language Description Languages for Computer Programming*, ed. T. B. Steel. Amsterdam: North-Holland Publishing Company, 1966, 139–47.

GERHART, S. L., "Proof Theory of Partial Correctness Verification Systems," *SIAM Journal of Computing*, 5 (1976), 355–77.

GORELICK, G. A., "A Complete Axiomatic System for Proving Assertions about Recursive and Non-recursive Programs," Technical Report no. 75, Dept. of Computer Science, Univ. of Toronto, 1975.

GREIF, I., AND A. MEYER, "Specifying Programming Language Semantics," Conference Record of the 6th Annual ACM Symposium on Principles of Programming Languages, 1979, 180–89.

GRIES, D., *Compiler Construction for Digital Computers*. New York: John Wiley & Sons, Inc., 1971.

GUTTAG, J. V., J. J. HORNING, AND R. L. LONDON, "A Proof Rule for Euclid Procedures," in *Formal Description of Programming Concepts*, ed. E. J. Neuhold. Amsterdam: North-Holland Publishing Company, 1978, 211–20.

HOARE, C. A. R., "An Axiomatic Basis for Computer Programming," *Communications of the ACM*, 12 (1969), 576–80, 583.

HOARE, C. A. R., "Procedures and Parameters: An Axiomatic Approach," in *Symposium on Semantics of Algorithmic Languages*, ed. E. Engeler. Berlin: Springer-Verlag, 1971, 102–16.

HOARE, C. A. R., AND P. E. LAUER, "Consistent and Complementary Formal Theories of the Semantics of Programming Languages," *Acta Informatica*, 3 (1974), 135–53.

HOARE, C. A. R., AND N. WIRTH, "An Axiomatic Definition of the Programming Language PASCAL," *Acta Informatica*, 2 (1973), 335–55.

IGARASHI, S., R. L. LONDON, AND D. C. LUCKHAM, "Automatic Program Verification I: A Logical Basis and its Implementation," *Acta Informatica*, 4 (1975), 145–82.

JENSEN, K., AND N. WIRTH, *PASCAL User Manual and Report*. Lecture Notes in Computer Science, no. 18. Berlin: Springer-Verlag, 1974.

KENNEDY, K., AND J. RAMANATHAN, "A Deterministic Attribute Grammar Evaluator Based on Dynamic Sequencing," *ACM Transactions on Programming Languages and Systems*, 1, no. 1 (1979), 142–60.

KNUTH, D. E., "Semantics of Context-free Languages," *Mathematical Systems Theory*, 2 (1968), 127–45. Correction in *Mathematical Systems Theory*, 5 (1971), 95.

KOSTER, C. H. A., "Affix Grammars," in *ALGOL 68 Implementation*, ed. J. E. L. Peck. Amsterdam: North-Holland Publishing Company, 1971, 95–109.

KOWALTOWSKI, T., "Axiomatic Approach to Side Effects and General Jumps," *Acta Informatica*, 7 (1977), 357–60.

LANDIN, P. J., "The Mechanical Evaluation of Expressions," *Computer Journal*, 6 (1964), 308–20.

LANDIN, P. J., "A Correspondence between ALGOL 60 and Church's Lambda-Notation," *Communications of the ACM*, 8, nos. 2–3 (1965), 89–101, 158–65.

LEDGARD, H. F., "Production Systems: or Can We Do Better than BNF?" *Communications of the ACM*, 17, no. 2 (1974), 94–102.

LEDGARD, H. F., "Production Systems: A Notation for Defining Syntax and Translation," *IEEE Transactions on Software Engineering*, SE-3, no. 2 (1977), 105–24.

LEE, J. A. N., *Computer Semantics*. New York: Van Nostrand Reinhold Company, 1972.

LEWIS, P. M., D. J. ROSENKRANTZ, AND R. E. STEARNS, "Attributed Translations," *Journal of Computer and System Sciences*, 9 (1974), 279–307.

LUCAS, P., "On the Formalization of Programming Languages: Early History and Main Approaches," in *The Vienna Development Method: The Meta-language*, ed. D. Bjørner and C. B. Jones. Lecture Notes in Computer Science, no. 61. Berlin: Springer-Verlag, 1978, 1–23.

LUCAS, P., AND K. WALK, "On the Formal Description of PL/I," *Annual Review in Automatic Programming*, 6 (1969), 105–52.

McCARTHY, J. ET AL., *LISP 1.5 Programmer's Manual*, 2nd ed. Cambridge, Mass.: The MIT Press, 1965.

McKEEMAN, W. M., J. J. HORNING, AND D. B. WORTMAN, *A Compiler Generator*. Englewood Cliffs, N. J.: Prentice-Hall, Inc., 1970.

MARCOTTY, M., AND F. G. SAYWARD, "The Definition Mechanism for Standard PL/I," *IEEE Transactions on Software Engineering*, SE-3, no. 6 (1977), 416–50.

MARCOTTY, M., H. F. LEDGARD, AND G. V. BOCHMANN, "A Sampler of Formal Definitions," *Computing Surveys*, 8, no. 2 (1976), 191–276.

MILNE, R., AND C. STRACHEY, *A Theory of Programming Language Semantics*. London: Chapman & Hall Ltd., 1976.

MOSSES, P. D., "Compiler Generation Using Denotational Semantics," *Mathematical Foundations of Computer Science, 5th Symposium*. Lecture Notes in Computer Science, no. 45. Berlin: Springer-verlag, 1976, 436–41.

NAUR, P., ed., "Revised Report on the Algorithmic Language ALGOL 60," *Communications of the ACM*, 6 (1963), 1–17.

NEUHOLD, E. J., ed., *Formal Description of Programming Concepts*. Amsterdam: North-Holland Publishing Company, 1978.

OLLONGREN, A., *Definition of Programming Languages by Interpreting Automata*. London: Academic Press Inc. (London) Ltd., 1974.

OWICKI, S., AND D. GRIES, "An Axiomatic Proof Technique for Parallel Programs I," *Acta Informatica*, 6 (1976a), 319–40.

OWICKI, S., AND D. GRIES, "Verifying Properties of Parallel Programs: An Axiomatic Approach," *Communications of the ACM*, 19 (1976b), 279–85.

PAGAN, F. G., "On Interpreter-oriented Definitions of Programming Languages," *Computer Journal*, 19, no. 2 (1976), 151–55.

PAGAN, F. G., "Formal Semantics of a SNOBOL4 Subset," *Computer Languages*, 3 (1978), 13–30.

PAGAN, F. G., "Algol 68 as a Metalanguage for Denotational Semantics," *Computer Journal*, 22, no. 1 (1979), 63–66.

PRITCHARD, P., "Program Proving—Expression Languages," in *Information Processing 77*, ed. B. Gilchrist. Amsterdam: North-Holland Publishing Company, 1977, 727–31.

Reynolds, J. C., "Definitional Interpreters for Higher-Order Programming Languages," *Proceedings of the 25th ACM National Conference*, 1972, 717–40.

ROCHESTER, N., "A Formalization of Two-Dimensional Syntax Description," in *Formal Language Description Languages for Computer Programming*, ed. T. B. Steel. Amsterdam: North-Holland Publishing Company, 1966, 124–38.

RUSTIN, R., ed., *Formal Semantics of Programming Languages*. Englewood Cliffs, N.J.: Prentice-Hall, Inc., 1972.

STEEL, T. B., ed., *Formal Language Description Languages for Computer Programming*. Amsterdam: North-Holland Publishing Company, 1966.

STOY, J. E., *Denotational Semantics: The Scott–Strachey Approach to Programming Language Theory*. Cambridge, Mass.: The MIT Press, 1977.

TENNENT, R. D., "The Denotational Semantics of Programming Languages," *Communications of the ACM*, 19, no. 8 (1976), 437–53.

TENNENT, R. D., "Language Design Methods Based on Semantic Principles," *Acta Informatica*, 8 (1977), 97–112.

VAN WIJNGAARDEN, A., "Recursive Definition of Syntax and Semantics," in *Formal Language Description Languages for Computer Programming*, ed. T. B. Steel. Amsterdam: North-Holland Publishing Company, 1966, 13–24.

VAN WIJNGAARDEN, A., ET AL., *Revised Report on the Algorithmic Language ALGOL 68*. Berlin: Springer-Verlag, 1976.

WATT, D. A., "The Parsing Problem for Affix Grammars," *Acta Informatica*, 8, no. 1 (1977), 1–20.

WATT, D. A., "An Extended Attribute Grammar for PASCAL," *SIGPLAN Notices*, 14, no. 2 (1979), 60–74.

WEGNER, P., "The Vienna Definition Language," *Computing Surveys*, 4, no. 1 (1972a), 5–63.

WEGNER, P., "Programming Language Semantics," in *Formal Semantics of Programming Languages*, ed. R. Rustin. Englewood Cliffs, N.J.: Prentice-Hall, Inc., 1972b, 149–248.

index

Abstraction (function), 169
Abstract machine, 133
  specification of:
    in Algol 68, 221
    in VDL, 135, 141, 145, 155–59
Abstract syntax, 76
  specification of:
    in Algol 68, 219–21
    in axiomatic semantics, 195
    in denotational semantics, 170–71
    informal, 76–77
    in two-level grammars, 101-2, 123
    in VDL, 141, 156, 159–60
Affix grammars, 49
Alagić, S., 215
Algol 60:
  correspondence with λ -notation, 99
  definition of, 7, 9, 21
  denotational semantics of, 193
Algol 68:
  as a metalanguage, 218–29
  official definition of, 50, 72, 229
allbutlast, 36
Ambiguity:
  with BNF, 10
  "dangling else," 13
American National Standards Institute, 167
Anderson, E. R., 135, 167, 227

append:
  in attribute grammars, 35
  in denotational semantics, 170
Application (of a function), 169
Apt, K. R., 215
Arbib, M. A., 215
Arithmetic expressions, 10
ASPLE, 5, 132
Assertion, 193–95
Assignment statement, 1–2, 49
Attribute, 27
  inherited, 30, 33
  synthesized, 30, 33
Attribute grammars, 27–49, 79–99
Automatic implementation, 4, 233
Axiomatic semantics, 133, 193–215
Axiom schema, 195

Backus–Naur Form (*see* BNF)
Basic, VDL specification of, 167
Belz, F. C., 235
Bjørner, D., 193
Blind alley, 57
Block structure (of Eva), 19–20, 124, 156–59, 184–88, 206
Blum, E. K., 235
BNF, 8–13, 15, 17
  variations on, 21–26, 50

Bochmann, G. V., 49, 99, 238
"Bottom," 168
Brady, J. M., 135, 193

Cartwright, R., 215
Clarke, E. M., 215
Cleaveland, J. C., 21, 26, 72, 132
Clint, M., 215
Cobol:
  standardization, 3
  syntax specification, 25
Cohen, R., 99
Compiler:
  automatic generation of, 4, 49, 99, 193, 233
  error checking in, 74
  syntactic and semantic processing in, 74
Compile time, 74
Complementary definitions, 233–34
concat, 35
Condition:
  in attribute grammars, 27
  invariant, 203
Consistent substitution, 53, 54
Context conditions (of Eva), 19
Context-sensitivity:
  of Eva, 19
  specification of:
    in attribute grammars, 31–34, 37
    in other formalisms, 49
    in two-level grammars, 56–59, 60
Continuations, 190
Control tree, 141, 143–45
Cook, S. A., 215, 234
Correctness of programs, 3, 195
Crowe, D., 49
Cunningham, R. J., 215

"Dangling else" ambiguity, 13
de Bakker, J. W., 215, 234
Deduction rule, 196
Definition, language, 2 (*see also*
        Specification, language)
Definition by processor, 134, 135, 218, 227
Denotational semantics, 133, 167–93
Derivation tree (*see* Syntax tree)
Dijkstra, E. W., 215
Distinguished symbol, 9
Domain, 168
  function, 169
  product, 168
  semantic, 167, 171
  sum, 168
  syntactic, 170
Donahue, J. E., 135, 193, 234
Dynamic semantics, 75

Elementary object, 136
Engeler, E., 236
Environment:
  in denotational semantics, 182
  in VDL, 156
Ernst, G. W., 215
Error:
  semantic, 74–76
  syntactic, 74
error, 148
European Computer Manufacturers'
        Association, 167
Eva:
  attribute grammar for syntax, 44–48
  axiomatic semantics, 214
  BNF grammar, 17
  denotational semantics, 190–92
  extended BNF grammar, 24
  informal description, 16
  semantic errors, 75
  two-level grammar for syntax 69–72
  two-level grammar for syntax and
        semantics, 125–32
  VDL definition of semantics, 162–66
Evaluation rule, 27–28
Extensional definition, 228–29

F (VDL), 140
Feldman, J. A., 99
field, 35
first, 35
Fokkinga, M., 215
Formal language theory, 8, 56
Formal Semantic Language, 99
Formal semantics, 133–215
Formal specification (*see* Specification,
        language)
Formal syntax. 7–71
Fortran:
  DO statement, 26
  Hollerith literals, 30
  identifier syntax, 25, 56
  standardization, 3
Function:
  in denotational semantics, 167, 169
  in VDL, 161
Function domain, 169

Garwick, J. V., 135
Gerhart, S. L., 215
Gilford, M. E. J., 215
Gorelick, G. A., 215
Grammar:
  affix, 49
  attribute, 27

Grammar (cont.):
  BNF, 8
  context-free (type 2), 8
  two-level (W-), 50, 54
Greif, I., 234
Gries, D., 21, 215
Guttag, J. V., 215

Harry, E., 99
hd, 170
head (VDL), 139
Hoare, C. A. R., 215, 234
"Hold," to, 57
Hollerith literal, 30
Horning, J. J., 237, 238
Hyper-rule, 52

Igarashi, J., 215
Implementation, automatic, 4, 233
Implementations:
  linguistic restrictions in, 75
  proofs of, 4, 233
Inherited attribute, 30, 33
Injection, 169
Inspection, 169
Instruction (VDL), 143
Instruction definition (VDL), 135, 143–44,
  161
Interpreter, automatic construction of, 4,
  223
Interpretive semantics, 99–132, 135–67,
  218–28
Invariant condition, 203

Jensen, K., 26
Jones, C. B., 193

Kennedy, K., 99
Knuth, D. E., 49
Koster, C. H. A., 49
Kowaltowski, T., 215

Lambda notation, 99, 169
Landin, P. J., 99, 167
Language, context-free or type 2, 8
Language design, 7, 193, 233
last, 35
Lauer, P. E., 234
Ledgard, H. F., 49, 238
Lee, J. A. N., 167
Left-recursion, 9
length:
  in attribute grammars, 35
  in VDL, 139

Lewis, P. M., 49, 99
Linguistics, natural, 8
Lisp 1.5, 228–29
List:
  in denotational semantics, 170
  in VDL, 139
London, R. L., 237
Lucas, P., 135, 167
Luckham, D. C., 237

McCarthy, J., 229
Machine, abstract (*see* Abstract machine)
McKeeman, W. M., 21
Marcotty, M., 5, 99, 132, 167
Mathematical semantics (*see* Denotational
  semantics)
Metalanguage, 5
Metanotion, 52
Metaproduction rule, 52
Metarule, 52
Meyer, A., 234
Milne, R., 193, 234
Mosses, P. D., 193
Mutation operator, 138, 160

Naur, P., 21
"Nest," 37, 60
Neuhold, E. J., 238
nil, 170
Nonterminal symbol, 8
Notion, 50
null, 146
Null object, 136

Object (VDL), 135–40
Object language, 5, 79
Ollongren, A., 167
Operational semantics, 133, 135–67, 218–28
Oppen, D. C., 215
Owicki, S., 215

Pagan, F. G., 167, 227
Pam:
  attribute grammar for syntax and
    semantics, 92–98
  axiomatic semantics, 204
  BNF grammar, 15
  denotational semantics, 178–80
  extended BNF grammar, 23
  informal abstract syntax, 76–77
  informal description, 14
  operational semantics in Algol 68, 224–27
  semantic errors, 75
  two-level grammar for syntax, 51

Pam (cont.):
two-level grammar for syntax and
    semantics, 116-22
VDL definition of semantics, 152-55
Parse tree (*see* Syntax tree)
Partial correctness, 195
Pascal:
    axiomatic definition, 215
    block structure, 20
    complementary definitions of, 234
    repeat statement, 205
    syntax specification, 26, 49
    variable declaration, 26
Perfect nmber, 15
PL/I·
    BEGIN block, 26
    block structure, 20
    semicolons in, 16
    standardization, 3, 167
    statements mixed with declarations, 21
    syntax specification, 26
    VDL specification, 167
Postcondition, 195
Pragmatics, 1-2
Precedence of operators, 12
Precondition, 195
Predicate:
    in two-level grammars, 57-58
    in VDL, 140
prefix, 170
Pritchard, P., 215
Processor as definition, 134, 135, 218, 227
Product domain, 168
Production rule, 8, 50
Production systems, 49
Programming languages as metalanguages,
    217-29
Projection, 169
Proof:
    of implementations, 4, 233
    of programs, 3, 193, 195, 201, 215, 233
Proof rule, 196
Proof theory, 193
Protonotion, 50

Ramanathan, J., 99
Recursion:
    in BNF, 9, 22
    in Eva, 18
Reference material:
    for implementers, 4, 233
    for language users, 3, 232
Representation table, 50
Reynolds, J. C., 167
Right-recursion, 9
Rochester, N., 26
Rosenkrantz, D. J., 238

Rule:
    abstract production, 171, 199, 205
    evaluation, 27-28
    hyper-, 52
    of inference, 196
    metal, 52
    production, 8, 50
Runtime, 74
Rustin, R., 239

Sayward, F. G., 167
Scope rules (*see* Block structure)
Scott, D., 193
Selector:
    Algol 68, 219
    VDL, 136, 156
Self-definition, 227-29
Self-replacing group, 144
Semantic domain, 167, 171
Semantic equation, 167, 171
Semantic error, 74-76
Semantic function, 167, 171
Semantics, 1-2
    axiomatic, 133, 193-215
    boundary with syntax, 74-75
    denotational (mathematical), 133, 167-93
    dynamic, 75
    formal, 133-215
    interpretive, 99-132, 135-67, 218-28
    operational, 133, 135-67, 218-28
    static, 75
    translational, 79-99
Side effects, 180, 194, 215
SNOBOL4, VDL specification of, 167
Specification, language:
    analogy with programming, 217
    applications of, 3-5, 232-33
    desirable qualities of, 3, 218, 223
Standardization of programming languages,
    3, 232
State, 133
    in Algol 68, 221-22
    in denotational semantics, 171, 182
    in two-level grammars, 100, 123
    in VDL, 135, 141
Static semantics, 75
Stearns, R. E., 238
Steel, T. B., 239
Stoy, J. E., 135, 193, 234
Strachey, C., 193, 234
Subject language, 5
Subscripts, 13, 72
Substitution:
    in assertions, 196
    consistent, 53, 54
Sum domain, 168

Syntactic analyzers, automatic generation
    of, 4, 21, 233
Syntactic domain, 170
Syntactic error, 74
Syntactic sugar, 76
Syntax, 1–2
    abstract (*see* Abstract syntax)
    boundary with semantics, 74–75
    formal, 7–71
Syntax tree:
    of abstract structures, 77–78
    with attribute grammars, 29–35
    with BNF, 9
    with extended BNF, 22
    with two-level grammars, 55
Synthesized attribute, 30, 33

T (VDL), 140
tail:
    in attribute grammars, 36
    in VDL, 139
Tennent, R. D., 193
Terminal string, 9
Terminal symbol, 8
tl, 170

"Top," 168
Translational semantics, 79–99
Tree:
    control, 141, 143–45
    syntax (parse, derivation) (*see* Syntax tree)
    for VDL object, 136–39
Two-level grammars, 49–71, 99–132

Uzgalis, R. C., 21, 26, 72, 132

Value-returning group, 144
van Wijngaarden, A., 72, 229
VDL (*see* Vienna Definition Language)
Vienna Definition Language, 135–67

Walk, K., 167
Watt, D. A., 49
Weakest preconditions, 215
Wegner, P., 167
W-grammar, 50, 54
Wirth, N., 26, 215
Wortman, D. B., 238